The Process of Constitutionalisation of the EU and Related Issues

AF770682

Europa Law Publishing, Groningen 2008

The Process of Constitutionalisation of the EU and Related Issues

Edited by Naděžda Šišková

Europa Law Publishing is a publishing company specializing in European Union law, international trade law, public international law, environmental law and comparative national law.
For further information please contact Europa Law Publishing via email: info@europalawpublishing.com or visit our website at: www.europalawpublishing.com.

All rights reserved. No part of this publication may be reproduced or transmitted, in any form or by any means, or stored in any retrieval system of any nature, without the written permission of the publisher. Application for permission for use of copyright material shall be made to the publishers. Full acknowledgement of author, publisher and source must be given.

Voor zover het maken van kopieën uit deze uitgave is toegestaan op grond van artikel 16h t/m 16m Auteurswet 1912 *juncto* het Besluit van 27 november 2002, Stb. 575, dient men de daarvoor wettelijk verschuldigde vergoedingen te voldoen aan de Stichting Reprorecht (Postbus 3060, 2130 KB Hoofddorp). Voor het overnemen van (een) gedeelte(n) uit deze uitgave in bloemlezingen, readers en andere compilatiewerken (artikel 16 Auteurswet 1912) dient men zich tot de uitgever te wenden.

© Europa Law Publishing, the authors severally, 2008

Typeset in Scala and Scala Sans, Graphic design by G2K Designers, Groningen/Amsterdam

NUR 828; ISBN 978-90-76871-87-5

Preface

The main objective of this book is to give an analysis of relevant parts of the European Union legal order with regard to some envisaged cardinal changes in the field of *acquis communautaire*, which are linked directly to the constitutional development at the supranational level.

The significance of the issues of EU constitutionalism is enduring and cannot be reduced merely to the process of formal creation of a Constitution for Europe. Although the Constitution for Europe, after the unsuccessful referenda in France and the Netherlands, seems to be at the moment put aside *ad acta*, actual constitutional development already exists in the form of concrete provisions and institutes, as well as indicated by general trends *de lege ferenda*, and thus it can be used as a guide for dealing with the key questions of constitutionalisation of supranational entities. In addition, the conclusions of the Brussels summit (June 2007) show that this document will serve as a source for the future and its substance will be used, but with certain modifications. This book reflects this fact. This publication, in the form of a collection of essays, was prepared by leading researchers from the universities of old and new EU Member States along with the participation of national authorities and representatives of European institutions.

This book commences with the issues of the constitutionalism in the field of human rights, which became the most significant impulse for the development of the whole constitutional sphere at the EC/EU level. The European Court of Justice's doctrine of fundamental rights, which found its inspiration in the constitutional traditions of member states and international treaties on human rights, became the foundation stone of the creation of the constitutionalism of the supranational entities.

This publication examines the mentioned factors, as well as the prospects for development in this field, including the analysis of future mechanisms for the enforcement of human rights of the European Union's standard and the questions of the binding character of the Charter of Fundamental Rights of the EU, and the eventuality of the accession of the EC/EU to the European Convention for the Protection of Human Rights and Fundamental Freedoms and its possible impact. The case-law of the European Court of Human Rights is examined as an element of the integration of human rights law of European states and the safeguarding of an equal minimal standard of legal protection of individuals.

Great attention is also paid to common constitutional values of Member states as a source of European constitutionalism and to the influence of national constitutional models on the development of European constitutional law. Great emphasis is also laid on the issues of the Europeanization of the term constitution in the EC/EU context and the analysis of the constitutional character of the existing Treaties.

Likewise, this publication focuses on the actual constitutional issues related to the European Parliament and national parliaments, the relationship between the European Court of Justice and constitutional courts of Member States, and the constitutional aspects of the European citizenship. Consideration is also given to other important questions (for instance, constitutionalisation of private law in Europe), where cardinal changes are envisaged.

This text is the main outcome of research project No. 407/06/0077 granted by the Czech Science Foundation, to which the authors would like to express their warm gratitude for its support.

December 2007

As. Prof. JUDr. Naděžda Šišková, Ph.D.

CHAPTER I

Actual Issues of the Creation of Constitutionalism in the Field of Human Rights at the EU Level and its Prospects

Naděžda Šišková

1 European Constitutionalism and its Human Rights Dimension

European constitutionalism is a multifaceted term used in many different ways.[1] This term can be expressed from the state-based approach, or, vice versa, in the sense of non-state conception as well as in other ways.[2]

Relating to the state approach, constitutionalism presupposes a constitution, which is characterised by these features: 1) a constitutive element of this document which defines the main organs of government and their powers; 2) its stable character; 3) its terms are usually enshrined in a written document; 4) constitutions are superior to law; 5) they are justiciable; 6) they can only be amended by special procedures; and 7) they express a common ideology.[3] It can be added, also, that modern constitutions contain not only the provisions related to state powers, but the catalogues of human rights as well, which create the basic values of society.

In the context of the EU, however, it is often spoken about the constitutionalisation of the Treaties.[4] 'It is certainly true that insofar as constitutionalism relates to the existence of a constitutional framework, several constitutional features are already clearly reflected in the basic Treaties of the EU. The main organs and their powers are defined; the principles of subsidiary, proportionality and attributed competence are listed, as are a certain number of citizens' rights, and of judicial and other remedies. Apart from the Treaties, other features of a basic constitutional framework are to be found in the jurisprudence of the Court of Justice on issues such as supremacy, direct effect, respect for fundamental rights and transparency... However, there may be other emerging forms of democratic practice in the EU, which support a more procedural conception of constitutionalism.'[5] In this respect, the work of the Convention and its output in the form of the Treaty Establishing a Constitution for Europe and later in the Treaty of Lisbon mean crucial progress has been achieved in the way from the

* As. Prof. JUDr. Naděžda Šišková, Ph.D. is the Head of the Department of European and International Law, Jean Monnet Professor on European Law, Vice-Dean of the Faculty of Law, Palacky University, Czech Republic and Vice-Director of the Institute of Legal Sciences of the Moravian College.

1 See G. de Burca, Aschenbrenner, B.: 'European Constitutionalism and the Charter', in Peers, S., Ward, A. (ed.): EU Charter and Fundamental Rights, Hart Publishing, Oxford and Portland Oregon, 2004, p. 9.

2 See, Shaw, J.: Postnational Constitutionalism in the European Union, (1999), 6(4), JEPP, 579.

3 See Raz, J.: 'On the Authority and Interpretation of Constitutions: Some preliminaries', in Alexander, L. (ed.): Constitutionalism, Cambridge University Press, Cambridge, 1998, p. 152-153.

4 Marcini, G. F.: 'The Making of a constitution for Europe', Common Market Law Review, 1989, 26, p. 595.

5 G. de Burca, Aschenbrenner, B.: 'European Constitutionalism and the Charter' in Peers, S., Ward, A. (ed.): EU Charter and Fundamental Rights, Hart Publishing, Oxford and Portland Oregon, 2004, p. 11-12.

international to constitutional legal order and the deepening of the process of constitutionalisation.

The aim of this contribution is to capture the process of constitutionalisation of the supranational entities in the field of human rights only, especially to explain how the regulation of these rights at the EC/EU level determines the whole development in the European constitutional sphere.

2 The Concept and Attributes of Human Rights; The Differentiation of Certain Terms

The first problem that must be solved is the question of the terminology, or better to say, a differentiation of certain meanings. In legal science as well as in the instruments of human rights (national and international), it is usual to encounter the following terms: *human rights, fundamental rights, fundamental human rights, human rights and fundamental freedoms, civil rights, rights of citizens,* etc.

The above-mentioned variety of expressions could be partially justified by the fact that human rights as a universal phenomenon projects into different scientific disciplines. However, when approaching this issue from the point of view of European law, which is our intention, we will find out that a confusion of meanings may occur even inside one branch. Certainly, the above-mentioned state is not satisfactory, and thus demands some corrections. First, we should like to determine the concept of human *rights* and *fundamental rights.*

Human rights are considered to be those rights and entitlements of the individual, which provide freedom and dignity for a human being and are insured by the institutional guarantees.[6] They are also 'the models of human behaviour' necessary for preservation of all living entities.[7] These rights are derived from the real essence of every individual as a human being. We can say that in their substance, they represent the rights which principally belong to every human being irrespective of nationality, race, colour of skin, sex, origin, religion, political or other conviction, social situation, genetic qualities and other individual characteristics. In this respect, we can speak about the universal character of these rights, their natural law lacks origin and non-discriminative basis. The inherent attributes of human rights are inalienability, indefeasibility, irrepealability and imprescriptibility.

The term *fundamental rights* in our opinion has two meanings. Firstly, as the 'hard core' of human rights[8] (classical rights and freedoms that are inherent in

6 Sudre, F.: Droit international et europeén des droits de l'homme, 'Press Universitaires de France', Paris (F), 1995, at p. 12.

7 Blahož, J.: Uvaha o podstate lidskych a obcanskych prav, 'Pravnik', (CZ), 1998, No. 10-11, at p. 875-877.

8 Sudre, F.: Droit international et europeén des droits de l'homme, 'Press Universitaires de France', Paris (F), 1995, at p. 131.

human dignity itself). Secondly, it is used according to the sources of their regulation. So it is possible to meet with the *fundamental rights* in the meaning of the 'human rights and freedoms guaranteed by the Constitution'[9] (at the national level) or on the contrary in relation to their regulation on the level of International law, namely, in the sense of 'human rights and freedoms embodied in international treaties and other norms of International law'.[10]

It is clear that fundamental rights in the scope of constitutional law do not have to correspond necessarily with their International law content or they may correspond only partially (in this context there is a differentiation between a *minimal standard of rights and a minimal international standard of rights*).

If we compare the concept of *human rights* and *fundamental rights* with regard to the above mentioned, we can unambiguously come to the conclusion that the concept of human rights is undoubtedly more extensive than the meaning of fundamental rights, as the concept of human rights represents natural laws' postulates and universal assets, which exceed the dimension of State formations, supranational entities, constitutions and instruments of International law.

While discussing the law of the EC/EU, we must mention that the concept of fundamental rights (but not human rights) was originally used by the European Court of Justice, which, as will be stated below, developed the *doctrine of fundamental rights*. Their incorporation into positive law was later projected in acts of primary law as well as in the Charter of Fundamental Rights of the EU. In this respect, it is necessary to stress that, although the ECJ started to use the term *fundamental rights* and later this term was incorporated in various sources of Community law, in fact, the meaning of this expression in the context of the *acquis communautaire* is much more extensive than the mere *hard core* of human rights. The analysis of different sources of the law of human rights at the EU level enables us to reach the conclusion that this corpus of law embraces the human rights and freedoms of all four generations, even including the so-called 'modern rights'.

Furthermore, we would like to point out the differentiation between *human* and *civil rights*. The differentiation is usually based on the criteria, whether these rights are somehow linked to the State; in other words, *human rights* are essentially understood as the rights of all human beings regardless of the country in which they live. On the other hand, *civil rights* result from the status of the individual as a citizen of a certain state. Naturally, this is only a general differentiation, because these concepts are often confused. If we apply the above mentioned in the sphere of EC/EU law, we can set apart specific rights that can be considered as *civil rights* in the sense of a connection between holders of these rights with the European Union, or better said, with European citizenship.

9 Gerloch, A.: Ustavni system Ceske republiky, 'Prospektrum', Prague (CR), 1999, at p. 288.

10 Stražnicka, V.: Clovek a jeho prava, 'Juga', Bratislava (SK), 1994, at p. 12.

With respect to civil rights, the question of the division of the subjective entitlements into the *rights and freedoms* according to the context also arises. The dividing line between them is even less evident, so by some authors or by the Charter of Fundamental Rights and Freedoms these terms are used in the same meanings. In this regard, we are inclined towards those representatives of jurisprudence, who consider *the freedoms* to be that part of human rights whose 'recognition and regulation by State was built in positive law'.[11]

From this point of view, *the human rights* undoubtedly have a much wider meaning because they are based on natural law and universal principles and thus, without any exemptions, belong principally to every individual regardless of their incorporation in positive law or existence of guarantees for their enforcement. However, even after summing up all the above-mentioned distinctive signs, we do not deny that the difference between *rights* and *freedoms* is sometimes hard to determine and can be considered in most cases as merely settled terminological custom.

In relation to *freedoms in the context of European law*, we must strictly differentiate between freedoms in the above-mentioned meaning (i.e. subjective entitlements of human rights nature and public character that are recognized and guaranteed by European Communities) and the freedoms in the meaning of basic structural elements of the Single Internal Market in the framework of the European Union area. The latter have a different nature, in particular, not all of them have the human rights dimension (for instance free movement of goods) and originally they occur as provisions ensuring the proper functioning of the Internal Market and the supporting of competition. Thus, the attributes characteristic for human rights cannot (with few exceptions) be applied to freedoms in the meaning of structural elements of area without internal frontiers in the framework of the EU. Thus, it is quite obvious that freedoms in this sense do not fit into our reasoning and therefore we will not deal with them, with the exception of some provisions, which comprise principles and norms of a truly human rights nature (e.g. free movement of persons and related prohibitions of the discrimination etc.).

Human rights can be further differentiated on the grounds that they are exercised by an individual separately or jointly with another person or group of persons. In this context, we distinguish *individual rights, collective rights* (rights of individual that are exercised collectively) and *group rights* (rights entitled to and exercised directly by groups of persons)

If this structure is applied to European law, it can be stated that while individual and collective rights are included in *acquis communautaire*, group rights are not included at all (even the specific regulation of rights through the institute of European citizenship does not include the group rights, so minority rights are completely omitted). This might seem like a certain paradox, because

---

11 Sudre, F.: Droit international et europeén des droits de l'homme, 'Press Universitaires de France', Paris (F), 1995, at p. 14.

the EC could be de facto perceived as a community of minorities, since none of the ethnic or national groups has a majority within the European union area.

The Generations of Human Rights

The differentiation of human rights is traditionally and inseparably linked with the theory of *generations of human rights*. While solving the 'generation question' from the point of view of the supranational entities, it can be stated that in the framework of the *acquis communautaire,* the rights of all four generations are represented. Especially interesting and original seems to be the European approach concerning the regulation of rights of the fourth generation, which in European law is named as 'modern rights'. As it will be demonstrated further, these rights in the latest EU instruments of human rights' protection are conceived as an immediate reflection of the recent scientific and technical progress and the actual development of the common policies of the EU.

3 The Evolution of the Protection Of Human Rights in the EC/EU: From Judicial Doctrine to the Charter of Fundamental Rights of the EU

The incorporation of the Charter of Fundamental Rights of the EU as the annex to the EU's new act of primary law – the Lisbon Treaty – creates an important change in the regulation of human rights at the level of supranational entities, confirming that the EU is not only an entity with primarily economic intentions but the Community of values as well.

This is especially significant as regards to the fact that the original Foundation Treaties did not have any mention or reference to human rights. This fact could be explained by two main reasons. First, it was considered for a long time that the Council of Europe, as a political organisation created especially for the protection of the principles of democracy in the society, would take care of human rights.

On the other hand, it was believed that the realisation of common policies would not exceed the economic dimension of European integration, so it would not interfere in the field of human rights; in other words, it would not lead to the violation of those rights. The first change in this attitude towards the issue of human rights can be found in the caselaw of the European Court of Justice. The elaboration of the Community doctrine of fundamental rights from the side of this judicial body of the European Communities was in its essence the forced reaction to the long lasting conflicts between the European Court of Justice and the Constitutional Courts of some Member States just in the field of human rights. Namely, these courts refused to recognise the supremacy of the Community Law with the reference to the fact that the EC law lacks its own regulation of human rights in contrast to the constitutional law of Member States.

It is quite obvious that the rejection of the supremacy of the Community law by means of the argument of the absence of the human rights regulation was able to threaten and jeopardise the existence of the whole project of the European integration, in which the Community law had always played the key role. Under such circumstances, the Luxembourg Court chose a very original solution to this problem, which consisted of the elaboration of the Community doctrine of fundamental rights as an integral part of the general principles of law. In *Stauder,*[12] the Court of EC declared, namely, that in spite of the fact that neither primary law nor secondary legislation have provisions relating to fundamental rights, nevertheless those rights are enshrined in general principles of the Community law. As such, they create the part of law, which the Court has to protect during the application and interpretation of the Treaty. In other cases, the European Court of Justice not only developed this doctrine, but also mentioned and named the main sources of its inspiration in the field of human rights. For instance in *Internationale Handelsgesellschaft*[13] the ECJ stated that even though it derives the force of its regulation solely from EC law, it is however inspired by national constitutional traditions common to the Member States. In other words, it declared the constitutional principles of national systems of law to be the basic source of the human rights concept in the Community.

In subsequent cases, the ECJ defined another source of its inspirations in human rights. In *Nold,*[14] *Rutili,*[15] *Hauer*[16] and other cases, it pointed out that international treaties concerning human rights, in which Member States participate, provide principles that should be followed in terms of EC law.

It is also possible to add to those sources of inspiration, without any doubt, the case-law of the European Court of human rights. The Strasbourg Court in the framework of the interpretation of the European Convention gives the binding definitions and explanation of the terms of the Convention, and thus enables this document to become 'the living instrument'.

So, the analysis of existing case-law of the Court makes it possible to indicate three basic sources of inspiration for the Community's concept of human rights as follows:

1) constitutional tradition of Member States;
2) international treaties in the field of human rights;
3) case-law of the European Court of Human Rights.

The creation and formulation of general principles of law could be in a simple way expressed in two phases:

- *Inductive* – when the Court sets off the general principle of law from the constitutional tradition of the Member States, international treaty or inter-

[12] ECJ Case 29/69 *Stauder* ECR [1969] 419.

[13] ECJ Case 11/70 *Internationale Handelsgesellschaft* [1970] ECR 1125.

[14] ECJ Case 4/73 *Nold KG v. Commission* [1974] ECR 491.

[15] ECJ Case 36/75 *Rutili v. Minister for the Interior* [1975] ECR 1219.

[16] ECJ Case 44/79 *Hauer v. Land Rheinland-Pfalz* [1979] ECR 3727.

pretation contained in the case-law of the ECHR;
- *Deductive* – when the Luxembourg court comes to a conclusion and to a specific solution in a concrete case by using the general principle of law.[17]

In this context, we would like to emphasize the fact that the existence of a certain general principle of law in the Constitution of single Member State does not automatically establish the claim to use this principle at the EC level, as it first has to gain the community's dimension in the decision-making of the European Court of Justice.

The general principles of law deduced in this way become an independent source of law within the *acquis communautaire*. The same applies analogically to cases of inspiration by international treaties (most often by *acquis* of the Convention), when the source of law became not the relevant provisions of the treaty (which remains a part of international law, i.e. a different law system) but the formulation of 'adopted' principles, that serve as guidelines in the case-law of the Court.

The ECJ defines and delineates the scope of these principles, sets up their limits and adjusts them to Community conditions. At the same time, the Luxembourg court confers on the general principles of law the qualities of *acquis communautaire*, namely, supremacy and direct effect, which function in cases of conflict with provisions of the national law as such. The general principles of law are the independent, autonomic and specific source of EC law.

When talking about constitutional traditions of Member States, it is necessary to stress that the concrete principle does not have to be explicitly included in the constitutional law of *all* Member States (though in most cases they are, especially, the classical principles). The Court adopted an approach that if a fundamental right does not contravene the goals of the Community and does not inhibit the realisation of the Community's policies, it can be declared as a general principle of law even if it is constitutionally guaranteed only in some or just one Member State. Practical demonstration of the mentioned approach can be observed in *Grogan,*[18] where the Court was examining the question of whether such a principle can be also found in the *right to life of an unborn child* in the sense of Article 40 (3)(3) of the Irish Constitution.

In other words, concerning the requirement of generality, it is not quite necessary that certain rights be commonly recognized in all Member States. This conclusion has a special significance as regards to the essentially permanent process of enlargement and extensive growth of the EC/EU, which implicates the accession of new Member States with different legal orders, cultures and traditions.

---

17 Hartley, J.C.: The Foundations of European Community Law, third edition, Clarendon Press, Oxford, 1994, p. 138.

18 ECJ Case C-159/90 *Grogan* [1991] ECR I-4685.

Regarding the international treaties in which the European Court of Justice looks for its inspiration in the field of human rights, it is essential to refer not only to the European Convention for the Protection of Human Rights and Fundamental Freedoms (hereinafter referred to as 'the Convention'), but to the European Social Charter as well and also the Convention No. 111 of the International Labour Organisation or the Covenant on Civil and Political Rights. This list cannot be considered as comprehensive and final, as it is to be expected that the ECJ's interpretation of the term *international treaties* will still be very extensive when looking for its inspiration.

However, if we analyse these sources of inventive inspiration for the ECJ, it is clear, that the Court does not do the reception of the national principles and norms of international treaties mechanically and without changes, but on the contrary, it approaches the mentioned postulates in the field of human rights very selectively. It is possible to say that the Court manifests great creativity and independence in choosing those principles and norms, which best serve the specific goals of the Community including the determination of the limits of their application.

The mentioned thesis can be demonstrated on certain differences between the case-law of the ECJ and European Court of Human Rights. For example, in *Musique Diffusion v. Commission,*[19] the ECJ stated that the Article 6 of the Convention (the right to a fair trial) is not applied to cases deriving from the competition law, because the Commission cannot be considered as a tribunal in the sense of this provision. Likewise, the Luxembourg Court in preference, took account of the goals of the Community in the field of competition law in *Orkem,*[20] where it drew a conclusion to reduce the scope of Article 6 of the Convention (the right to a fair trial including the protection from self-incrimination) only to natural persons, but not to corporations.

On the contrary, the European Court of Human Rights (hereinafter referred to as ECHR) stated expressly in *Funke*[21] that 'special features of customs law (...) cannot justify (...) the infringement of rights of anyone charged with a criminal offence within autonomous meaning of this expression defined in Article 6, to remain silent and not to contribute to incriminating himself.'

Further inconsistencies in the judicial practice of the Luxembourg and Strasbourg Courts occur in interpretation of the inviolability of the home on the basis of Article 8 par. 1 of the Convention. For example, the ECJ stated in *Hoechst*[22] that the protection under the mentioned article is related only to the individual freedom of people and therefore cannot be extended to companies. Furthermore, it concluded that the right to exercise the competences vested in the Commission including the entrance to the company area ensures the observance of the

---

[19] ECJ Joint Cases 100-103/80 *SA Musique Diffusion v. EC Commission* [1983] ECR 1825.

[20] ECJ Case 374/87 *Orkem* [1989] ECR 3283, at 3350.

[21] Case *Funke*, ECHR (1993), Series A, Vol. 256 – A.

[22] ECJ Case 46/87 *Hoechst* [1989] ECR 2859-2924.

rules of competition and it is necessary for the prevention of the violation of economic competition. The ECHR maintained an absolutely different opinion on the application of Article 8 (1) of the Convention in *Niemietz,*[23] which involved the search of a lawyer's office in the absence of an independent observer. The ECHR stated that the interpretation of the terms 'private life' and 'residence' within the Convention, which contain the professional or business activities or business areas, is in compliance with the essential aim and purpose of Article 8 of the Convention, namely the protection of an individual against arbitrary intervention of the public authority.

The analysis of the chosen cases of the European Court of Justice and their comparison with the case-law of the ECHR reflects that, when in doubt, the ECJ often followed the principle *in dubio pro integrationem*; in other words the Luxembourg Court preferred the common goals of EC over the private interests of individuals.[24] However, the latest development in the ECJ's decision-making shows some positive tendencies directed to acceptance of the position of the Strasbourg Court. As an example, it is possible to mention the ECJ decision in *Familiapress,*[25] where the Luxembourg Court expressly followed the conclusions of the ECHR in *Lentia.*[26]

A brief summary of the above-mentioned cases makes it possible to draw certain conclusions. Concerning the rights deriving from the Convention, application of their substance as a general principle of law by the ECJ became an irrevocable precedent; in the case of the binding interpretation by the ECHR, it is not always axiomatic. It stands for a rule that the ECJ ordinarily draws inspiration from the case-law of the ECHR; in all circumstances, it examines whether relevant decisions of ECHR could be used as guidelines for the ECJ's decision-making in the field of human rights.

In terms of taking advantage of the ECHR's conclusions by the European Court of Justice, the different interpretation exists only in certain areas, such as competition law or custom law, where the European Court of Justice at the beginning refused to recognize the argumentation of the human rights and applied restrictive interpretations in favour of ensuring of the effectiveness and efficiency of common policies of the EC. However, the last decisions of the Luxembourg Court indicate that it tries to keep in line with the ECHR concerning the minimum standard of human rights contained in *acquis* of the Convention.

Theoretically, nevertheless, the different interpretation cannot be completely excluded, because the Luxembourg Court modifies the *acquis* of the Convention to fit the EC's conditions and in addition, it is not formally bound by the Conven-

23 Case *Niemietz*, ECHR (1992), Series A, Vol. 251-B.

24 See Spielmann: 'Human Rights Case-law in Strasbourg and Luxembourg Courts: Conflicts, Inconsistencies and Commentaries' in Alston, P. (Ed.): 'The EU and Human Rights', Oxford, 1999, p. 770.

25 Case C-368/95 *Familiapress* [1997] ECR I-3689, para. 26.

26 Case *Lentia*, ECHR (1993), Series A, No. 276.

tion. The most effective and from a legal point of view also the 'purest' way to avoid eventual differences in the interpretation of the Convention and inconsistencies in the case-law of both European judicial bodies is the formal accession of EC/EU to the Convention. But this measure is not simple and may collide with a number of legal and political problems (see below).

The judicial doctrine of fundamental rights since the time of its appearance (the end of the 60's) until now has created a wide and extensive corpus of cases, which formulates the concrete rights, as well as determines the conditions for its realization and certain restrictions, given by the Community specifics. Nevertheless, at the end of the 90's, the European Communities and the Union were still missing their own coherent and binding catalogue of human rights that enabled individuals to identify simply their rights and to enforce them effectively before the Courts.

The Charter of Fundamental Rights of EU, elaborated by the Convention under the leadership of Roman Herzog, and approved by the Intergovernmental Conference in Nice in December 2000, partially eliminated this disadvantage, as it adopted the first Bill of rights of European Unions standard, but at that time without any binding character. Due to the fact that the Charter was intended and drafted as a very rich and generous instrument, as far as it deals with the great number and wide scope of the protected rights (not only the rights of personal and political character, but the social, economic, cultural and modern rights) the opinion prevailed that the Charter would hardly obtain the binding status in a short time.

Nevertheless, the evolution in the framework of the preparatory works of the Convention under the leadership of Valéry Giscard d'Estaing and the holding of the International Conference in Rome of December 2003 brought a result, which surpassed the expectations to a great extent. The consensus achieved namely enabled the most optimum solution – not only to incorporate the Charter into the text of the Constitutional Treaty, but also enabled it to occupy a dignified and important place inside this constitutional instrument. The Charter was integrated into part II of the Treaty Establishing a Constitution for Europe, which followed the main important institutional and constitutional provisions, instead of the originally proposed eventuality of its incorporation among the Protocols.

In this respect concerning the issues of constitutionalisation, certain conclusions can be made. Firstly, the Charter became an impulse for the elaboration of the whole document – The Treaty Establishing a Constitution for Europe. In other words, it prepared the foundations for the creation of constitutionalism in the formal meaning at the EU level. Secondly, the Charter belonged to those parts of the Constitutional Treaty, due to its briefness and clarity, which were closer than other chapters of this document to the meaning of the Constitution as the Basic Law, as being the real Bill of human rights. This fact is quite apparent in comparison with other parts and provisions of the Treaty, which de facto cumulated the norms both of the constitutional and technical character that were often criticised for their opacity and low clarity.

Unfortunately, the Charter had to follow the destiny of the whole document. So, the failure of the approval of the text of a Constitution for Europe on the national level of Member States did not enable to realise, in our opinion, the best solution concerning the legal life of the Charter.

The Treaty of Lisbon brings a new option, less cardinal and unambiguous. Instead of the incorporation to the text of the Treaty itself, the Charter obtains the autonomous status again, accompanying by the declaration in the Article 6(1), that: 'The Union recognises the rights, freedoms and principles set out in the Charter of Fundamental Rights of the European Union of 7 December 2000, as adopted at Strasbourg, on 12 December 2007, which shall have the same legal values as the Treaties.' In this respect, the great expectations are connected with the European Court of Justice, which must ensure through its authoritative interpretation that the Charter will be applied correctly.

The Charter of Fundamental Rights, in its English version, contains only about three and a half thousand words, and creates, with no doubt, the document par excellence as regards to its material scope. This modern list of human rights of the 21st century brings the catalogue of rights protected at the EU level, namely it embraces not only the classic rights, that were already declared in the framework of the other instruments, but also formulates and develops the new entitlements of the individual, which can be realised inside the supranational entities only.

In this respect some new provisions could be mentioned that do not appear in other catalogues of human rights, such as for instance Article 3 containing *the right to the integrity of the person*, including *the prohibition of reproductive cloning of human beings, the prohibition of eugenic practices in particular those aiming at the selection of persons and prohibition of making the human body or its parts a source of financial gain*, the so-called bio-political provisions. Later on, *the right for good administration* (Article 41 Charter) could be mentioned or the specific rights connected with the institute of the European citizenship (for instance, the freedom of movement and residence inside the Single European Market without restrictions or the right for the consular protection etc).

These new and specific norms are represented in the Charter together with the traditional entitlements of the individual, which belong to the classic human rights and *hard core* of these rights. So, it is possible to conclude that the Charter is really a coherent, original and modern catalogue of human rights, which reflects scientific progress and is influenced by the specific Union conditions.

4 The Issues of the Enforcement of the Charter

Nevertheless, the legal effects of this progressive document, especially its impact on the status of an individual, do not enable us to be too optimistic. That is due to the fact that despite the considerable generosity of this European Union's Bill of Rights as regards to its material provisions concerning concrete rights, it lacks its own specific control mechanism in the form of the institutional provisions and procedural guarantees of enforcement of those rights.

This fact is striking especially in comparison with the European Convention for the Protection of Human Rights and Fundamental Freedoms, which contains an effective control mechanism comprising the institute of individual complaints that enables private persons to appeal directly and to invoke their claims of a human rights nature within the Strasbourg proceedings.

While analysing the particular possibilities of an individual to appeal directly for the rights declared in the Charter in the present state and under current legal prerequisites, including the envisaged perspectives given by the Reform Treaty, it must be concluded that the conditions for the enforcement of those entitlements are rather difficult and demand certain modifications.

The analysis of the construction of norms contained in this catalogue of the EU human rights standard shows a number of vague formulations and provisions of *program character,* especially concerning the economic and social rights, where a direct effect can be hardly anticipated. The provision of Article 31, para 1, can serve as an example: '*Every worker has the right to working conditions which respect his of her health, safety and dignity*'. So, the concrete content of this right is not defined clearly. In addition, the Charter in many of its places refers to provisions contained in the secondary legislation, international treaties and national law of Member States, as can be demonstrated in Article 16: '*The freedom to conduct a business in accordance with Union law and national laws and practices is recognised.*'

Based on the aforesaid, it can be stated that the Charter from its own nature as a brief document of the constitutional character is capable of articulating the rights in a very general way, whereas it leaves the filling of the contents of such generally declared rights to the secondary legislation, national laws, and the authoritative interpretation by the European Court of Justice.

With regards to the above-mentioned peculiarity of the Charter and considering the wording of the restrictive clause of Article 51, para 2, of the Charter, especially: '*This Charter does not extend the field of application of Union law beyond the powers of the Union or establish any new power or task for the Union, or modify powers and tasks defined in the other Parts of the Treaty,*' it is hardly possible to anticipate enforcement of these above-mentioned norms by individuals directly before the national courts of Member States in all the cases.

Concerning the application of the vague provisions of the Charter at the Community level, i.e. before the European Court of Justice or the Tribunal of First Instance, certain problems must be mentioned. Namely, within the proceedings before the European Court of Justice in the cases of the infringement of those human rights, contained in the acts of the secondary legislation, the individual as unprivileged plaintiff has a very hard position being an object of some restrictions. It is due to the fact that under the current wording of Article 230 TEC, the natural or legal person must prove that this act is of direct and individual concern to him or her. It is just the word *individual* that causes certain problems in practice. Especially it can be considered as the source of unnecessary limitations as regards to individuals, namely in the cases of directives, as the acts of general nature and normative character where it is rather difficult, if not impossible, to prove that those acts are of individual concern to private parties. This is the point where the deep deficit in the Community system of human rights protection can be seen. The necessity to remove those restrictions has been pointed out many times in jurisprudence,[27] as well as by the representatives of the judiciary.[28]

The Constitutional Treaty and after it the Treaty of Lisbon tried to reduce to some extent these restrictions. In this respect, three eventual options were discussed at the meeting of the Working Group II of the Convention, namely:

a) an introduction of a special remedy based on alleged violations of fundamental rights;
b) a relevant amendment to Article 230(4) TEC;
c) enshrining an obligation of Member States to provide for effective rights of action before their courts.[29]

The second option was chosen as the result of the discussion, so the new wording of the provision of Article 230(4) was incorporated into the text of the Constitution and later on into the Lisbon Treaty as follows: 'Any natural or legal person may, under conditions laid down in the first and second paragraphs, institute proceedings against an act addressed to that person or which is of direct or individual concern to them, and against a regulatory act, which is of direct concern to them and does not entail implementing measures' (Article 263(4) of the Reform Treaty). It is expected that this wording would serve to

---

27 Ward, A.: 'The Draft EU Constitution and Private Party Access to Judicial Review of EU Measures', p. 212-214. Ward, A.: Access to Justice, in Peer, J., Ward, A (ed.), 'Hart Publishing', Oxford and Portland, Oregon, 2007, p. See Jacobs, E.: Human Rights in the European Union: The Role of the Court of Justice, (2001), 26 E.L.Rev., Sweet and Maxwell, at 333.

28 See Case C-174/01 *Jégo-Quéré and Cie v. Commission* [2002] ECR II-2365, Opinion of Advocate General Jacobs in Case C-50/00 *Union de Pequenos Argicultures v. Council* [2002] ECR I-6677.

29 Working Group II, Working document 021 from 1.10.2002: 'The question of effective judicial remedies and access of individuals to the European Court of Justice', http://european-convention.eu.int/docs/wd2/3299.pdf.

solve the problem of 'self-executing' legal acts, which under current rules cannot be contested before the Court of First Instance and where an individual must break the law before he can have access to the Court.[30]

The primary intention of this norm, as it was reasoned by the Working Group of the Convention, is to ' to alleviate the rigidity currently resulting from the conditions of ' individual concern' in Article 230, where an applicant wishes to challenge self–executing Community acts of general application,'[31] and 'to preserve to global division of work between courts on European and national level, and to remedy only such exceptional situations were currently there is no protection at either level.'[32] This very cautious solution could be hardly justified by the purpose of improvement of the judicial protection of individual rights, but rather by the anxiety of the extreme increase in the number of cases caused by the relaxation of the conditions of *locus standi* for private parties.

The scope of possibilities to bring an action from the side of an individual under the new wording of the Article 230(4) is influenced by the type of act, which is to be revised, (determining in this respect is not a form but a substance of the act, as it can be followed from the case *JBM*[33]). So, in practise this norm will have a very selective impact, which can be demonstrated in three main situations, where the private applicants would be able to challenge:

1) Acts of general application (regulations or decisions having no addresses) which do not require implementing measures. In this case, there would be real progress, the gap in the legal system would be removed and the problem of 'self-executing regulations' existing today would be resolved. This would mean the victory of Advocate general Jacobs and the judges of the Court of First Instance ruling in *Jégo – Quéré*. Nevertheless, the requirement of direct concern' would still apply and would require interpretation.[34]
2) Acts not addressed to them, but which concern them directly and individually. Here the difference with the current situation is that this definition encompasses the 'legislative' acts, which under some circumstances may be of individual and direct concern for the applicant. This possibility has been recognized by the Court since *Codorniu* but now it would be explicitly written in the Treaty. Thus, in case of general acts concerning the applicant individually, there would be an extension of the standing with regard to the wording of Article 230(4) but not with regard to case-law (*Codorniu*)[35].

---

[30] Biernat, E.: 'The Locus standi of Private Applicants under Article 230(4) EC and the Principle of Judicial Protection in the European Community', New York University School of Law, New York, 2003, p. 51.

[31] Working group WG II Working document 21 from 1.10.2002, p. 4-5.

[32] Ibidem, p. 6.

[33] Case 60/81 *JBM v. Commission* [1981] ECR 2539, par 9.

[34] Biernat, E., supra note p. 54.

[35] Ibidem.

3) Acts addressed to them (e.g. Commision decisions in the field of competition law). Whether this new wording would relax the conditions of admissibility with regard to individual acts would depend on the interpretation of the notion of 'individual concern'. If it were to be interpreted according to *Plaumann,* then there would be no change with regard to the current situation.[36]

The analysis of the above-mentioned situations confirms that the chosen solution is half-hearted and is capable of causing confusion and other problems in practise; besides under all circumstances, it needs the relevant interpretation by the European Court of Justice.

More rational, effective and generous towards an individual are the other proposals, which were also discussed through the work of the Convention. For instance, the test proposed by the Court of First Instance in the case *Jégo – Quéré* can be mentioned, according to which an individual could seize the Court also (i.e., besides the case of individual acts) against a Community measure of general application 'that concerns him (i.e. the applicant) directly if the measure in question affects his legal position, in a manner which is both definite and immediate, by restricting his rights or by imposing obligations on him.'[37]

This option wasn't accepted by the Working Group II[38] as well as in the exhausted argumentation of Advocate General Francis Jacobs given in his Opinion in *UPA,*[39] according to which the private applicant 'is individually concern by a Community measure where the measure is or is likely to be substantially prejudicial to his interest, 'or under his opinion in the case *Union Pequenos,* 'the applicant is individually concern by a Community measure where the measure has, or is liable to have a substantial adverse effects on his interests.'

Two other proposals of the Convention Members – to convert the conditions of 'direct' and 'individual' into alternative criteria (i.e. 'direct or individual concern)[40] or simply delete the words 'an individual'[41] – were also refused. The reasoning of the rejection of all these proposals was that it 'could lead to a rather significant opening-up of direct access of individuals to the Court of First Instance and thus to a shift in the present division of tasks.'[42]

While evaluating the discussed options, it must be stressed that in our opinion the risk of increasing the number of cases and the overloading of the judicial body cannot be a strong reason for the continued existence of restrictions for private parties in the future. An adequate measure for the solution of this

36 Case *Plaumann.*

37 Case C-177/01 *Jégo-Quéré and v. Commission* [2002] ECR II-3239.

38 WG II, Working document 21, 1.10.2002, p. 5-6.

39 Opinion of AG Jacobs Case C-173/98 *UPA v. Council* [1998] ECR I-983, para 87-90.

40 The proposal of Jurgen Meyer, WGII, Working Document No 17.

41 The propsal of Cannes Farnleitner, Coc CONV 45/02 CONTRC 8 25.

42 WG II, Working document 21, 1.10.2002, p. 6.

problem could be found in the possibility of the omission of the word *individually* from the text of the mentioned provisions. This would enable individuals to appeal for the review of those acts of secondary legislation that have the human rights dimension. In this respect we share the opinion expressed in jurisprudence concerning that 'it is inconsistent with the charge of current mood for the Community to uphold outdated and paternalistic view of the rights of individuals to bring annulment proceedings.'[43]

While solving the question of the effectiveness of enforcement of concrete provisions of the Charter, the nature of the particular right is determining. In this sense, it is important to distinguish if they are personal and political rights or rights of an economical and social nature. The latter ones, considering the difficulties in the effort to reach consensus among Member States when incorporating those rights into the Charter, have been divided into social rights and social principles (aspirations).[44] In other words, some rights are understood as subjective enforceable entitlements, while the others as mere provisions of the programme character or definitions of objectives to be reached.

An illustration in this respect can be given in the Article 36 of the Charter, which states: '*The Union recognises and respects access to services of general economic interest as provided for in national laws and practices, in accordance with the Treaty, in order to promote the social and territorial cohesion of the Union.*'

This provision of programme and aspiration character defines an objective to be reached, as opposed to the provision of Article 32 of the Charter (prohibition of child labour and protection of young people at work), which can be defined as a directly applicable norm, which contains directly enforceable rights.

Regardless of the changes suggested herein, it is eligible and worth considering introducing a special procedure for violating of rights granted by the Charter. This proceeding could be structured either in the form of the incorporation of a new provision on breach of human rights protected by the Charter or by the extending the Charter itself, in Chapter VI 'Justice', which will contain the provisions dealing with the control mechanism. The latter mentioned version will reach the analogical solution as in the case of the European Convention for the protection of human rights, which also has provisions of procedural character incorporated in the text of the instrument itself.

In this connection, it is necessary to mention that the similar option in the form of the introduction of a new action (fundamental rights complaint) was refused by the Convention (mostly for the reason that the issues of fundamental rights arise within the other proceedings, and the relationship between such a 'special' constitutional action and the ordinary system of remedies in Article

43 Biernat, E., supra note 30, p. 57.

44 For a detailed differentiation of rights and principles within the Charter's provision see Updated Explanation relating to the text of the Charter of Fundamental Rights, Conv. 828/03, Brussels, 9.July 2003, at 1-52.

230(4) Treaty could be difficult to establish.'[45] On the other hand, it is worth recalling in memory that institution of constitutional complaints exists in the constitutional law of Member states, where it creates an effective mechanism and important warrant for the protection of fundamental rights of the individuals.

The eventuality of the introduction of a new special action enabling individuals to challenge Community acts, including those of general application, was already proposed several times and was mentioned in the report of the Court of Justice of May 1995.[46] The proposed solution would allow to leave intact the 'normal' system of direct actions as established by Article 230(4) focusing on individual acts of administrative character, and to add a special remedy of truly constitutional character.[47]

In our opinion, the introduction of a new procedure for violation of rights granted by the Charter will mean creation *of the European Union's sub-regional system of human rights protection,* which would contain a binding catalogue of human rights combined with an effective control mechanism for its enforcement.

5 Eventuality of the Accession of EC/EU to the European Convention of Human Rights

The next way to achieve effective protection of human rights at the Community and Union levels consists in the accession of the EC/EU to the European Convention on Human Rights and the submission of the Communities/Union to the Strasbourg control machinery, in other words, a linking of supranational entities with the system of human rights protection with a pan-European territorial scope.

Although the fact that in the text of the Constitutional Treaty and later on in the Treaty of Lisbon appears the provision of Article 6 (2), which declares: 'The Union accede to the European Convention for the Protection of Human Rights and Fundamental Freedoms', the implementation of this norm in practise is not so clear.

The solution of such a cardinal problem as the question of the possible accession of the Communities/Union to the European Convention of Human Rights belongs to the most complicated issues in the *acquis communautaire*. This problem also belongs in *acquis communautaire* to so called 'evergreens', if we take the numerous attempts of its sufficient solution into account.[48] The difficulties with

[45] Supra note 29.

[46] See, WG II. Working document 21, p. 4.

[47] Ibidem.

[48] See, for instance Memorandum on the accession from April 1979, or the Opinion A 2/94 of European Court of Justice from March 1996, Memorandum on the accession of the European Communities to

the proper solution are caused by the fact that many arguments in favour of the accession as well as against this step exist.

Some of the advantages can be briefly defined as follows:

- the accession will formalise the status of the Convention in the Community legal order;
- the accession will significantly strengthen the protection of the rights and freedoms of the individuals and their legal certainty;
- the accession will precisely define the limits of the responsibility of the EC/EU institutions for their actions, which interfere in the areas dealing with the human rights;
- the accession will exclude different interpretations of terms in the field of human rights from the side of the two European judicial bodies – Luxembourg and Strasbourg Courts;
- the accession will increase the democratic legitimacy of the EC/EU and of its actions;
- the accession will ensure the development of the protection of human rights in the whole of Europe without dividing lines;
- besides, the respect for human rights will become the basis for the future construction of the whole of Europe.[49]

On the other side, the accession will necessarily be accompanied by a number of legal and other complications, especially considering the following into account:

- the submission of the Court of the Communities to the judicial body of another international organisation;
- the danger of a threat to the autonomy of the Community legal order;
- the unclear relation between the European Convention on Human Rights and the Charter of Fundamental Rights of the EU;
- the eventuality of the delays caused by the accumulation of litigations and the prolonging of the whole length of the proceedings;

It is necessary to stress that none of these problems was yet satisfactorily solved neither by the *acquis communautaire*, nor by the *acquis* of the Convention.

The relevant act at the side of the Union is the Protocol relating to Article 6(2) of the TEU On The Accession of the Union to the European Convention, which was annexed to the Treaty of Lisbon. This document, which contains three paragraphs only, envisaged the preparation of the agreement for solving merely 2 groups of issues: 1) the Union's participation in the control bodies of the European Convention and 2) the mechanism necessary to ensure that the proceeding by non-Member States and individual applicants are correctly addressed to Member States and/or the Union as appropriate.

---

the Convention for the Protection of Human Rights and Fundamental Freedoms of 4th April, 1979, Bulletin of the European Communities, Supplement, 2/79.

49 Betten, L., Grief, N.: EU Law and Human Rights, Longman, London and New York, 1998, at 116.

On the side of the *acquis* of the Convention, the relevant norm is the Protocol No 14 to the Convention, which is even briefer concerning the accession of the Union, while shortly declaring only in Article 59(2) that 'European Union may accede to this Convention.' Although some further modifications were proposed in the Reflection paper of the Secretariat in the Document DG – II (2001)02[50], their incorporation into the Protocol No 14 wasn't possible at the time of the drafting of this Protocol due to the lack of relevant competences on the side of the supranational entities and the absence of the legal personality of the Union.

Attention must also be paid to the question of whether the European Convention, which was adopted more that a half a century ago, remains to be the very instrument which is capable of ensuring the proper protection of the individual's rights in the framework of the EC/EU.

The final decision concerning the accession of the Union to the Convention will be conducted by political reasons and will be influenced to a great extent by the contractual conditions which the representatives of the Union will be able to achieve, while negotiating about the accession, including the satisfactory solution of all mentioned legal and political issues.

5 Conclusions: Future Direction of the EU in the Field of Human Rights

It is just the mentioned eventuality of delays caused by the accumulation of litigation, which is able to cause the greatest problems, if we take into account that an applicant under the wording of Article 35 of the Convention would have to exhaust all domestic remedies (including a reference to Luxembourg Court in the cases of the preliminary rulings) before bringing his or her case to Strasbourg.[51] In this respect, it is worth reminding that litigation takes approximately 18 to 23 months before the European Court of Justice and even longer before the European Court of Human Rights.[52] Under such circumstances, the way from Luxembourg to Strasbourg for the attainment of justice would not necessarily mean the straight route, but could be changed in the travelling roundabout. The proposed solution[53] in the form of the introduction of a special procedure under which the ECJ would be authorised to request an interpretation of the Convention from the European Court of Human Rights would hardly improve the situation with the lengthiness of the procedure, besides it is capable of overloading the EHCR.

---

50 Accession of the European Union to the European Convention on Human Rights, Reflection Paper prepared by Secretariat, Strasbourg, 8.2.2001.

51 For details see Accession of the European Union to the European Convention of Human Rights, Reflection paper prepared by the Secretariat, Strasbourg, 8.2.2001, D 6-II /2001/, 02, at 8.

52 Bown, 'The First Five Years of the Court of the First Instance and Appeals to the Court of Justice, Assessment and statistics', ECML Rev., 1995, No 32, at 743-749.

53 Supra note 50.

Regardless of those controversial questions and the methods for their solution, there remains the question of the effectiveness of that step as such. The eligibility of the accession was discussed for the first time in the late 1970's, i.e. almost 30 years ago, in the time when neither the Charter nor a mere coherent list of human rights protected at the EC level existed. The European Convention, in principle, does not regulate economic, social, cultural and modern rights, and less so the EU citizens' rights. On the other hand, the Charter within its factual effectiveness brings in a new standard of the protection of the entitlements of the individual, which considerably reaches beyond the *de minimis* standard envisaged by the Convention. Under these circumstances, the question of accession to the European Convention of Human Rights and Freedoms should definitely be considered in connection with the EU Charter of Fundamental Rights.

Under all circumstances, it is necessary to keep in mind that the importance of the accession of the Communities/Union to the European Convention, although it is a document which is less modern and embraces fewer categories of human rights, remains still very significant, especially if we take into account that it brings the standard of protection of human rights *de minimis* in the pan-European region. The creation of the mechanism for the enforcement of the Charter of the EU in the form of special proceedings in this connection seems to be a proper step for the construction of the highest standard of the protection of the individuals' rights in the European Union area.

Nevertheless, should it be only accession to the Convention, without the Charter's own specific control mechanism being created, the significance of the Charter would be rather political than legal. If both these steps were carried out simultaneously, i.e. the introduction of a control mechanism at the EU level and the accession to the Convention, then certainly an undesirable duplicity would appear. In the case of ensuring an effective control mechanism at the EU level, the accession to the Convention would be unnecessary, because the Charter itself cumulates nearly all the rights comprised in the Convention and besides its own norms that reach beyond the scope of the minimum standard guaranteed by the Convention.

It is apparent that a successful solution to this dilemma is actually a political issue rather than a legal one, namely, on the future direction of the Union, especially about what level of human rights protection do the supranational entities intend to ensure and if those rights will create a real priority and basic value, as declared in the Preamble of the Charter and in Article Ia of the Treaty of Lisbon.[54]

---

54 Article I a of the Treaty of Lisbon provides: 'The Union is founded on the values of respect for human dignity, freedom, democracy, equality, the rule of law and respect for human rights, including the rights of persons belonging to minorities. These values are common to Member States in a society in which pluralism, non-discrimination, tolerance, justice, solidarity and equality between women and men prevail.'

In this respect, it is indisputable that should the Charter become an effective instrument for human rights protection (and not merely a declaration of objectives, values and principles), it requires certain modification to its material provisions, as well as the creation of its own mechanism of the judicial control. This judicial procedure may be designed alternatively. One option is a special proceeding for violation of the rights granted by the Charter as a new kind of action (incorporated into the text of the Treaty of Lisbon). Another possibility is the enlargement of the Charter itself, so that it will include provisions of a procedural character to regulate procedures for violation of rights protected by this catalogue of human rights at the Union level.[55] Such a solution would be analogical to the European Convention of Human Rights, which also regulates procedural questions within this instrument of rights as such.

The absenting possibility of effective enforcement of the rights articulated by the Charter in all cases of their infringement, respectively hindering conditions for their enforcement in certain cases, does not ensure a sufficient level of individuals' rights protection, and consequently would even mean a weakening of the democratic dimension of the Union, which could be in the future perceived as a key problem within the framework of the still deepening European integration.

[55] For details see Šišková, N.: Dimenze ochrany lidskych prav v EU, 'ASPI', Prague (CZ), 2003, at 199-200.

CHAPTER 2

Fundamental Rights in the European Union

Rainer Arnold

I The Protection of the Fundamental Rights is the Nucleus of Contemporary Constitutionalism: the Anthropocentric Approach

The legal orders of the European Community and of the European Union have become *constitutional orders*.[1] Even if this term is not used by the Reform Treaty of Lisbon, which shall enter into force instead of the European Constitution by the next European Parliament elections in 2009, the existing structure of the EC/EU strongly differs from that of a traditional international organisation. One of the main reasons for such a characterisation is the fact that supranational law has a direct effect on the individual's freedom.

Neither the EU nor EC are states but in many respects the structure of these orders are similar to that of a state. National competences have been largely transferred to the supranational level where they are exercised by multinational institutions in a Europe-wide dimension. The transfer of these competences (called in some constitutional orders 'transfer of sovereignty')[2] has opened the formerly closed state systems[3] and by this given way to a direct vertical impact of supranational power on the individual.

Modern constitutionalism in its anthropocentric approach[4] requires as its primary finality the observance of the Fundamental Rights as the very basis of the personal and social existence of the individual. The need for protection corresponds to the fact that public power – state power as well as supranational power – is able to affect the individual's freedom. Therefore, the EU Treaty (with the EC as its supranational Pillar I) has to establish and maintain an efficient Fundamental Rights protection system which satisfies all modern requirements.

II Unwritten Fundamental Rights as General Principles of Community Law

Neither the EC nor the EU Treaty has laid down written Fundamental Rights. This was due to the fact that at the beginning these treaties were regarded rather as technical, executive agreements. This can also be seen from the terminology used for the legal acts as regulations or directives, terms more characteristic for the executive than the legislative sphere. At that time, the

* Prof. Dr. Rainer Arnold is a Jean Monnet Professor on European Law and holder of the Chair of Public Law and Economic Administrative Law at the University of Regensburg, Germany.

1 See R. Arnold, 'European Constitutional Law – an emerging concept in the second half of the twentieth century', in: Tulane Civil & European Law Forum, New Orleans, 1999, p. 49-64

2 As Articles 23 and 24 of the German Basic Law do; see also R. Arnold, Právní rozhledy (Evropské právo) 1998/1, p. 2-4.

3 Expression used by the German Constitutional Court, vol. 37, 2711.

4 For this term, see R. Arnold, Profili di giurisprudenza costituzionale – I sistemi Tedesco, austriaco e francese, Trieste 1990, p. 3.

dynamism inherent to European integration and the development of a Common Market was not esteemed to affect seriously the individual freedom.

However, in the sixties, the idea of the Fundamental Rights was taken up by the judges of the European Court of Justice. This period coincided with the recognition of the very particular structure of the supranational order: in 1964, the famous *Costa/ENEL* decision[5] made clear that the EEC legal order was of a constitutional character. The decision did not use the term of the constitutional law but nevertheless outlined the very structures of such a type of order. Soon after this statement, the *Stauder* case[6] raised the question of whether a guarantee of dignity of man exists in the EEC legal order. In this case, a regulation requiring the disclosure of personal data for getting cheap butter as a support for poor people had to be interpreted according to dignity as a fundamental right. This decision gave the signal for a rich jurisprudence developing a great number of fundamental rights in the form of unwritten principles.

III The Inspiration Sources for the Judicial Development of Fundamental Rights

The judges of the European Court of Justice stated in a number of decisions that Fundamental Rights exist as unwritten principles in Community law. These principles were derived from the Member States constitutions as well as from international instruments protecting humans' rights. The common constitutional tradition in Europe was regarded as the ideological basis for finding such rights in the unwritten supranational legal order.[7]

The judges considered these rights as a part of the invisible legal order of the Communities, which had to be explicitly formulated in their judgments. The argument of the judges was clear: the Communities composed of Member States have autonomous constitutional spheres but are historically, ideologically and legally integrated, linked together with a homogeneous cultural context. In history, the French Revolution and the Declaration of 1789 created a fundamental rights tradition. By the example of the Belgium Constitution of 1831, the fundamental rights idea spread all over Europe.

Therefore, it is justified to speak, as the ECJ judges did, of a common constitutional tradition in Europe.[8] This has been an adequate basis for stating that the fundamental rights in the Member States' constitutions must be common in their concepts with the unwritten fundamental rights of the community. National constitutional law was not regarded as a legal source applicable on the supranational level but as a *source of inspiration* which legitimized the Luxem-

[5] Case 6/64, ECR 1964, p. 1151.

[6] ECR 1969, p. 419.

[7] ECR 1978, p. 629.

[8] See ECR 1969, p. 1419.

burg judges to take over national law concepts in the field of fundamental rights for their own legal order.

The judges used, as a second source of inspiration, the international instruments, in particular the European Convention of Human Rights,[9] as an expression of a common European legal conviction binding the Member States.[10] Indeed, this Convention has binding force on all the Member States.

IV The German Federal Constitutional Court and its Relation with the European Court of Justice in Fundamental Rights Matters

The Federal Constitutional Court of Germany describes its role with respect to EC/EU law as a partner in a cooperation process with the European Court of Justice. In the *Maastricht* Decision,[11] the German court underlined this cooperation link with the Luxembourg court which had been determined, in the field of Fundamental Rights, by the *Solange II* Decision:[12] it is up to the ECJ to control supranational legal acts under the supranational Fundamental Rights while the task of the national constitutional court is to control, abstractly, the existence of an adequate Fundamental Rights protection for the individual at the EC/EU level.

A further question of the relations between these two courts in this field is the problem of whether the Federal Constitutional Court underlies the obligation to address the Luxembourg Court in the context of Article 234 of the EC Treaty. Until now, the Constitutional Court has not yet practised a preliminary question under this provision. It is commonly said that the Court is reticent to do so. However, it must be said that the Constitutional Courts are courts in the sense of Article 234 III of the EC Treaty whose decisions are definite and cannot be challenged by an appeal. The Court itself has confirmed, in two decisions, that it underlies this procedure, in the first *Solange* Decision of 1974[13] as well as in the so-called 'Perhaps (*Vielleicht*)' Decision of 1979.[14] In summary, it can be said that the Federal Constitutional Court is obliged to launch preliminary questions to the European Court of Justice in order to get an authoritative interpretation of EC law whose application is the object of a constitutional dispute.

---

9 See ECR 1979, p. 3727.

10 The binding force results from international law while the internal effect of the Convention is regulated by national constitutional law.

11 Report, vol. 89, p. 155.

12 Report, vol. 73, p. 339.

13 Report, vol. 37, p. 282.

14 Report, vol. 52, p. 187-202; Franz C. Mayer, Das Bundesverfassungsgericht und die Verpflichtung zur Vorlage an den Europäischen Gerichtshof, WHI-Paper, 20-02(2002), (http://whi-berlin.de/vorlagen/httm, p. 15-17).

The Constitutional Courts of Europe are divided on this question. In line with the Community position are the Austrian and the Belgian Constitutional Courts while the Italian and Spanish Constitutional Courts seem to be more hesitant to undergo the Article 234 procedure.[15]

It should also be mentioned that the Federal Constitutional Court in Germany has stated a violation of the German Constitution by the Federal Administrative Court (a violation of the guarantee of the legal judge embodied in Article 101 Basic Law) because this Court failed to make preliminary rulings. The specific argumentation of the Constitutional Court was that by omitting to address the ECJ, no adequate consideration of the supranational Fundamental Rights had taken place. The German Administrative Court had applied only a national perspective without reference to the EC Fundamental Rights. Thus, the Constitutional Court stated that the case was not well treated by applying only the national perspective without consideration of the supranational law, methods and in particular Fundamental Rights. The fact that the Luxembourg Court had not been involved under Article 234 EC Treaty had as a consequence that the EC Fundamental Rights were not sufficiently respected. In this decision, a direct link between the protection of Fundamental Rights and the preliminary rulings procedure had been pointed out.[16]

V Fundamental Rights as Primary Law

General principles of Community law embodying fundamental rights have the same rank as primary law, superior to secondary law. This means that all the actions of the EC institutions have to comply with these fundamental rights. In particular, legislative acts as regulations or directives must be in conformity with these rights. In case of controversy, the European Court of Justice and the EC Tribunal of First Instance have to review these legal acts and may have to annul them.[17]

---

[15] See. Karl Korinek, Die Praxis der österreichischen Gerichte mit dem Vorabentscheidungsverfahren; R. Arnold, Die Beziehung der Verfassungsgerichte der EU-Mitgliedstaaten zum Europäischen Gerichtshof der EG; S.Pross, Das deutsche Bundesverfassungsgericht und das Vorabentscheidungsverfahren; L.TIchy, Vorabentscheidungsverfahren vor dem EuGH und die tschechischen Gerichte; sowie B. Banaszkiewicz, Zum Verhältnis von nationaler Verfassungsgerichtsbarkeit und EuGH, in: Das Vorabentscheidungsverfahren und die nationalen Gerichte, Sammelband, Konferenz des Verfassungsgerichts der Tschechischen Republik, 3.12.2004, Praha 2005; see also The position of the constitutional courts following integration into the European Union, International Conference, Slovenia, Bled, 30.09.-2.10.2004, Ljubljana 2005.

[16] Federal Constitutional Court, decision of 9th of January 2001 (1 BVerfG 1036/99), Europäische Grundrechte Zeitschrift 2001, p. 150.

[17] See Article 230 EC Treaty.

VI From Unwritten to Written Fundamental Rights

1 Article 6 § 2 of the EU Treaty

In 1993, the Treaty of Maastricht created the European Union and modified the name of the European Community transforming it from the European Economic Community into the European Community. The Treaty establishing the European Union introduced Article 6, which is of a real constitutional character. This article establishes in its para. 1 a clause of homogeneity which prescribes that the EU and Member States have to be based on common fundamental values: Democracy, Rule of Law and Fundamental Rights. Para. 3 of the same Article guarantees the identity of the Member States. What is important in our context: This Article establishes in its para. 2 the obligation for the EU/EC institutions to observe the European Convention of Human Rights as well as the general principles of the Community law which have been developed by the supranational judges in the field of fundamental rights.

It shall be noted that the European Community as a legal subject has not been able to join the Strasbourg Convention in lack of any competence for such a step. The European Court of Justice denied, in an advisory opinion made under Article 300 § 6 of the EC Treaty, the possibility of a formal adherence.[18] But Article 6 para. 2 of the EU Treaty establishes the unilateral obligation for the supranational institutions to observe the ECHR and in particular follow its interpretation by the European Court of Human Rights. Thus, no formal international law obligation has been created so that the judgments of the European Court of Justice are not submitted to the review by the Strasbourg Court.[19]

But what has been even more important is that Article 6, para. 2, EU Treaty established in primary law the obligation to apply the general principals as developed by the Luxemburg judges. Similar to the traditional style of the English judges when formulating common law, the Luxemburg judges 'discovered' the common Community principles, but did not 'invent' them.

This was a first step towards written fundamental rights. No detailed catalogue of rights has been introduced into the EU Treaty but the obligation to apply these general principles has been established in primary Community law.

2 The Elaboration of the Fundamental Rights Charter by the First Convention

A further step in positivising the fundamental rights protection in the European Union was the creation of a so-called Convention with the task to elaborate a written Fundamental Rights Charter. This Convention, consisting of preponderantly parliamentarians from the European Parliament and especially from the member and candidate states, worked out under the presi-

[18] ECR 1996, I-1759.

[19] Article 6 para. 2 of the Lisbon Reform Treaty gives way for a formal adherence of the EU to the ECHR.

dency of the former Federal President of Germany, Professor Herzog, a Charter containing over fifty articles. Although not yet in force, the Charter already exercised important influence as an inspirational source within the European Union.

A second Convention elaborated the text of a Constitution for Europe; part two of this document should have been this Charter of the Fundamental Rights proclaimed in December 2000 in Nice, at the occasion of a European Council Summit. The Constitution, already signed by all the Member States, failed as a consequence of the negative votes in the French and Dutch referenda.

In June 2007, the European Council in Brussels decided to prepare, instead of a Constitution, a Reform Treaty which makes a reference to the Fundamental Rights Charter proclaimed in Nice and, seven years later, proclaimed again by the European Parliament.[20]

The hitherto purely informal character of the Charter would be transformed into a legally binding text in the moment when the Reform Treaty enters into force. With the exception of Great Britain and Poland, the Member States have already declared acceptance of it. The Charter should bind the EU institutions as well as the Member States when applying or executing EU/EC law.[21]

VII The Charter of Fundamental Rights Charter of the European Union and its Basic Characteristics

1 The Charter as a European Document

The EU Fundamental Rights Charter is inspired by various sources of European instruments of fundamental rights. Thus, the national constitutional tradition, the European Convention of Human Rights, the European Social Charter as well as the Community law itself have influenced the contents of the Charter.

Chapter I on human dignity seems to be essentially inspired by Article 1 of the German Basic Law as well as by the Article 3 of the European Convention of Human Rights prohibiting torture and degrading treatment. Chapter II on the classic freedoms seems to have been modelled after the constitutional guarantees of the Member States as well as the jurisprudence of the European Court of Justice, which has taken over from the Member States many of their fundamental rights concepts. Furthermore, Chapter IV on social rights has drawn much inspiration from the European Charter of Social Rights and Chapter V on the European Union Citizenship reaffirms the rights laid down in the written EC Treaty. Finally, Chapter VI on justice is quite similar to the core provisions, Article 6 and 7, of the European Convention of Human Rights.

[20] Proclamation by the President of the European Parliament, the Council and the Commission on Dec. 12, 2007, OJ of Dec 14, 2007, C 303/1.

[21] See Article 51 para. 1 of the Charter.

It can easily be said that the Charter is an expression of a common European fundamental rights tradition, which has grown during the second half of the XXth century.[22] However, it is clear that the Charter is a part of the European Community primary law and as such an autonomous legal source with its exclusive normative basis in Community law itself. The interpretation of the Charter must basically follow Community standards but must also adequately take into consideration, according to the harmonization clauses of the Charter, Article 52 para. 3 and 4, the jurisprudence of the European Court of Human Rights as well as the constitutional concepts of the Member States insofar as rights drawn from these sources are concerned.

2 The Fundamental Rights Charter as an Anthropocentric Document which Fulfills the Requirements of Modern Constitutionalism

The modern, anthropocentric approach of the Charter reflects various facts: thus, the Preamble places man at the centre of all public power activities so that the final objective of Community as well as Member States' activities is the protection of the dignity, autonomy and freedom of the individual. Furthermore, the individual's protection as effectuated by the Charter is a very efficient one: the Charter covers all the modern dangers for the individual (biomedicine, data protection, environmental protection etc.)[23] and limits the restriction of the fundamental rights in an essential way. Thus, fundamental rights can only be limited, according to Article 52 para. 1, by public authority acting with the authorization of a law, respecting the principle of proportionality and the very essence of the fundamental rights. This modern safeguard of this sphere of liberty is very similar to that of the German Constitution which has been assumed on the Community level by the European Court of Justice[24] and which is now confirmed by the Charter.

3 The Charter as an Expression of the Modern Concept of Rule of Law

The modern concept of the Rule of Law as developed in continental Europe is essentially based not only on legality of executive action but, in particular, on the constitutionality of legislation. Thus, the primacy of the Constitution over whatever public power activity is recognized. Besides that, the Rule of Law of today is closely linked to the fundamental rights themselves. Thus, the concept of the Rule of Law is value-oriented.

---

22 See R. Arnold, 'A Fundamental Rights Charter for the European Union', in Tulane Civil & European Law Forum, New Orleans, 15/16 (2000 – 2001), p. 43-59.

23 See Article 3 (2), Article 8 and Article 37 of the Charter.

24 ECR 1979, p. 3727.

The Rule of Law as developed by the European Court of Justice[25] is mentioned in the Charter and some of its elements, as for example, the right to good administration (Article 41), have been introduced into the Charter itself.

4 Supremacy of the Fundamental Rights Protection Instead of Supremacy of Community Law

The Charter contains a clause, which confirms that the most far-reaching protection shall apply even if other documents different from the Charter, for example a national Constitution, should be applied. This clause of 'optimalization' can be seen in Article 53 of the Charter and be regarded as an important contribution to the effectiveness of the fundamental rights idea.

5 The Application and the Entry Into Force of the Charter

The Charter binds, according to Article 51 para. 1, the EC/EU institutions in a broad sense (that is, not only the organs enumerated in Article 7 para. 1 EC Treaty) as well as the Member States when executing Community/Union law. As it is known, the great majority of Community legal acts have to be executed by national authorities, so that the application of the Charter will be far-reaching.

The Reform Treaty of Lisbon makes reference to the Charter,[26] which has been proclaimed on the 12th of December 2007 by the European Parliament, a document which shall replace, with the entry into force of the Reform Treaty, the Charter proclaimed on the 7th of December 2000 in Nice (Article 54 of the Charter 2007). The proclamation in Nice did not give any legal effect to the Charter, yet it has proved to be an important inspirational source. The Tribunal of the First Instance of the European Communities as well as the Advocates General have repeatedly referred to the Charter while the European Court of Justice itself avoids arousal of the impression that it is acting *ultra vires.*

The Charter as proclaimed by the EP will obtain a normatively binding character with the entry into force of the Reform Treaty. It will be incorporated functionally into this Treaty by reference.

VIII The Charter More in Detail

The complex contents of the Charter cannot be completely analyzed here. Nevertheless, some remarks seem to be important.[27]

1. Dignity of man as laid down in Chapter I is the basic value, the fundament of the individual's autonomy and freedom. The Community recognizes

---

[25] See R. Geiger (note 12), Article 220 notes 25-31.

[26] Article 1 (8) referring to the new Article 6 of the EU Treaty.

[27] See also R. Arnold (note 18).

this fact and obliges the public power to protect this value. Dignity must be seen as a real fundamental right and not only as a very general orientation concept, as it is disputed in the Member States. Of course, the contents of dignity are not precisely definable and must be conceived in the light of the Member States constitutional jurisprudence. The constitutional jurisprudence of the new democracies in Central and Eastern Europe will have great influence on the interpretation of this basic guarantee by the European Court of Justice because most of these countries, in contrast to the Western systems, have embodied dignity into their constitutional texts.

Dignity is not restricted. Human dignity is intangible; therefore, no restriction is possible nor the weighing up of dignity with another value. The same must be said for the prohibition of torture and degrading treatment, which are specific expressions of human dignity. The jurisprudence of the Strasbourg Court on Article 3 of the European Convention of Human Rights as well as the interpretation of the Biomedicine Convention will have much influence on Chapter I. Besides that, the right of life including the prohibition of death penalty is embodied in this First Chapter because it is closely linked to human dignity. It is not excluded that controversy on whether the embryo is protected by the guarantees of human dignity as well as of life will reappear on the Community level.

2. Chapter II reflects the fundamental rights tradition as developed in the Member States as well as on the Community level by the jurisprudence getting inspired by national constitutional law. In this chapter the classic rights as freedom of expression, Article 11, of assembly or of association, Article 12, the right to property, Article 17, etc. are guaranteed.

3. Chapter 3 on *equality* has three dimensions: a *traditional* one, which forbids arbitrariness and discrimination, Article 21; a *modern* one in a sense that 'positive' action is allowed for promoting the position of a disadvantaged gender (Article 23) in order to compensate this deficit by preferential treatment. A further *modern* dimension reflects from the fact that equality is also understood as a basis for the protection and promotion of persons who are potentially weaker than the average members of the society: the handicapped, the aged person and children (Article 24-26).

4. *Solidarity* – a term which derives from the French legal culture – is a Chapter (Ch.4) on social rights essentially oriented towards the Council of Europe Social Rights Charter in force since 1965 (with revised version, in force since 1999). It has been very controversial whether to introduce this type of rights or not. Great Britain and the Scandinavian states were sceptical (the latter for not undermining their own high social standards), but in particular France and Germany supported this intention. Thus, the Fundamental Rights Charter is the first international document, which combines individual freedoms and social rights. These guarantees address predominantly the Member States obliging them to fulfill the requirements laid down in this Chapter. This is an appeal to the national legislature to complete social standards according to the Charter

and to avoid the reduction or even the elimination of such rights. Seen from the German standpoint, no major issue of this Chapter is unfulfilled in Germany. This is a Charter, which guarantees a common social standard as a minimum.

5. Chapter V reassumes what has been laid down explicitly by the EC Treaty (Article 17-22) as rights of the *European Union citizens*: the right to have his/her domicile in whatever Member State of the European Union (Article 45), to be treated equally with the nationals of where the domicile has been chosen, Article 21 para. 2), to participate in local and EP elections in an active and passive way (Article 39 and 40), being protected by the European Ombudsman (Article 43), having a right to diplomatic and consular protection from whatever Member State (Article 46) etc. Article 41 of the Charter is an important provision which is regarded as a citizen right: the right to good administration. This Scandinavian type of right is conceived, for example in Germany, as an element of the Rule of Law but has been formulated in the Charter as a subjective right which includes the right to be adequately heard by the administration, to get a motivated act if it encroaches on the individual's freedom, to have access to the documents of personal concern (Article 42) and so on.

6. The Chapter VI on *justice* reassumes the guarantees developed by the Member States and laid down in particular in Article 6 and 7 of the European Convention on Human Rights: fair trial (Article 47), nulla poena sine lege (Article 49), ne bis in idem (Article 50), the right to be heard before the courts, the presumption of innocence (Article 48) and so on. These fundamental rights have their importance for Pillar III of the European Union. They are completed by rights formulated in secondary law e.g. as a Pillar III Framework Decision on the rights of the suspects, which is in preparation.[28]

IX How to Realize Fundamental Rights Protection

Judicial realization of the Charter rights is possible in particular with the action for annulment of a Community legal act, which is not conforming to the Charter (Article 230 EC Treaty). The preliminary ruling mechanism of Article 234 EC Treaty is also relevant as well as other instruments in this context. If national courts are involved, the Charter must be respected as directly applicable primary law of the Union. It is evident that the principle of supremacy of Community/Union law over national law applies.

[28] In 2004, a Commission proposal was elaborated upon but had not been accepted until now.

X General Principles of Community Law and Written Fundamental Rights: A Parallelism

The European Court of Justice will continue to develop unwritten fundamental rights in the form of general principles of Community law. The existence of the Charter will not exclude this judicial action. Rights which are not written in the Charter can be developed by jurisprudence. Furthermore, Great Britain and Poland though not having accepted the Charter will be bound by this judge-made law in the field of fundamental rights.

XI The Accession of the European Union to the European Convention of Human Rights

The most vigorous document of fundamental rights protection in Europe is the European Convention on Human Rights with its additional protocols. As it is known, the attempt of the European Community to adhere to the Convention was stopped by the European Court of Justice explaining that for such a step an explicit competence should be written in the EC/EU Treaty.[29] In the Constitution Project and now in the Reform Treaty such an authorization will be laid down. The Additional Protocol XIV to the European Convention of Human Rights enables the Community/Union to adhere to the ECHR.

Article 6 (2) of the EU Treaty contains the unilateral attachment of the European Community/Union to the Convention by obliging the Community institutions to follow it. This unilateral obligation to obey the Convention does not imply the possibility for the European Court of Human Rights to control ECJ decisions. After a formal adherence of the European Community/Union, the competences of the European Court of Human Rights will extend to revise the Luxembourg Court decisions.

XII Convention Rights as an Examination Criterion for Community Law?

The European Court of Human Rights has repeatedly stated that the Council of Europe Member State's obligations to respect the Charter do not end with the entry of the State into the European Community/Union. The transfer of competences from a state to the supranational level does not exempt it from the observance of the Convention rights.[30] Thus, State authorities when executing Community law can be controlled by national Constitutional law and Community law as well as the law of the ECHR. The position of the Strasbourg

---

[29] See note 14.

[30] *Matthews v. UK*, para. 32, 34.

Court is very clear in this respect. But it shall be mentioned that the *Bosphorus* case of 2005[31] declared that EC acts are presumed to be in conformity with the EC fundamental rights and therefore not revised under the ECHR except in evident cases. Thus, the EC protection is deemed to be equivalent to that of the ECHR.

Mutual confidence towards fundamental rights systems of the EC on the one hand and the ECHR on the other hand is necessary for harmonizing the protection levels throughout Europe. Confidence is also justified by the fact that the protection standards are similar and converging more and more. It seems that this concept is very close to that of the *Solange II* developed by the German Constitutional Court.[32]

XIII Fragmentation or Confirmation of Fundamental Rights Protection in Europe?

National authorities of Member States, which execute Community/EU law, are submitted to the complex variety of guarantees: national constitutions, the European Convention of Human Rights, the Charter of Fundamental Rights of the European Union, international covenants, and probably also regional constitutions in federal systems.

It is important to harmonize the procedures as well as substantive protection standards. The European Union Charter contains, as already mentioned, harmonization clauses as to the rights derived from the ECHR and the Member States Constitutions (Article 52 para. 3 and 4).

If the harmonization process is going on with success, the multiplicity of fundamental rights in Europe is an element of confirmation and not of fragmentation weakening the protection idea. The convergence of the standards leads, especially in the field of fundamental rights and of the Rule of Law, to the emergence of *transnational constitutional principles* throughout Europe. The body of these transnational principles constitutes an important part of a newly developing European Constitutional Law.

31 Dec. ECHR June 30, 2005, 45036/98.

32 ECR 73, p. 339.

CHAPTER 3

European Constitutional Law

Rainer Arnold

1 The Reform Treaty of Lisbon

When addressing the subject of European Constitutional Law, the first question must be: can this term be further used? Is this possible despite the fact that the project of a Constitution for Europe has failed? The answer is affirmative. Though a formal European Constitution has not been adopted, the basic provisions and principles of European Community Law did not loose their character as *substantive* Constitutional Law. Even the Reform Treaty of Lisbon, avoiding the use of the terms Constitution and Constitutional Law, contains, in its substance, Constitutional Law. Therefore, it is justifiable to continue with reflections on the existence and the features of European Constitutional Law.

2 European Constitutional Law – An Emerging Concept Without a Commonly Accepted Definition

As it is well known, the debate on using the term of Constitutional Law for supranational norms has been launched by the European Court of Justice. In its decision Les Verts[1] and its opinion on the European Economic Area,[2] the Court qualified EC law as *constitutional* and has incited many authors, especially in Germany, to reflect on a general transfer of this term, the use of which was traditionally limited to states, to the supranational level. It shall also be pointed out that the German Federal Constitutional Court, long before the quoted jurisprudence of the ECJ, denominated the EEC Treaty as a sort of 'Constitution'.[3]

It is not surprising that the particularities of the EC legal order have accelerated this process. The three elements of supranationality – the autonomy of the EC legal order, the direct validity of EC law and its supremacy over national law – are phenomena, which cannot be found, in principle, at the level of international relations between sovereign states but only in the internal order of a state. Though neither the European Union nor the European Communities can be qualified as states, state – like mechanisms and structural elements of a state can be found in the supranational order. This seemed to be the reason for using the term of Constitutional Law in this respect, a perspective which has been vehemently disputed but which has found an increasing number of adherents.[4]

---

* Prof. Dr. Rainer Arnold is Jean Monnet Professor on European Law and holder of the Chair of Public Law and Economic Administrative Law at the University of Regensburg, Germany.

1 Case 294/83 [1986] ECR 1339, note 23.

2 Opinion 1/91 [1991] ECR I-6078, note 21.

3 In 1967, see Court Reports volume 22, pp. 293, 296.

4 BVerfG, Court Reports volume 22, pp. 293, 296; see also Christian Calliess in Calliess/Ruffert EUV/EGV, Commentary, 3rd Edition 2007, Art. 1, notes 25-38; R. Arnold, 'European Constitutional Law: Some Reflections on a Concept that Emerged in the 2nd Half of the Twentieth Century', in: Tulane European & Civil Law Forum, vol. 14/1999, pp. 49-69.

3 Formal and Substantive (Functional) Constitutional law

Before reflecting on the legitimacy of naming EC/EU law a sort of 'Constitutional Law', the difference between formal and substantive (functional) Constitutional law shall be taken into consideration. Formal Constitutional Law has a specific character in contrast to ordinary law with reference to its *form*. Substantive or functional Constitutional Law is specific towards 'normal' ordinary law for its *content*. Which particularities does *formal Constitutional Law* have?

a) The three elements of a formal Constitution

'Formal' in this sense has a specific meaning which has been developed by the continental Constitutional Law: Three elements are linked to this term, a formal, a functional and a genetic element: (1) The Constitution must consist of one or more 'formal' documents which codify the main part of Constitutional Law, (2) its hierarchical rank must be superior to ordinary, daily legislation, and (3) it must have been created by the constitution-making power, normally the people.

First of all, a formal Constitution is embodied in one or several documents which have a legal force superior to ordinary legislation. The type of a formal Constitutional Law is common to most states. This is a result of the growing recognition of Constitutional Law as the 'supreme law of the land', the primacy of the Constitution having been accepted as an indispensable element of Rule of Law.

As history shows, the model of a Constitution being normatively equivalent to the ordinary legislation was also known, for example in the Italian Statuto Albertino.[5] And there are countries such as Great Britain without a formal Constitution so that ordinary Acts of Parliament with an important institutional impact build up a multiple, parliament-made Constitution. This is substantive, not formal Constitutional Law. This type of law is written, formalized in Acts of Parliament, and with a constitutional content.

However, in principle, it can be stated that formal Constitutional Law is characterised by its formalized content, its superiority to ordinary legislation, and by the fact that it is created by the '*pouvoir constituant*'.

b) The characteristics of a formal Constitution in detail

(1) The element of form

Formal Constitutional Law does not require the existence of one unique document, a Charter which comprises all the constitutional norms. This is a solution found in Germany, but in Austria, for example, the formal Constitution consists of a multiplicity of Constitutional Acts. Or, to quote the example of the Czech Republic, where besides an institutional document –the Constitution- a Fundamental Right Charter, the *Listina základných práv*, exists. Those two documents constitute the formal Czech Constitution.

---

5 See G. de Vergottini, Diritto costituzionale, 2nd ed., 200, p. 115-123.

There are also systems, such as Spain or France, in which a formal Constitution, laid down in a single text, is completed by so-called Constitutional Acts (lois organiques, leyes orgánicas). This type of legislation does not form part of the formal Constitution. They belong to the sphere of ordinary legislation, though they have, for their function to implement institutional and value concepts laid down in the Constitution, a particular status.

(2) Hierarchy

A further point seems to be important in this context: Constitutional Law is not submitted to the *lex posterior rule,* which governs the relation between the different Acts of Parliament as ordinary law. Formal constitutional law is hierarchically superior to ordinary law. If there is an incompatibility between formal constitutional and ordinary law, the latter is void or annullable by (Constitutional) Courts. Normally, qualified requirements exist for the reform of formal Constitutional law. There are various forms of reaction in case of controversy between constitutional and ordinary law. In summary, formal constitutional law has to be considered as the 'supreme law of the land' linked to the concept of normative hierarchy.

(3) The *'pouvoir constituant'*

A further element of formal Constitutional Law seems to be its adoption by the constitution-making power. While normal legislation is created by Parliament in a daily political process, the Constitution as a formal basic legal order of a social entity, normally a state, is created in a specific time period by those who are entitled to exercise the 'pouvoir constituant'. The concept of people's sovereignty, which has evolved as a basic legitimizing concept of the state is also relevant in our context. The adoption of a formal document as the basic legal order by the people is able to create the formal Constitution.

However, it must be stated that some of the new Central and Eastern European Constitutions have been adopted only by Parliament.[6] And, it is well known that the German Constitution of 1949 has not been submitted to the consent of the people. The reason was that the population in the Eastern German parts could not participate in the voting so that the Western part created a Basic Law as a preliminary Constitution until a general vote on a new Constitution by the united German population could occur. The Basic Law developed towards a real Constitution and was extended as such without the creation of a new Constitution in 1990 to the new Eastern parts of the former German Democratic Republic. The peoples' legitimizing will was seen by the western doctrine in an implicit process: the acceptance of the institutional system laid down in the Basic Law seemed to be expressed by the people of Western Germany when they participated in the first elections to the German *Bundestag.* The Basic Law as such was adopted by the Parliaments of the then existing Länders, the Member States of the Federation.[7]

---

6 See for Czech Republic V. Pavlíček/J. Hrebejk, Ùstava a ústavní rád Ceska Republíky, 1.dil, 1994, p. 7-10.

7 See R. Zippelius/Th. Würtenberger, Deutsches Staatsrecht, 31st ed., 2005, p. 17-20.

These are some examples of Parliaments creating formal Constitutions. The adoption of a formal Constitution can also be realized by an *international treaty*. In such a case, the fusion of several states takes place, necessarily on the basis of the international treaty which creates the formal Constitution. National Parliaments are involved in the ratification process by giving their consent to the treaty; these Parliaments can be qualified as creators of the Constitution. This would have happened if the 'Constitution of Europe', formally laid down in the international treaty, had been ratified by all the Member States of the European Union. The people's consent would not have been required except in those systems where referenda are foreseen in these matters. In states where such an obligatory requirement does not exist, a voluntarily organized referendum could have been a directly democratic support, which would have been in line with the classic aspect of people's sovereignty. It seems that the Reform Treaty of Lisbon will not be submitted to the people for consent except where a referendum is obligatory.

In summary, it can be said that the making of a formal Constitution is up to the people as an expression of sovereignty, while constitutional practice in Europe also shows models of Parliament-made constitutions accepted without protest by the people.

A different question is whether a formal constitutional document, which is part of an international treaty and adopted by national Parliaments through the ratification of the treaty, would get the peoples' consent *tacitly*. Sovereignty of the people comes hereby into effect by the acceptance of the institutional process, e.g. by participation in elections and by obeying the law, without protest and political abstention. Therefore, it can be said that the making of a formal Constitution is up to the people as an expression of its sovereignty, while the constitutional practice in Europe also shows models of parliament-made constitutions.

4 The Notion of Substantive or Functional Constitutional Law

The concept of substantive Constitutional Law, which is known in all national orders, refers to the *contents* of the provisions laid down in legal acts. If the contents are of particular importance for the institutional structure of a society and its finalities as well as its values, their constitutional character is evident.

The word 'Constitution' means to constitute a society by making it a state or, what is in nowadays also relevant, to integrate a plurality of societies into a supranational body such as the EC. This means to regulate three *aspects* essential for constitutional law: an institutional system, finalities and values. As a minimum set, it would be sufficient to determine the institutional fundaments. This is a historical type of Constitution while modern types expressly declare values especially in form of Fundamental Rights. The modern Constitutions contain, in explicit provisions, a sufficient institutional framework including organs, instruments of action, and rules on the territorial organisation. Beside that, they express, in accordance with the modern anthropocentric concept of Constitutional Law, values protecting the individual. If they are not written, which is seldom in Constitutional systems of today's Europe, the judges develop them as an unwritten part of Constitutional law. The main finalities of the state are normally expressed by the orientation of a state or a supranational body as democratic, Rule of Law oriented and so on. Therefore, these finalities are to be an addition to democracy, to realise the supremacy of the law, especially of constitutional law, often combined with details on constitutional jurisdiction, etc. Increasingly, the finality of the state to promote international relations or even to adhere to a transnational cooperation is expressed by specific provisions.

If not formal constitutional law but ordinary legislation contains rules on these issues, they have constitutional character.

Two systems where substantive constitutional law is of importance can be distinguished: the systems where formal constitutional law determines the main institutional structures and values, but leaves open, as often, important issues which are indispensable for an adequate functioning of the institutional system. Here, substantive constitutional law has a complementary function, to determine those parts of the system, which are indispensable for a coherent institutional and value system of a society. Thus, we can speak of substantive constitutional law in a *narrow sense,* which is indispensable for the determination of the basic structure of a state or a supranational body.

Substantive constitutional law in a *wider sense* are those provisions, which are not necessary for determining the institutional law and value structure but give important indications to the framework laid down in the formal Constitution. This framework is as such coherent but needs further definition. This definition can be made by the formal Constitution itself but is often entrusted to the legislator acting either in the form of normal, ordinary legislation or, observing qualified requirements, in the form of particular laws (organic laws).

5 Is the Term Constitution or Constitutional Law Limited to a State?

Is the use of the term Constitution and Constitutional Law for non-state bodies justified? Can this notion be extended beyond its traditional field of application? To give an answer to this question it is, first of all, necessary to make clear how terminology comes into existence.

A term as a word or a combination of words has the function to identify a certain phenomenon existent in reality. If there is a legal definition, a certain term is fixed with binding force. If a multinational treaty is called a Constitution, as it was foreseen for the project of a Constitution for Europe, this term is legally binding for the treaty partners after the entry into force of this treaty.

If no such definition is made by law, it is a *convention* of the society to find a name for a certain concept. Convention means that the actors of a society which are co-involved in this matter agree, explicitly or implicitly, to use this term in this context. For legal terminology, the main actors in this sense are jurists, academics, practitioners as well as politicians. Of course, the process of building up a terminological convention undergoes, for a certain time, uncertainties.

It is possible, and it has been the case with the term of Constitution in the context of supranational law that no common acceptance can be reached in a short time. It can be a long time before a due terminology will be consolidated. A striking example is the debate on whether it is possible to use the term of Constitution and Constitutional Law for the supranational institutions.

6 The Functions of a State Constitution and their Transfer to Supranational Level

The main functions of a state constitution are:
1) the creation of institutions and
2) the determination of values.

Institutional values are those which are established by a constitution as well and which combine these two categories. Thus, Democracy and Rule of Law are value-related institutional concepts: Democracy by the institution of Parliament and Rule of Law by the institution of a well-functioning justice, expressing and realizing the political self-determination of a person as well as supremacy of law as main finalities of a state.

The transfer of state powers to the supranational organs has shifted the functions of a state constitution to the multinational level. While the national constitutions are relevant for the matters remaining in the hand of the EU Member States, the relations between the EC/EU central power and the Member States or individuals are governed by primary and secondary law of the supranational EC. There is a parallelism of the functions of a constitution of the Member States and within the supranational order. The EC primary law has founded a set of institutions and a range of instruments to act and has described the effects of these actions. Beyond this institutional side, fundamental rights as values have been developed by the jurisprudence of the European Court of Justice and now written in a single document, the European Charter of Human Rights, which itself is not yet in force.

Furthermore, concepts as the 'Community of Law', an analogy to the Rule of Law clause of a state, have been developed.[8] We can observe that the legislative field, which had been under the regime of the national constitution, is now, to a great extent, transferred to the EC/EU. For all these reasons, it seems justified to use the term of constitution and constitutional law for the supranational organs.

[8] See R. Geiger, EUV/EGV Commentary, 4th ed., 2004, Art. 220, 25-31.

7 The Different Dimensions of European Constitutional Law

a) The three-level-model

European Constitutional Law is often used as a synonym for the EC/EU law but its notion seems to be wider: it comprises *three levels* of constitutional law in Europe.[9] *The first level* is that of constitutional law of the European states, not only of the EU Member States, but also of the Council of Europe Member States. *The second level* is that of EC/EU law insofar as the basic norms and principles are concerned. *The third level* is the European Convention on Human Rights, which can also be qualified as a sort of constitutional law though its form is that of an international treaty.

These three levels are autonomous, independent each of the other, but there is an internal connection between them creating *vertical* and *horizontal* mutual influences. An example of this influence in the *vertical relation* between EC/EU and Member States is the supremacy of supranational law on the national normative order including national constitutional law. At the same time, national concepts have been adopted by the ECJ when formulating fundamental rights on a basis of a common constitutional tradition.

The *vertical influence* of the European Convention of Human Rights on the Member States is also evident as the national fundamental rights protection is influenced to a great extent by the Strasbourg Convention, which requires the conformity of the Constitutional Courts' decisions of the Council of Europe Member States with the Convention. Less significant is the adoption of national concepts by the Strasbourg judges, which gives impulses to the interpretation of the convention.

The *horizontal influence* can be found in the relation between the EC/EU and the Strasburg Convention. Though the supranational institutions are not formerly bound by the European Convention of Human Rights (the observance of which results from a unilateral declaration to follow this Convention, by Article 6 II EU Treaty) the Strasburg concepts are taken into account by the jurisprudence of the ECJ and the First Instance Tribunal. Reciprocally, the Strasburg Court respects the EC/EU developed fundamental rights as it was clearly expressed by the *Bosphorus decision* of the Strasbourg Court in 2005.[10] These mutual influences lead to a considerable *convergence* within the three orders, in particular in the field of Fundamental Rights and of Rule of Law. These *transnational European principles* of Constitutional Law are emerging and form a nucleus of European Constitutional Law. Thus, we can define this body as the totality of principles common to the European Constitutional Levels.

9 See R. Arnold, The emergence of European Constitutional Law, General Report, XVIIth Congress of the International Academy of Comparative Law, ed. by K. Boele-Woelki/S. van Erp, Brussels/Utrecht 2007, pp. 763-769.

10 ECHR 2005-VI (30.6.05), number 45036/98.

8 Constitutional Law at the EC Level

It is important to look at Constitutional Law insofar as it is expressed by the EC law. What are the constitutional norms and principles in this context? A short analysis shall follow here. Let us begin with the Fundamental Rights. As it is well known, such rights have been developed since the 60's by the ECJ. With reference to a common constitutional tradition of the Member States and the European Convention of Human Rights, the Court has elaborated a long line of rights for the protection of the individual.

A judge-made Fundamental Rights Charter was created containing unwritten principles of EC law and has been assured by Article 6 II EU. This provision imposes the duty for the EU institutions to observe these general principles. The elaboration of a written EU Fundamental Rights Charter has been a certain step towards positivisation of Fundamental Rights.[11]

Not only Fundamental Rights but also aspects of Rule of Law have been developed by the jurisprudence. The requirements of a modern concept of Rule of Law as known from the Member States can also be found in EC law.[12] This modern concept is mainly based on supremacy of the Constitution, which means also primacy of the EC over national law as well as primacy over secondary EC law. While the primacy of the national constitution is assured by the national constitutional jurisdiction, the ECJ has similar competences to those of national constitutional courts. In particular, the competence to review the conformity of secondary community law with primary law and with Fundamental Rights is of great importance. Fundamental Rights are a constituent part of the modern, substantive concept of Rule of Law which goes beyond a merely formal concept valid in former periods.

9 Constitutional Law Convergence

The main fields of constitutional convergence can be found with clarity in these two areas of Fundamental Rights protection and the Rule of Law. However, there are also further elements of converging principles: one of the many examples is the principle of *subsidiarity* which is, in its basic idea, common to all EU Member States such as Germany, France, Italy, Spain or Poland. This mechanism with great importance in differentiated systems, in particular in regional and federal systems, can also be qualified as such a common European constitutional principle.

---

11 See R. Arnold, Los derechos fundamentales comunitarios y los derechos fundamentales en las Constituciones nacionales, in: F. Javier Matia, La protección de los derechos fundementales en la Unión Europea, 2002, p. 51-59, 54-55.

12 See German Constitutional Court, vol. 88, p. 310.

10 Conclusion

As it can be seen from the above explanations, it is justified to use the term Constitutional Law for the basic norms and principles of EC/EU law. These norms constitute a body of substantive constitutional law and also the Reform Treaty of Lisbon contains provisions of constitutional character. In consequence, European Constitutional Law consists of the constitutional norms and principles of three orders: the national constitutions, EC/EU law and the ECHR.

CHAPTER 4

Europeanization of the term "Constitution"

European Court of Justice and the Establishing Treaties of EC/EU

Nora Chronowski

'Our Constitution is called a democracy because power is in the hands not of a minority but of the whole people.'

(Thucydides)

'Democracy is the end; states as we have known them are but means. Achieving a stateless democracy has been one of mankind's most recurrent and noblest dreams.'

(G. F. Mancini)

'Democracy, dear friend, is not the end. Democracy, too, is a means, even if an indispensable means. The end is to try and try again, to live a life of decency, to honour our creation in the image of God, or the secular equivalent. A democracy, when all is said and done, is as good or bad as the people who belong to it.'

(J. H. H. Weiler)

The principle of democracy appears as the central element in the Antique motto and the above quoted polemics by Mancini and Weiler[1] used in the draft version of 'The Treaty Establishing a Constitution for Europe'. In my exposition on the subject, however, I could have chosen a train of thought linked to the problems of the 'constitution', 'sovereignty', 'the role of the state', 'human rights' or 'the power of the state', demonstrating the diversity of possible approaches for the reason that the European integration process makes and even forces the representatives of science to re-evaluate and update the terminology and relations regarding numerous constitutional principles, institutions and dogmas.

The content of specialised terms tends to be of a pluralistic nature. Thus, the task before the science of constitutional law is 'merely' to provide a flexible and up-to-date framework of interpretation to enable the theoretical and practical explanation of the content in a way that regarding the 'essence', it shall function as a consensus-based point of orientation. That given it is virtually irrelevant whether a particular principle, institution or term is placed as a purpose, an instrument, a subject or a predicate in the sentences we write. The conceptual culture of the so-called European constitutional law is currently evolving and as such poses a challenge for the classical dogma of constitutional law. However, the concepts of constitutional law can be applied in the European Union's constitutional law, and integration-process affects the content of the constitutional law of the Member States. This volume illustrates the previously mentioned mutual influence through issues forming part of the areas of constitutional law that – due to the integration process – need to be revised.

The theoretical issues under review are as follows: To what extent can the community jurisdiction be regarded as constitutional and what expectations should the constitution for the European Union meet? How can the division of power and the principle of democracy be interpreted in the European integration

---

* Dr. Nora Chronowski, Ph.D. is associate professor at the Faculty of Law, University of Pécz, Hungary.

1 G.F. Mancini: Europe: 'The Case for Statehood.' European Law Journal March 1998 p. 42., J.H.H. Weiler: Europe: 'The Case Against the Case for Statehood.' European Law Journal March 1998 p. 60.

process? How does the protection of fundamental rights develop on a European level?

1 Concept of the Constitution

The science of public law has related the concept of the constitution to that of the state, defining it as the norm to establish the basic legal order of a society organised as a state. For this reason, the use of the concept of a constitution related to the European Union, whose integration has not yet developed enough to achieve the status of a state[2], may need some further explanation. However, one has to consider that legal definitions are not everlasting, cohesive or indisputable. The concept of a constitution itself might contain several layers of connotation, depending upon which attributes of it the emphasis is placed. The word constitution can signify a set of norms as well as a political status quo or organised group of functions, but it can also be the document itself.[3] Therefore, constitution in its broader sense might be connected to entities not being considered as a state but being based upon and working according to a settled fundamental agreement.[4]

Thus, one might venture the presumption that a European Constitution is replacing the contractual basis of the EU. Presently, considering the treaties of Maastricht, Amsterdam and Nice as well as the successes of the European Convention, or the results of the Treaty of Lisbon, this presumption is not utopian.[5] However, in the case of European integration the difficulty is not only the ambiguous definition of the constitution, but also the different constitutional traditions inside the integration[6], as well as the lack of consent in the necessity of the constitution. Thus, the question cannot be separated from the preconceptions of constitutional politics.[7]

---

2 Roland Bieber – Jürgen Schwarze: Verfassungsentwicklung in der Europäischen Gemeinschaft. Nomos, Baden-Baden 1984, p. 20.

3 Christoph Möllers: Verfassunggebende Gewalt – Verfassung – Konstitutionalisierung. In: Armin von Bogdandy (ed): Europäisches Verfassungsrecht. Springer Verlag, Berlin-Heidelberg 2003, p. 1.

4 The dispute is not finished at all, because there are several reasons for the concept of constitution being related to states only. See Summary of Gilbert Gornig's speech when being conferred an honorary doctor. Judit Zeller: Szükség van-e európai alkotmányra? Díszdoktori előadás kritikai felhanggal [Is there a real need for a European Constitution? Presentation of Professor Gilbert Gornig on the occasion of his 'honoris causa' doctoral ceremony] Európai Jog issue 2003/3, p. 28.

5 Péter Paczolay: Az Európai Közösségek Bíróságának politikai legitimációja. [Political legitimacy of the ECJ] Politikatudományi Szemle issue 1999/4, p. 15. 'Two major characteristics of establishing constitutionalism are: the legitimacy of the government is based on the people's consent and public power not based on the constitution shall not exist.'

6 Roland Bieber – Jürgen Schwarze: op. cit. pp. 15-16.

7 Möllers: op. cit. p. 1.

2 Treaties as Constitution in the ECJ's Case-Law

From the aspect of public law, it is a key question whether the European Union and the complete regulation of the Communities, the *acquis communitaire* might be considered as a constitutional system. However, legislation in the Communities still lacks the participative mechanisms of modern democracies.[8] Whilst acknowledging that the debate cannot be finished yet, still, there are many reasons[9] for the treaties establishing the European Communities and the European Union and the treaties of Amsterdam and Nice modifying them to be considered a constitution. This approach is in accordance with the opinion of the European Court of Justice.[10] The progress of the treaties' 'constitutionalisation' manifests itself in the fundamental values of the law and order of the communities (Union), in the existence of state organizational functions and having many traditional competences of a state.

The system of the EC/EU might be described as an *integrative federalism*, which indicates a constitutional system aiming to create convergence instead of divergence between states earlier being independent or confederative.[11] The activity of the efficient central government affects the life of citizens directly, but respects both the competency of the Member States pluralism.[12] Accepting

---

8 Deirdre Curtin: 'The Constitutional Structure of the Union: a Europe of Bits and Pieces'. CMLRev 1993, pp. 62-63 and 69: There is no real constitutional concept behind the EC treaty. The fact that communication between the governments is secret and uncontrolled by the public risks the *acquis communautaire*.

9 The constitutional nature of the abovementioned treaties is sustained by several rulings. Article 6 of the Maastricht Treaty declares that the Union shall respect fundamental rights as stated in the European Convention for the Protection of Human Rights and Fundamental Freedoms and as the result for constitutional traditions common to the Member States. Furthermore, it declares that the Union shall respect its Member States' identity. Article 5 guarantees this when acknowledging the principle of exercising powers under the conditions and for the purposes provided for. The Treaty of Amsterdam completes these constitutional values with liberty, democracy, rule of law and other principles, which are common to the Member States.

10 The European Court of Justice identified the Treaty of Rome as the constitution of the Communities, which has the form of an international treaty but created a new legal system, in the verdict 'Le Verts'. On behalf of this new legal system, the Member States restricted their rights, and its subjects are not only the Member States but also their citizens; Case 294/83 *Partie Ecologiste Les Verts v. European Parliament* [1986] ECR 1339.

11 However, the status of the Union under public law is debated. Under the terminology of traditional international law – which has been adopted by the functionalists – the EU is a supranational international organization. Other approaches take the EU as a pre-federal formation, which is developing towards becoming a state. The third approach considers it unnecessary to define the EU-integration process under political science. A. Weber: Zur künftigen Verfassung der Europäischen Gemeinschaft. Juristenzeitung (JZ) 1993, p. 352.

12 The constitutional system of the transferring, decentralising federalism divides the early-unified power of state among its components, which get autonomous status in their authorities. Zsuzsanna Horváth:

the Treaty of Rome (which has developed towards a central legal system being in a federation relation with the legal system of the Member States) as a constitution makes it possible to define the supranational system of the Community as a federation system.[13] Federation stands for a system where the national or the supranational constitution assures the divided sovereignty of the states and the supreme court of the common law and order guards this constitutional balance; in addition, in the case of a conflict between the rights of the federation and the members of the federation the former one prevails over the latter.

The Community is characterised by high-grade normative supra-nationality.[14] The special principles of the supranational law of the Community became constitutional principles, and the *European Court of Justice* became a 'constitutional court' practising norm control,[15] due to its practise developing the principles of the direct effect and supremacy. Therefore, the case-law of Luxemburg is one source of the efforts towards 'constitutionalisation', though not the only source. The other active character in the process of constitutionalisation is the *European Parliament*, coming up with several draft constitutions since 1984.[16] Of course it is a directly legitimated, upward-striving 'integrative' institute that considers itself capable and suitable to give the initial impulse for the constitutionalisation, though obviously it can not be the only one being in charge of the All-European constitutionalisation.[17]

Az EK joga (review of Francis Snyder /ed/: European Community Law, Aldershot 1993). Jogtudományi Közlöny issue 1994/4 p. 181.

13 In the case of the Union, the supranational aspects are less dominant because of the pillar-like structure of it. However, Armin von Bogdandy uses the expression supranational federation to define the Union. Bogdandy: 'The European Union as a Supranational Federation: A Conceptual Attempt in the Light of the Amsterdam Treaty'. Columbia Journal of International Law Vol. 6 No. 1. 2000.

14 The normative supranationality defined by Weiler, indicates that the states establishing supranational organizations acknowledge the existence of these organizations, obey their authorities, accept the mechanisms of decision-making, acknowledge their decisions as binding and support their effectiveness through their preserved national authorities. Supranational law is a system of principles, values, rules, prohibitions set in international treaties or based on international practice, norms of the organizations established by the treaties and precedents of the international courts explaining and applying them. Kelsen's theory of legal stairs and the practice well-proven in the international practice prevails and defines the legislation and implementation, provided that the states acknowledge it implicitly or explicitly in their constitution and support it in their constitutional practise.

15 The Court is not only controlling if the Member States imply and interpret correctly, but also the legislative and executive performance of the communities' bodies. 294/83 *Les Verts v. European Parliament* [1986] ECR 1339.

16 The most elaborated version is the one made by the European Parliament for 1996 IGC. See more in Nóra Chronowski-József Petrétei: Az Erópai Unió alkotmánytervezete. [Draft Constitution of the EU] JURA issue 2001/1 pp. 103-117.

17 These two tendencies are also referred to in Péter Paczolay: Fórum – Hozzászólás az Európai Alkotmányról folyó vitához. [Some Remarks to the Debate on European Constitution] Fundamentum issue 2003/2 pp. 64-65.

The starting point of the European Court of Justice is that integration does have a constitution in the form of an establishing treaty. This principle has been explicitly set in the practice of the ECJ: The European Economical Community is based upon the rule of law; therefore, neither the Member States, nor its institutions can evade examining whether their provisions are in accordance with the constitutional chart, the Treaty...The *EEC Treaty*, thus it has the form of an international treaty, is still the *constitutional charter* of a community based upon the rule of law.[18] The ideas deliberately taken from the case-law showing a courageous improvement of law define the primary sources of Community law as a constitutional system based upon the principle of the rule of law. Obviously, transgressing the competence of law implementation, the European Court of Justice aims to prove the uniformity of the Community law through a teleological explanation, which has no connection to the text of the treaties and the set objectives and principles. However, adopting the concepts well known in the Member States' constitutional laws (such as constitution, rule of law) helped the Court define itself and control the operation of the Community's legal and institutional system. As for this concept (of its mission), it anticipated the goals taking form in the future and the development of the integration, in accordance with the logic of the judicial improvement of law.

Various *components* of the constitutional interpretation – such as the necessity of protecting fundamental rights by the Community, securing an institutional balance and unfolding the layers of loyalty to the Community – occurred earlier in the practise of the Court.[19] Actually, the consequent emphasis and enforcement of these principles resulted naturally in setting the demand for constitutionalism and the rule of law, because the former ones are formal and established elements of the latter ones.

The evolutions of the *principles* of direct effect, supremacy[20] and emphasis on the autonomy of the Community's legal system have served as preconditions of the constitutional interpretation.[21] These doctrines expressed that the European

18 First sentence: 294/83 *Partie Ecologiste Les Verts v. European Parliament* [1986] ECR 1339, second sentence: Opinion 1/91 on the EEA Agreement [1991] ECR I-6079.

19 Some valuable cases: Fundamental rights: 29/69 *Stauder v. Stadt Ulm* [1969] ECR 419; Institutional balance: 138/79 *Roquette v. Council* [1980] ECR 3333. Institutional co-operation: 44/84 *Hurd v. Jones* [1986] ECR 29.

20 'Direct effect, supremacy and pre-emption are known as the main principles by the constitutionalisation of the treaties.' G. F. Mancini: 'The Making of a Constitution for Europe.' CMLRev 1989, p. 603 or 'The constitutionalisation of the Community's legal system developed based upon four doctrines, not set in the treaties. These are the direct effect, supremacy, implied powers and securing fundamental rights.' See Zenon Bankowski – Andrew Scott: 'The European Union?' In: Richard Bellamy (ed.): Constitutionalism, Democracy and Sovereignty: American and European Perspectives. Avebury Ashgate Publishing, Aldershot 1997, p. 83-84.

21 The concept of constitualisation may mean that the Community's legal system established the vertically integrated legal system of sovereign states based upon the above mentioned principles and mean a legal system providing judicially enforceable rights and duties for subjects of civil and public law. Ulrich

Court of Justice deems itself to be the highest guard of the Community's legal system and will not stand other or higher courts having effect on the Community's matters. The way the ECJ interprets its own role explains the Court's interpretation of the relation between Member States and the European institutions, Community law and national law, explanation of Community law, its origin and legitimacy. All of these naturally cause the European Court of Justice to consider the treaties as a basic and hardly modifiable constitution.[22]

The *consequence* of the European Court's practise is that, although the Member States dominate the treaties,[23] their power is necessarily restrained by the judicial constitutional interpretation, in spite of the body from Luxemburg setting the legal limits of constitutionalisation such as transferred powers, unique authorities, tacit prohibition of treaties' modification through supplementary competence and implying the principle of supremacy only for the Member States' law.[24] The European constitution, appearing in the practise of the European Court of Justice as a binding autonomous basic order, floats indefinably above the secondary law of the Community, moreover, in some cases above the Member States' constitutions. Therefore, one might conclude that the 'masters of the Treaties' have fulfilled their mission with the establishment and got in subordination with their obligation. To counterbalance this tendency, the constitutional courts of the Member States restored their powers in safeguarding the constitution; this means correcting the constituent treaty theory, sometimes against, sometimes with the European Court of Justice.[25]

3 Constitutional Character of the Establishing Treaties: Pros and Cons

While examining the constitutional character of the existing Treaties, the reality of the European Union has to be taken into consideration.[26] Presently, the founding treaties of the (original) three Communities (ECSC, EEC and EURATOM) and the treaties modifying them, as well as the Maastricht

Haltern: Pathos and Patina: The Failure and Promise of Constitutionalism in the European Imagination. European Law Journal Vol. 9 No. 1 February 2003, p. 15.

22 Hans Heinrich Rupp: Ausschaltung des Bundesverfassungsgerichts durch den Amsterdamer Vertrag? Juristen Zeitung issue 1998/5, p. 215.

23 The dogmatic of the German constitutional court made the concept popular. See BverfGE 75, 242. (*Kloppenburg Entscheidung*).

24 Opinion 2/94 (28 March 1996) *Accession by the Community to the European Convention for the Protection of Human Rights and Fundamental Freedoms* [1996] ECR I-1759.

25 Rupp: op. cit. p. 215.

26 Europe has a constitution without being a state. The founding treaties include all the significant components of a constitution. These are the possibility of fundamental rights' deduction, organisational law and regulation of secondary legislation. Hauke Brunkhorst: Constitution without a State – A European Constitution in Making. Source: http://www.arena.uio.no/events/papers/Brunkhorst/paper.pdf.

Treaty on the European Union, and to some extent the treaty of Amsterdam, Nice and Lisbon are deemed to be the constitution of the integration process.

3.1 Pros for Constitutional Character

The first aspect, giving constitutional character to the treaties, is that they are situated on the *highest level of the hierarchy of the EC/EU legal system*. The majority of the European Courts' competences guarantee exactly the supremacy of the treaties. The ECJ supervises whether the acts of the Community's institutions are lawful.[27] The supervision covers not only lawfulness of legislation, but also the lawfulness of administration. The ECJ also stated that the national courts have no right to render the acts of the Community's institutions being void.[28] This has two reasons: on one hand, the requirement of a unified community law, on the other, the necessary coherency of the legal protection's system established by the EC Treaty.[29] Constitutional supervision provides the reason for the court's desire to possess the exclusive right in decisions about the validity of the act on the Community.[30] This judicial practise originates in a case regarding an administrative decision, not about a norm having general binding force. However, the EC Treaty differentiates between the rights to propose an action against acts having a generally binding force or an individual effect. Above all, the Member States and the Community's institutions have the right to bring an action against generally binding decisions of the communities. In spite of this, individuals might occasionally sue for acts having general force (decisions) being declared unconstitutional, if they are directly and individually affected.

The other constitutional aspect of the Treaties is that they *define precisely the competences* of the Community and the division of competence among Community's institutions. The considerable number of actions regarding conflict of competence made the constitutional character of regulations dealing with the institutions' authorities clear. There is no special procedure for handling conflicts of authority, thus the action for nullification – and to some extent the action of nonfeasance – turned out to be an adequate means to settle judicially conflicts between institutions or institutions and Member States.[31]

The Community/Union (unlike sovereign states) does not have general authority, only the powers transferred to it by the founding treaties. Generally, the difference between international organisations and the Community/Union is the dimension and intensity of conferred competences, namely, that it possesses extensive legislative, executive and judicial authorities, which belong

27 EC Treaty Article 230 (ex Article 173).

28 Case 314/85 *Foto-Frost v. Hauptzollamt Lübeck-Ost* [1987] ECR 4199.

29 See the reasoning of the judgment.

30 Gil Carlos Rodrigues Iglesias: Zur Verfassung der Europäischen Gemeinschaft. In: EuGRZ 1996. Issue 5-6. p. 125.

31 EC Treaty Article 230-233 (ex Article 173-176).

traditionally to the states' sovereignty, that is they are exclusive rights of a state. The means to share powers between the Community and the Member States are the treaties, i.e. the Community's constitution. The conflicts of competences between Member States and the Community are therefore constitutional debates. There are two procedures to settle them judicially: the action for nullification and the procedure against a Member State for breach of treaty.[32]

Further constitutional regulations of the Treaties are the *'basic freedoms'*, which are not only economic directions for the Member States but also safeguards of citizen's fundamental rights on the common market.[33] Besides, the citizens against the acts of Community institutions have also used these economically orientated fundamental rights. The principle of subsidiarity and the concept of respecting national identity have constitutional character as well. The criteria of convergence became an internal part of the Community constitution after Maastricht.[34]

Formally, the treaties are the constitutional law of the EC/EU. From a *material point of view* though, it is not restricted to the treaties but also consists of the general principles common in the Member States' law. The general principles elaborated by the ECJ – being so significant that these principles are said to be the *'ius cogens'* of the Community law – has to be mentioned as well. The constitutional character of these fundamental principles reveals in their supremacy above the Community's acts and above the acts of national authorities related to the implementation of Community law. The Court examined in several cases whether the Community's decisions might suit the principles of saving confidence and proportionality.[35]

The principles regarding fundamental rights[36] have outstanding significance among general principles, since the Union's primary law acknowledges the protection of fundamental rights with positively normative binding force. The ECJ elaborated the protection of fundamental rights step-by-step and ranged them with the general principles of Community law. The base of the protection is the common constitutional traditions of the Member States and those international treaties dealing with human rights of which the Member States are participants or contributors.[37]

---

32 Iglesias: op. cit. p. 127.

33 EC Treaty Article 43–49 (ex Article 52–59) about the right to settle down and services, Article 28 (ex Article 30) about the prohibition of quantitative limitation.

34 EC Treaty Article 121 (ex Article 109/J). The four criteria: stability of prices, low rate of budgetary deficit, stability of exchange rate, long-term rates of interest.

35 The latter one became primary slaw in the Article 5 paragraph (3) (ex Article 3/B) of the EC Treaty. Iglesias: op. cit. p. 128.

36 P. Pescatore: Die Gemeinschaftsverträge als Verfassungsrecht – ein Kapitel Verfassungsgeschichte in der Perspektive des europäischen Gerichtshofs. In: Festschrift für H. Kutscher, Nomos Baden-Baden 1981, p. 323.

37 The charter of fundamental rights accepted in Nice is not part of the founding treaties; therefore, it might not be grouped either with the communities or with the Unions legal system. Erzsébet Szalayné

3.2 Cons for Constitutional Character

However, the Community's *constitutional order is limited,* as it differs from the model of states' constitutions.

The formal constitution of the Community/Union is originally an *international treaty.* This international character is extremely obvious in a crisis. The Founding Treaties do not regulate how Member States can quit the EC/EU. Consequently, this is only possible on the legal ground of the Vienna Treaty about international treaties from 1969.[38] Politically the chances of a Member State being forced to stay in the Union against the will of its government and citizens are modest.[39]

The EC and EU Treaties are not only treaties by their names and origins, but also their *modification* postulates the contribution of all Member States, expressed through their ratification.[40] In other words, to get back to the constitutional analogy, constitution-making power of the Communities/Union originates from the Member States and stays there. Member States affirm the modifications of the founding treaties following their own constitutional rules, according to their legal sovereignty. Therefore, each change of quality in the integration process, i.e. all constitutional modifications, has to be compared with the requirements of the Member States' constitutions.

Another speciality of the Treaties is that their *subject* consists of the integration process, the final goal of which is neither politically, nor legally finally set yet. The basic aim is of course to bring the nations of the Union closer to each other; still this aim is not explicitly set as a political goal. However, there are legally consistent goals among the *economic* aims, such as establishing the common market based on the Treaty of Rome and realisation of the internal market as set in the Single European Act.

Sándor: Gondolatok az Európai Unió alapjogi rendszerének metamorfózisáról. [Thoughts about the Metamorphosis of the Human Rights' System of the EU] Európai Jog issue 2003/2, p. 11.

38 Article 60, par. (2) of the Vienna Treaty: breaching a multilateral treaty entitles other parties to partly or fully suspend or finish the treaty. Article 62: Basic changes in the surroundings – under set circumstances – are reason for finishing or quitting the treaty.

39 The possibility to quit the Union is debated strongly in the science. The traditional reasons from the international law – according that treaties signed by states might be abolished with the same act- formally prove the possibility of quitting. On the other hand, the EC/EU has developed into an organization of its own right;; therefore, it does not belong under the jurisdiction of the Member States. However, it might be doubted whether the integration really reached that level of development. Existence 'on own rights' is only true when an independent constituent power exists, abolishing the fundaments originating in an international treaty. That is not yet the case in the EU. See Christian Tomuschat: Die Europäische Union unter der Aufsicht des Bundesverfassungsgerichts. EuGRZ 1993. Dezember Heft 20-21, pp. 494-495.

40 Iglesias: op. cit. p. 129.

After all, taking the arguments pro and contra into consideration, applying the concept of constitution to the reality of the Union and the Community[41] nowadays does not lead to confusion,[42] because the Community's constitution differs basically from the Member States' constitutions such as the Community/ Union differs from the classical meaning of a state.[43]

From a political point of view, the constitutional character of the founding treaties is more problematic. Despite the European Parliament's demands, the development has not reached the process of real European constitutionalisation for a long time.[44] The Member States applied the inter-governmental model again and again, and changes in this area are not likely. Constitutionalisation has two advantages to the traditional inter-governmental model: transparency and (most probably) the increasing homogeneity of political integration. The pre-condition of appointing the constitution-making power, would require a closer political union than the present one.

---

[41] As already mentioned at the beginning of this chapter, the concept of constitution is not obvious at all. Regarding the present and future constitution of the integration, two historical definitional approaches have to be synthesised. The American-French approach defines the constitution as legal outlining a new political order and powers, while the English and the German approach it as the legalisation of an already existing order of power. For establishing the theory of a supranational European constitution, both traditions are needed. Möllers: op. cit. p. 4.

[42] In his speech, when accepting his honorary title, G. Gornig comes to the opposite result. In his opinion, the word constitution is confusing, because on one hand the Treaties do not fulfil all the constitutional functions; on the other, the word might confound European citizens. See Zeller: op. cit. p. 29. Accepting the Treaties as a constitution depends on where the emphasis is put in the system of arguments. Also, one has to take into consideration that in the case of a supranational constitution other functions might get in the foreground.

[43] Roland Bieber – Jürgen Schwarze: op. cit. pp. 21-23.

[44] The concept of political society imminently contains the theory of constitutionalisation. The Union becoming a political community leads to the necessary call for a constitution. The question is whether the Union's political society is integrated enough and whether it can make good use of the three-hundred-year-old tradition of European constitutionalism. Ulrich K. Preuss: 'The political meaning of constitutionalism.' In: Bellamy, Richard (ed.): Constitutionalism, Democracy and Sovereignty: American and European Perspectives. Avebury Ashgate Publishing, Aldershot 1997, p. 11.

4 The European Constitution in the Future

4.1 Factors Influencing the Drafting of a Constitution for Europe

In the 1990's, the question arose evermore frequently of whether a European constitution would exist, and if so, when it would be created and what would its relation to the national constitutions be, explicitly from the point of view of constitutional law. On the eve of the 21st century, the intention of creating a new, written constitution as an assurance of the Union's further development seemed to become more and more definite. Politicians as well as scientists suggested the topic, different drafts were written, political declarations for and against were stated and several dozen articles, studies, and even monographs tried to address the problem.[45]

Since the integration is first of all not a legal but a political problem, politics must be taken into consideration when defining the European Union's constitution's requirements.[46] Law – and therefore the legal meaning of the constitution as well – might only aim to give the political intentions and aspirations a formal outline to support political ambitions. This statement is not only appropriate regarding the future constitution, but is also necessary and reasonable.

Behind legal debates about the Union, there are usually *political controversies*. The law might be capable of finding the optimal solutions for the Union's development, but only if there is political accordance in the background. Judging by the necessity of constitutionalisation, the means of creating it and the solutions it might offer all require a basic political agreement. However, this seems to be quite intricate, because the questions appearing in different legal solutions and regulations, regarding the further development of the EU, originate in the various political goals of the Member States. The legal nature of the Union, sovereignty or attribution of powers and the concept of the Union's development has to be examined from this perspective. Is it going to be a confederation or federal state? Will the strengthening of political integration follow the intensification of the economic co-operation? Or will the Union remain what it is now: a special supranational organisation and legal community without development of a common European state, at least not in the near future?[47] Therefore, the ques-

---

45 At the conference of heads of states and governments in October 2001 in Gent, Belgium, the convocation of the Constitution-making Convention was decided. This resulted in the conference of Laeken. Until now, this has been the most resolute step of the European institutions in order to begin the constitutionalisation.

46 Möllers: op. cit. p. 4.

47 The lack of statehood makes it relative to what type of constitutional norms are needed and whether they really want a European constitution. Antje Wiener: 'Evolving Norms of Constitutionalism.' European Law Journal Vol. 9. No. 1 February 2003 p. 2. Some consider the constitution to be the proof of becoming a federal state. See Géza Kilényi: Fórum – Hozzászólás az Európai Alkotmányról folyó vitához. Fundamentum issue 2003/2, p. 76.

tion of the EU outrivals the constitutional concept. Only after answering these questions can one respond to how a constitution, serving as a tool for developing the process of becoming a community, should be formed, i.e. the nature of the European Union's constitution.

However, reaching political agreement does not seem simple, because of the Member States' conceptions and so their opinions about constitutionalisation diverge considerably:

- Member States judge the future of the Union/Community differently: some of them wish to strengthen the co-operation and establish the political union that is converting it into a confederation or federation, while others do not want to change the nature of co-operation;
- the 'own constitution' concept of a particular Member State influences not only the need for a constitutional charter, but also the process of creating it;[48]the Member States' concepts of state[49] significantly influence the possible content of the constitution and the way they see the Union's future (either looking at it as an economical or as a more intensively political co-operation), since it is not all the same which organisational structure or decision-making mechanism will be established by the new constitution;
- the hybrid nature of the integration has also to be taken into consideration: already it is more than a confederation but less than a supranational organization, it does already have some kind of partial international legal entity, but it is not a sovereign entity yet. Moreover, its operation allows three models: the traditional intergovernmental, the *'sui generis'* model of the communities and the supranational centralist model;[50]
- there is a significant opinion denying the necessity of the Union's constitution, because the Union's present development does not require it.[51]

Of course, on the present level of development, creating the supranational constitution would be too early. Because of the enlargement, there are several structural, theoretical and attitude-related problems to solve, not only theoreti-

[48] This influence prevails formally and in its content horizontally, moreover vertically. The difference in formal opinions influenced the document's type and name. The influence on the content contains the possibility of dissent in the subject of constitutional norms. Vertical problems may arise from different opinions regarding the volume of constitutionalisation and legislation. Antje Wiener: op. cit. p. 5.

[49] Is it a unitary and centralised state or a decentralised federative one, where Member States' independence may give an example for the future European political union?

[50] F. W. Scharpf: What a European Constitution Could and Could Not Achieve. Source: http://www.ces.fas.harvard.edu/working_papers.

[51] In Gilbert Gornig's opinion a constitution is only necessary if Europe really aims to become a state. Zeller: op. cit. p. 31. In Haltern's opinion, the EU's law materializes some kind of consumer's identity, it lacks emotional-cultural identity, and a written constitution will not help this. Ulrich Haltern: Pathos and Patina: 'The Failure and Promise of Constitutionalism in the European Imagination'. European Law Journal, Vol. 9. No. 1 February 2003, p. 14.

cally but also practically. The problems of democracy deficit[52] require solutions, because legislation is only legal if the European Parliament, as a representative body, exercises real powers and gets internal legitimacy from Europe's nations. Formal legitimacy already materializes in direct elections. Internal legitimacy would mean real powers exercised in favour of European nations.[53] Division of competence among the Community/Union institutions has to be rationalized, accepting the concept of sovereignty conforming to the differentiated integration. Differentiated integration is based on the divisibility of state sovereignty – if sovereignty means partially transferable prerogatives – and accepts the fact that Member States contribute based on their capacities. Transferring competences has not only two dimensions, between the supranational entity and Member States, but also more differing dimensions on different layers. [54] Through developing the federative structure, the present two-faced character – originating in the pillar-like structure combining intergovernmental and supranational solutions – could be abolished.[55] Writing an explicitly supranational constitution is only achievable in the remote future, because of the present structural problems and differing opinions of Member States, but conclusions about its functions and contents are possibly based on the attempts and aspiration already made.

4.2 Functions of a Supranational Constitution

It is worthwhile to approach this problem from the aspect of the functions of a supranational constitution. Setting requirements for the real European Constitution may help to outline the character and nature of the legal (normative) constitution, unless there is no chance for a long-term political union.

First of all, it has to be stated that constitutions are always a result of historical development and, in each phase of this development, the contents and functions of the constitution have always been elaborated by the political situations: in the case of legal funding of contemporary structures, or in the case of improving them or in the case of the reactions to these structures.[56] In accord-

52 Tibor Navracsics: A demokrácia problémája az Európai Unióban. [Problematic of democracy in the EU] Politikatudományi Szemle 1998, issue 1 pp. 53-55.

53 A. Weber: Zur künftigen Verfassung der Europäischen Gemeinschaft. Juristen Zeitung (JZ) 1993, p. 330.

54 N. Walker: 'Sovereignty and Differentiated Integration in the European Union.' European Law Journal 1998, December pp. 355-356.

55 A. Weber: op. cit. p. 327. Furthermore, the problem originates in the EC being a supranational organisation, the communities' law has a character similar to a constitutional structure, but this is not true in case of the EU. The EU's constitution may not be mentioned until each policy becomes community policy and the pillar-like structure of different areas of co-operation is abolished.

56 Dimitris Th. Tsatsos: Bemerkungen zur Gegenwartsfunktion der Verfassung. In: Verfassung – Parteien – Europa. Nomos Verlagsgesellschaft, Baden-Baden 1998/1999.

ance with the European development, the constitution has to express the regulative founding of the European integration. Since the functions of a constitution are continuously in the process of historical change and transformation, today – in Europe – the basic question regarding a constitution arises: what functions should the Union's constitution fulfil?

To answer this, summarising the essential functions of national constitution is reasonable. National (state) constitutions have two levels: on one hand, the constitution serves the establishment and preservation of state unity; on the other, it affects the state-organised society's life. A constitution is a fundamental legal orientation of social existence.[57] On the state's level, it creates decision makers, competences and processes that establish a normative foundation for the acts of state organs. In a pluralistic society, a constitution also fulfils the function of making the permanent integration of persons and interests possible through the openness and stable values of the political processes.[58] The political and legal order of communal existence does not only exist through its abstract acceptance and in the sense of the fundamental consent transmitted by the constitution. The constitution is only capable of establishing unification and legitimizing the operation of state power – at the same time and on the same level – if it is able to express the freedom, openness and ability to develop the political process.[59]

Several ideas exist about the special requirements of what the European Union's constitution, as a supranational basic norm, should fulfil and what functions above the national constitutions it should complete. A summary of these is given below.[60]

a) The European Union's constitution has to be a *treaty-like constitution*. This sets the requirement of the constitution as being based on the agreement of all Member States; moreover, it should be legitimized directly by the Union's nations, or rather by the political will of the union's citizens. This is because, as a political union, neither the European Union, nor its institutions could provide Europe's nations more communality than what the 'European people' could establish through creating the constitution. Naturally, the European constitution has to be created by European people, regarding themselves as Europeans and having their roots not only in national states, but also in the European Union. This political identity can neither be forced rapidly, nor stated in political proclamations, because politics does not have power over this. This can only be the outcome of the Union's establishment as a communicational, experimental and

---

57 Tsatsos: op. cit. p. 572. 568.

58 Ibid.

59 Ibid.

60 See T. Läufer: Zur künftigen Verfassung der Europäischen Union – Notwendigkeit einer offenen Debatte. Integration issue 1994/4 pp. 208-211. See also Nóra Chronowski – József Petrétei: Fórum: 'Európai alkotmány – szuverenitás – legitimáció' Fundamentum issue 2003/2, pp. 67-72.

remembering community, that is, to let the collective identity emerge, stabilise and become inherited tradition.[61] The political foundations of the European constitution can only originate in the rooting, entwinement and relations of this common identity, including not only the present institution building, but also nation building and democracy building.[62] However, it has to be stated that for this European community, identity is in a very initial stage of development.[63] For the citizens of the Member States, the political attachment to the Union is only related to the European Parliamentary elections; emotional identity has not yet emerged. This derives from the specialties of the European integrations, from the economic character of the co-operation and the democracy-deficit mentioned so many times regarding the organisation's operation. However, increasing the European identity is not hopeless, because some beginnings, some seeds already exist and when spearing these, it might lead to the forming of the 'European people' and its conscious acceptance. These are:

- first of all, the cultural heritage, which has a significant effect on the acquaintance[64] of belonging to Europe as a historical community, even alongside restoring national diversity and its continued existence;
- besides the diversity of values, the existence of common fundamental values – such as peace, safety, co-operation, democracy, tolerance, freedom, equity, justness and so on – the protection and improvement of which is a common aim of all European nations;
- the development of European law and its results, which means the Europeanization of law, in its entirety and in different areas, common European civil law, common European law of constitution in its broader sense, but also there are ambitions regarding European labour law and social law; and
- the constant amplification and enrichment of 'community achievements', which might strengthen the identity as well and might encourage the Member States inhabitants to make common efforts.

Naturally, the process does not end in a day. It is essential to improve the democratic elements of the Community's/Union's operation and increase subsidiarity as well as regional co-operation.

b) The European Constitution, similar to the European citizenship, has to be a *complementary* one, meaning a 'basic norm' completing the Member States' constitutions, influencing and supporting those constitutions in the sense of the European Union's structural and material homogeneity as well. The European

---

[61] Haltern: op. cit. pp. 29-30.

[62] Läufer: op. cit. p. 208.

[63] Tibor Navracsics: Az uniós állampolgárság és az európai civil társadalom. [The union citizenship and European civil society] Comitatus 1999, November pp. 9-11.

[64] Mancini: Europe: 'The Case for Statehood.' European Law Journal, March 1998, pp. 37-38.

treaty-like constitution, as a complementary constitution, is the most important means to establishing the common European constitutional law in its restricted sense, that is, of the legal development – as legal framework of order – aiming for a common legal culture and common base of values.[65] The basic nature of a European constitution has always been similar in many senses: sovereignty and representation of people, principles of rule of law and distribution of power, acknowledging and guaranteeing fundamental rights, and so on. Consequently, each Member State's constitution fulfils the requirement of the democratic rule of law. [66]

c) The European constitution has to be an *integrative* one, that means one including goals regarding the intensification of becoming a community and deepening the integration to – as stated in the preamble of the Maastricht Treaty – achieve 'an ever closer Union among the Peoples of Europe'. The integrative functions of the European constitution include transparency and close relations with citizens, establishing of democratic processes, which might generate democratic legitimacy to the acts of institutions made suitable to the Union and its specialities. The complicated legitimacy problem of the European Union cannot be solved either, only with reference to the Parliament or one-way, for example through transferring the methods a democratic participation and control developed in the national states.[67] More elements and processes related to the legitimacy belong to the integrative components of a European Constitution before 'democratisation bound to a system' of the European Union can be achieved.[68]

d) The supranational constitution has to be a *flexible* basic norm, which means one that supports the dynamic process of becoming a community and guides this consciously, based upon its finality. Especially this function makes the European constitution different from state constitutions, because this flexibility is related directly to the upgrading process of the European Union. This corresponds to the speciality of the European constitutional grade being based more and more strongly on development and change, while at the same time it has to remain open to the definition of the integrative policy's goal, if it does not want to be the main obstacle of transformation and change.[69]

e) The supranational constitution has to be an *incorporating* constitution, which means the regulations about the European Union have to take into consideration the European territories, being affected by the European Union,

[65] Läufer: op. cit. p. 209.

[66] This can be more or less be proven in the case of the English historical constitution as well.

[67] See Weiler: The Constitution of Europe. 'Do the New Clothes Have an Emperor?' and other Essays on European Integration. Cambridge University Press, Cambridge 1999, p. 265.

[68] Läufer: op. cit. p. 209.

[69] Flexibility would not be effective without being embedded in a constitution, because it requires the Member States' goals of community building and international interest to go along with the constitution. From a procedural point of view, this means that the future union's constitution has to include accordingly rules for development and improvement, which are necessary to direct this process.

and political or economic reference points for it. The incorporating function does not only refer to the candidates, to the other Central and Eastern European states and associated partners, but also to the forming of the European Union's relation with international and regional organisations.[70] This is true in particular for organisations in which the Union is a member or contributor.

f) The European constitution has to be a *federative* constitution, that is, it has to complete the clarification and re-definition of the European Union's federal character, taking into consideration the shaping future construction as a polycentric, opened and novel bearer of the sovereign rights, entwined closely with Member States' action plans. In order to define this function and principle of structure, the hierarchical structure of the Union has to be abolished in the sense of state law and structural law.[71] As a federal constitution, the future constitution of the Union would also be a structural and value-based constitution.[72]

g) Finally, it has to be a *strategic* constitution that means determining the steps necessary to becoming a community and the periods of time, stages of it. On a certain level, besides setting the direction towards full integration, the constitution has to contain the schedule of execution and has to direct the union exactly toward this. The constitution decides the debate about the 'the right way' and gives a scale to measure whether the proved direction of integration is kept, or whether it has to be modified. As a structural constitution, the new European constitution has to contain, alongside the strategic aspect of integration, the elements of institution building and development processes. Here belong the goals, the deadlines and the process to reach all of these, such as distinctive projects (for example internal market 1992, currency union 1999, political union 2000). There are two possibilities competing regarding the pace of the integration: the pragmatic policy of small steps and the 'big jump', where the optimal situation of being a community is already given. The European constitution will most probably contain a policy-mix, since not all the options have the same strength and effect; moreover, not all of them might be introduced at the same time.[73]

---

70 First of all OSCE, GATT/WTO, UN, European Council, G7, OECD etc. See Läufer: op. cit. p. 210.

71 Ingolf Pernice: 'Multilevel Constitutionalism in the European Union.' ELRev., 2002 October pp. 511-513

72 This character brings the constitution of EU closer to the state constitutions as well, but without proper regulatory contents it would be something else: as a value-based constitution it would serve by transmitting the final level, basic values and decisions entirely and independently, as a structural constitution it had to set coherent distribution of functions and competent , moreover it has to establish an effective net of different grades between the Member States and the Union and its different centres of operations. Läufer: op. cit. p. 210

73 Läufer: op. cit. p. 211.

4.3 Contents of a Supranational Constitution

Based on the functions, one might make certain conclusions about the contents of the Union's constitution. In all probability, the fundamental order of the European integration will appear as a constitutional treaty laying down a minimal consent, with European people as parties, instead of the Member States' governments.[74] The constitution has to incorporate the following most essential value-based decisions – deriving from the treaties or completing them:[75]

- realistic general and specific integrative *aims* have to be set, for example creating Europe's political identity, building federal structure, safeguarding international peace and safety, assuring continuous economic and social development, reaching complete employment, increasing protection of the environment, maintaining a borderless legal and economic community, common intervention in international relations;
- fundamental *principles* expressing common values of European nations have to be listed, such as liberty, equity, solidarity, human dignity, democracy, rule of law and safeguarding human rights;
- the principle of the Union's *openness*, which means that every European country having a democratic structure and accepting the *acquis communitaire* may join, has to be articulated. It would be practical to specify the requirements of joining the EU in the treaties, taking into consideration the necessary geopolitical, economic and cultural decision – which should be made as soon as possible – about Europe's and the EU's frontiers;
- principles of the EU institutions and their operation ought to be constituted: *subsidiarity*[76] completed with guarantees for regions and local authorities, proportionality,[77] flexibility, which came into the primary community law with the Amsterdam Treaty[78] and basically takes the Member States' ability to adapt with accepting differentiated integration;
- acknowledgement of Member States' constitutional systems and their

---

74 H. Abromeit – T. Hitzel-Cassagnes: 'Constitutional Change and Contractual Revision: Principles and Procedures.' European Law Journal 1999, March pp. 43-44.

75 F. G. Jacobs: 'The Community Legal Order – A Constitutional Order?' In: Towards a New Constitution for the European Union? ERA, Volume 21. Bundesanzeiger 1997 p. 34-35 and EP Resolution on the Constitution of the EU, ibid. pp. 167-182.

76 Subsidiarity was incorporated in the Single European Act in order to save the Member States' legal systems.

77 Proportionality in this aspect means that the Union's acts and operations shall not override the necessary degree for reaching the aims set in the constitution.

78 Treaty of Amsterdam Article 1, 12. Title VI a (new) Provisions on closer cooperation, Article 2, 5. Presently TEU Articles 43–45. A core of the Member States can integrate more deeply in certain areas – based on their interests. The advantage of this is that Member States unwilling or unable to co-operate deeper do not hinder the development of integration any more.

national identity, historical, cultural traditions and languages should be guaranteed in the Union's constitution;

- the constitution has to regulate the *sources of the legal system*[79] going together with the federative structure, has to define the relation between a constitution and founding treaties plus the principles of primacy and supremacy as specialities and guarantees of implementing, for the *acquis communitaire* have to be laid down;[80]
- in a separate chapter, the *institutions* of the EU should be listed and their role in the whole organisation of the integration process; and the core norms about their creation and competence should be outlined, based on fundaments of constitutional law and the treaties. By doing so, limited competences, Community loyalty, subsidiarity and proportionality have to be taken into consideration. The aim should be a way of regulation making the distribution of powers unambiguous, horizontally – inside the Union – and vertically – between the Union and Member States – as well;[81]
- including *fundamental rights* and providing them judicial assurance would fill in an old deficiency.[82]

The European Union's constitution has to be in a special co-ordinated, *adjunctive relation* with the Member States' constitutions. Until the European federative structure has been established explicitly, it can not prevail over Member States' constitutions as a super-norm, but it has to respect Member States transfer of powers and it can only set organisational, competence norms for the Union's organisations. A basic requirement towards the supranational constitution has to leave the Member States' constitution untouched regarding a democratic form of government, the essential principle of state organisation and safeguarding fundamental rights. The supranational constitution has to create and express common European values: the values in the Member States' constitutions, then the ones improved in their constitutional traditions should not be summarized on their smallest common denominator but on their largest common multiple.

79 Based on the EP's concept, there would be constitutional, organic and simple acts, with the Council taking part in its making, furthermore the regulations made by the Council and the individual decisions would still exist. Towards a New Constitution... pp. 174-175.

80 Tamás Kende: Európai közjog és politika. Osiris-Századvég, Budapest 1995 p. 331 and László Kecskés: EK-jog és jogharmonizáció, Közgazdasági és Jogi Könyvkiadó, Budapest 1999, p. 131.

81 See Towards a New Constitution... p. 171-176. It has to be considered, whether the Member States should remain in charge of implementation of community law with indirect control of the Committee, or it would be worth giving the Council more effective rights to sanction the disobedient country – based on the new Article 7 of the Treaty of Amsterdam – in order to increase the enforcement of implementation.

82 More and more people urge it, so the EU has finally to accept – furthermore in a legally binding form- the chart of community human rights. Gábor Kardos: Az emberi jogok védelme az Európai Unió keretében. Acta Humana 1994, No. 14 pp. 42.

An essential aspect is that law – and so the European constitutional law – is not only a complexity of norms, but also a social practice. The constitution might gain its entirety through the European people's practice.[83]

5 Summary

As for the Treaty of Lisbon, it can be concluded that it is rather a step back than a step forward in the course of EU constitution-making. The fall of the Draft Constitutional Treaty for the EU exposed that there is not yet a European nation with a common European identity. This leads us to the problem of a democracy deficit. However, the Treaty of Lisbon has saved some definitive developments of a Constitutional Treaty (e.g. more clear separation of competences, regulation of the legal status of the Charter of Fundamental Rights, dissolving more or less the controversies of the pillar structure, standard regulation of the legal personality of the EU). The big jump for a constitution has not happened at the EU level, but by the Treaty of Lisbon, European citizens are a little bit closer to a basic norm.

83 Antje Wiener: op. cit. p. 11.

CHAPTER 5

The Constitutional Nature of the European Union

The Theoretical Premises of European Constitutionality

Karel Klíma

I The Constitutional Specialties of EC/EU in the Development

The phenomenon of the EC/EU needs investigating, which would use the best methods of public law and political science, and would address the legitimacy and identity of the process of European integration and at the same time would show the possibilities of the further development of the European Union. The complete investigation is tending now towards exploring the specialty of the European Union as an international organisation and at the same time as a sovereign complex state, The Union cannot be stripped of the elements of national entities.

The investigation is followed by the logic of the constitutionalisation of Europe. It is a lasting dilemma, whether a new multilateral pact or constitution accords to the situation. However, the conception of the possible constitution has established itself mainly because of the fact that the present character of the EU makes the Union to be a complex system of usual constitutional elements.

A review on a normative basis of the law of the European Union enables us to find out its constitutive elements, or those elements, which have already partially become the substantive material legal content of the Constitution of the European Union. The discussion should also present the broad public legal character of the European Union.

The development of the investigation of constitutional aspects is the constitutional problems of the present and mainly the future. It creates pillars, which respect national identities and are generating new divisions of competencies.

The Union is not a finished system. It is a system, which depends on the further development of integration, and also on the development of common European policy. A system, which includes (implicates) Member States is being created. At the same time, its federative nature becomes clearer. On this basis and in the relation to those elements the Union becomes a subject of constitutionality, which is identifiable and sortable under the constitutional rules.

The process of integration creates law, which has changed the relationships between states and people. The integration of the Union can be defined as a process, which is directed politically – through increasing exchange between diverse societies (states) of member subjects during the passing of time. The reality shows a creation of a center, which distinguishes the integration from the traditional cooperation between states. The organisation of cooperation has the harmonising of external competences of Member States as its aim. It aims for the execution of international politics in a common way, which is normally done separately in an isolated way. The progression of integration transcends – from the institutionalised cooperation to – constitutional integration. The constitutional nature of integration is formed by structural elements of relations between states and people, when it concerns common higher interests

* Hab. Prof. JUDr. Karel Klíma, CSc. is professor of Constitutional Law and the Head of the Department of Constitutional and European Law, University of West Bohemia in Pilsen, Czech Republic.

above partial interests, with an emphasis on common economical and political interests.

The sense of integration gains an anachronistic space (not limited by time), which one can find out from the following elements, which at the same time give the Union the so-called supranational character, namely with constitutional elements:

1) the transition of competences, to the exclusively union or concurring ones;
2) the passing of independent decisions of Union organs;
3) special (own) Union rights, which enter the legal systems of Member States;
4) judicial enforcement of rights, especially against a state, which does not respect common norms.

The European Union as a certain association of states has a common system basis in the systems of power, which are based on commonly respected constitutional values like freedom, democracy, respect towards basic human rights and freedoms, and the binding nature of law (state of law). The European Union has a common standard of constitutional values according to Article 6, 1 of the EU Treaty. There are acting 25 legally independent constitutions and one 'roof' institutional system. The European Union is in that sense a protector of a certain common order of relations. One can also say that the European Union is a constitutional system of several stages.

II The European Union as a Sovereign System of Power

The development of the present Europe, the rights of the European Union, European politics and further related aspects is not only a question of political, economical, human or commonly legal relations, but it displays also more obviously the question of the so-called 'new sovereignty", or of the relation of the single legal (public legal systems) of Member States of the European Union and the public legal system of the Union as such and that also from the viewpoint of its further development.

The problems connected with the solution of the new shape of the system of organs of the European Union, or the questions about the catalogue of basic human rights, which are binding as civic rules for citizens of each Member State, the questions of the development of the democratic basis of the EU system are of course constructional questions of the public legal system and of the complexity of relations, which by their subject form the usual basis of constitutional systems of sovereign states. Looking at the stage of development of cooperative relations of the Member States of the European Union and also looking at the deliberation about the development of the so-called European policy (also with respect to the future EU enlargement), one surely has to consider questions, which are already today part of the debate about the present objective constitutional basis of the European Union, or which could potentially enter this object and would be formulated in the text as the complete constitution of the EU at a certain stage of development of Europe.

The institutional elements of the new system were undoubtedly built through the creation of common organs of the European Union, even when the European Union is still a commonwealth of states by its nature, which means a creation of mostly a confederative type, even when the classical definitions of confederation, federation and Unitarianism are today insufficient, as V. Klokočka states.

Even if it mainly concerns the market, monetary, financial and judicial coordination of state systems or harmonisation of national legal norms, the sovereignty of ground, civil and national organs are being kept intact. The binding nature of common decisions, which is ensured mostly by national organs that keep their sovereignty in many further national cases, means that there is a mingling of traditional state sovereignty with the mediated influence of the new system. That means, in fact, that some competencies are executed together:

- in the area of creating norms (the national law and common acts function together);
- in the executive area (the measures in the customs, economical, monetary, economical, agricultural and other areas of politics are mingling);
- in the judicial area (the judicature of common courts and national justice, including the influence of supranational judicature, start to mingle).

III The State-Legal Nature of European Union

Even when one cannot fully apply the traditional encyclopedic divergence of the so-called states into the confederative or federative ones of the European Union, still the analytical view of this categorisation still remain instructive. From this viewpoint are:

a) the confederative moments of the EU, in that:
   -the primal founding treaties are by their nature international documents, with whose change all the members must agree;
   -the basic (democratic) decision processes are a constitutional privilege of the single Member States, when the European Parliament has the legitimate power based on the voting in single countries, but the creation of legal norms is usually a privilege of delegated organs;
   -further transferring of the sovereignty of national states depends on the common (of international legal nature) and on their own constitutional decision.
b) the federative moments of the EU, in that:
   -the primal treaties and partially also the so-called secondary right is binding the Member States directly;

-in many areas of law and state policy, the integration of economy, social and legal policy is being followed;
-the EU acts towards the outside as a fixed organised system, which sets the rules of entry for other countries and decides upon their acceptance by general consensus;
-the citizenship of the EU exists, which is derived from the legality of citizenship of Member State;
-there exists certain limited aerial basis of the Union, which consists of the single areas of the Member States.

From a general encyclopedic outlook, there are traditional variants of conception and organisation of state sovereignty and so three categories, which can be considered to be three legal categories. The gradation goes from the confederation, which is not sovereign and belongs to the international public law to the federation, which is sovereign and subordinate to the inner law. These variants are of course 'borderline' ones, because the confederation is usually too 'loose' and the federation too 'fixed and centralized', when the common organs ensure together the unity between Member States. The criteria of legal subjectivity, mediation or non-mediation of right and further of single opinion or majority by decision making make these two forms different.

The European Union corresponds in a special way to the usual three criteria of statehood: the ground, population and the existence of power. It has a ground, where the community law is being applied, the population is under the European citizenship and certain mechanism of public power exists.

The view of the European Union as a federation is not unequivocally accepted, usually also more in a controversial way. The political tendency is to create 'a Community of states and people', which will not change into a state. One can say that at present, the Union oscillates between a federation and federative union.

From the viewpoint of usual development of federative states, however, the European Union shows such transition to federalisation, when originally fully independent states are united by a treaty and they create in a certain form common organs. If they do not lose all their sovereignty and their common organs are operating in certain functions for them (especially towards the outside), one can speak about a certain type of confederacy. In the case of the European Union, a system of structured power is being created, both through a common legal order, which is directly binding in all states (to the laws), and through the direct decisions and the binding nature of decisions of some common organs of the Union (European Court), and also through the territorial equivalent possibility of application of some basic human rights (the freedom of movement and place of living, free movement of goods, the reciprocity of freedom of procedural application), in which the centre has a certain superiority, and of decisions based upon a certain contractual territorial fundament with the transition of protection to outer borders.

IV The European Union as a Combined Constitutionality

According to the constitutional basis of Member States of the European Union, the principle of integration of the Union forms the legal system of the Union as a constitutional order. The community law is an organised, wide and structured system of legal rules with its own sources, institutions and procedures. The treaties are creating a certain constitutional Charter, while the usual rules of international public law are becoming parallels. The community law disposes with certain autonomy in the area of norms of international law, but at the same time, it can outsource from the sources of internal law of Member States.

The constitutionality of European integration in relation to constitutions is (was) always certified and many changes in the constitutions were needed for the development of integration. The acceptance of community law (its criteria) usually does not interfere with the sovereignty of states. It however has no 'supra-national' authority in the typical sense of the word.

The legal order of the European Union belongs still to the international order; however, its experiences started a process of special centralisation. It still does not have the qualities and values of a positive law of state and it remains a 'special constitutional order'.

The process of integration has caused from the start the constitutional adaptation of Member States. Generally, it does not cause transcribing of texts of constitutions and follows pragmatically and peacefully. It of course depends on the nature of the national constitutional system. The effect of constitutional integration is: the execution of competences and activity of European institutions influences the inner separation of powers. The transition of competences has made and is making the executive power of state stronger; that can influence the position of national parliaments, and so the inner separation of powers. It is much more obvious in the area of rights, with an impact on economical and monetary policy.

The revisions of constitutional texts did not mean changes in the constitutions; however, they represented modernisations from the viewpoint of European integration. Nevertheless, these revisions have shown that it is a constitutionally and institutionally innovative process, which for the time being does not accept the classical mechanisms of a federative state. The statehood is considered as a 'dualist' one, which derives from the constitution itself, in the context with the founding treaties of the EC/EU and the treaties with states.

The modern constitution, in its almost 200 year long development, is an expression of state sovereignty. It represents in that sense a territorial sovereignty, institutional sovereignty – the legitimacy of power, the sovereignty of state's citizenship – rights, freedoms and the protection of a citizen.

If the constitutions were created as a certain self-organization, self-regulation of nations and systems, they have expressed and still are expressing their inner untouchability (for example the keeping of the form of government and democracy) but also a possible relation to outer systems – supranational orders or institutions. In relation to the internationalisation of international life, especially after World War II, in some constitutional systems the elements of parallel or cooperation with supranational systems, but also the subordinance to supranational law or even supranational systems (the UN, the European Union) or institutions (the European Court of Human Rights) and similar, start to appear.

The constitutional systems, especially those of the Member States of the European Union, are becoming the so-called open systems when the constitutions reflect not only the supranational law, but also the creation of common supranational institutions. The constitutions have not lost the character of national document, which captures (in fact conserves) the system. The ruling of a process is slowly asserting itself into the texts of constitutions of the countries in the European Union, through which the country applies for the new supranational power, including the possible transition of sovereignty.

From the viewpoint of constitutional law, the constitutions of Member States are still describing the community law more than an international law than their own law, even when they accept it as a directly acting law, which prevailed before the laws. All changes in international treaties (in this sense of those, which we consider to be primal community rights at present and in the future) from the viewpoint of content are bringing a lasting challenge of possible changes in their own constitutions resulting from entering such 'strong' international unions and also from the viewpoint of the possible direct binding nature (and in the future direct enforcement) of plights. In the final result, these constitutional changes can point towards the issue of the change of the form of state itself (unitary, confederative, and federative).

The question of 'sovereignty of a state' does seem to be usable as a criterion for the legal qualification of the European Union. However, the question of 'sovereignty' plays an important role in the discussions about the constitutionality of European construction: The international law acknowledges expressively the restriction of the sovereignty of a state.

V Common Constitutional Values of Member States as a Source of European Constitutionalism

The states are traditionally basing their political identity upon the constitutional philosophy (culture), which can be called constitutionalism: this culture has elements of stability and durability. It sets up an order and constitutional institutions.

The European Union tries to define its own constitutional culture according to its identity. The new constitutional order is based upon the constitutional national traditions and cultures. The constitutional value of national states is considered a basis of the value of integration, because it is also created by law (principles).

The modern constitutionalism is related to the birth of the state. This basic relation between the state and modern constitutionality causes that the development of constitutionality depends on the development of statehood. The development of the Union however builds upon the keeping of statehood of Member States. The integration is based upon the preservation of states. That preservation is considered to be a premise and condition of integration. From the international legal view, one needs to imagine the parallel existence of the state and the Union.

The current constitutions are an expression of national identity; they are a testimony of an era. The national statehood is a basis for modern constitutionalism. The non-existence of the so-called European Nation does not mean that the principles of constitutionality cannot be used for the construction of the Union.

The constitutionalising of the Union in general is strongly based on the development of law. It depends, however, on the development of politics and the progress of integration. The law has until today 'covered up' the lack of political decisions. The constitutional development of the European Union is based on the initiatives, interpretation of constitutional texts, and the changes of constitutions of Member States. The interpretation of the treaties as a 'constitution' on the basis of the inner legal orders is the basis for the constitutionalising of treaties.

The characteristics of the constitutional nature of the European Union are of crucial importance in considering the common constitutional values of the Member States. It enables us to see the Union as a homogenous legal and procedural legal system. Connected with the recognition of these political legal values is the recognition of the Union in relation to the Member States, which are its members. In that sense, one can speak about the common constitutional 'property' of Member States. Through the development of the Union, it comes to the constitutional convergence of constitutional sources of the states and the Union.

The community law in its international legal origin also has ties to the natural sources of international public law, which contain constitutional values. It concerns mainly the long-term development of human rights and democratic principles (see further). At the same time, human rights become a part of international law and especially in the way of custom law and, on this basis, became a law recognized by civilised nations. It does not mean that the common international law would include all components of human rights, but it includes the relations to humanitarian norms and to the international criminal law.

The internationalisation of the concept of the state of law and democracy is another source of the norms of the constitutional nature.

The international European system is represented strongly by the 'dominance' of the European Court of Human Rights; the organs of the Court themselves have spoken out in the sense, that the 'Court aims to be considered a constitutional tool of the European order'. Legally, the matter and content of the activity are classifiable as constitutional ones. The entire European treaty is inspired by national texts of founding states. The Court contributes to the homogenisation and to the fixing of the normative European space. The Court has practically defined the minimal standard of the protection of human rights.

Mostly it happens so in the relation to the communication between the national constitutional courts and the Court. The Court in Strasbourg contributes to the development of judicial monism and to the federalisation of Europe.

The constitutional law of the Member States of the Council of Europe is confronted more and more with the content and interpretation of the Convention. The Court can judge the constitutional norms with the Convention and its interpretation on the basis of incidental control in relation to single cases. It can speak out temporarily first after the decision of the highest constitutional judicial institutions, which are applying and explicating their own constitution. The decisions of the Court can lead to the nullification or to the re-interpretation of laws, jurisdictional decisions, especially those of constitutional courts. Generally, one can say that the time after World War II is typical for its convergence of the constitutional sources of the single European states and the EC/EU. In particular, the Treaty of Amsterdam strengthens the nature of the European Union. One can also speak about a 'common European constitutional culture', and about a legal property heritage. This culture is common to the Member States, it has formed itself and it was formalised.

The convergence of the constitutional values of Europe is based mainly on the spreading of these values in the single states of Europe. This expansion was typical for the period after World War II, and the acceptance of constitutions was inspired by a common philosophy accepted by the states when they were overcoming the totalitarian systems. First it was Germany at the end of 1940's, then in the 1970's Greece, Portugal and Spain and in the 1990's, it was the changes of constitutional systems in Middle and Eastern Europe. It shows more and more that the constitutions are tending towards the characteristics of a reciprocal influence, so to the assimilation and internationalisation of constitutional rules. A certain mingling of European constitutionalism, or its values, demonstrates itself similarly then in the European Union and strengthens the thought of a commonwealth of ideas in it.

The common constitutional values of Europe are based on the philosophy of the values of liberal democracy, which consists of a certain 'hierarchy' of this philosophy: the democratic system, state of law, basic rights. Upon these values, the so-called western democracy is built.

The democracy itself is represented by the principles of sovereignty, participation of inhabitants, representation, votes, and pluralism. It is a method of ruling, which was developed into the current form. This way of ruling represents more and more the state as a state based on law, where the law is a basis of democratic ruling.

VI The Europeanisation of National Constitutions

The general political homogeneity of Member States cannot ignore the diversity of Member States. However, this diversity is followed by the 'Europeanisation' of national constitutions.

Since the Maastricht Treaty, integration interferes massively with the constitutional texts. Germany, France and Portugal have decided that they will signify their European incorporation with a special constitutional basis. Germany has incorporated a special 'European article', France speaks in point XVI about the European Community and the European Union, and Portugal has incorporated a complimentary paragraph into the point, which concerns international relations (Art. 7, Paragraph 5). In relation to the constitutions of Greece and Spain, whose text supposes this type of article, neither are they out of the discussion about the so-called 'European Ruling'.

The situation of Member States, which have joined after the Maastricht Treaties, has meant a revision of constitutional texts (Sweden, Austria). The constitutionalisation of the Union has reacted with the necessity of creating a necessary constitutional basis in the single Member States. The so-called candidate countries have followed a similar way. The constitutionalisation of national constitutional texts revaluates the joining of a single state in the European integration. The new constitutional basis follows the new position of a state as a Union member.

The texts of national constitutions are supposing the specifics of the European Union; the term 'international constitutional law' appears also. The constitutional dimension of the Union is based on the enlargement of constitutional relations between the Union and its members and the recognition of a new loyalty of members towards the Union. The constitution-giving power also in some constitutions is binding to a new 'respect'. The incorporation of this element into the constitutions of the member or candidate states is a part of development of European constitutionality and it also shows that this process cannot follow without the constitutional systems of Member States. The development of integration and the revision of constitutional texts, which are relevant, influence the role of 'national constitutional power'. The incorporation of the so-called integration clause shows the protection of constitutional identity of a state in a new light. Part of the change is also the incorporation of procedures, which are related to possible transition of competencies to the new entity. These articles are strengthening the monist theory, even if they are protecting the identity of the constitutional order at the same time.

Part of the procedures of incorporation into the European Union and also of the possible transition of competencies or the changes of constitutions tied to it can be also a referendum.

The constitutional texts, despite formulating differences, which concern the possible transition of competencies, are not setting up the limits of this transition (also its broadness), neither its 'final version'. The absence of this final form is not considered to be a failure, because it would for many reasons assume something, which will be developed further.

Some constitutional texts are setting up certain legal conditions for the integration of the state. So, the so-called 'Europa-Artikel' of the German constitution states that Germany contributes to the development of the European Union, which is based on democratic social and federative principles.

A further source of constitutional values is the activity of constitutional courts. The constitution is unifying the legal order, constitutional law is coordinating the relations between the legal branches, and the judge of constitutional court interprets, rationalizes and explains the basic constitutional questions. The relation of the Community law and the national constitutional systems is one of the many material problems, which are being solved by constitutional courts. There is a positive effort in the activity of constitutional courts in the Member States to bring the national constitutional values closer to the values of the Union. This strengthens even further the mentioned loyalty of constitutional texts. At the same time, the relation of 'national' constitutional systems and Community law was judged by constitutional courts of originally candidate states.

From the viewpoint of the past decision-making activity of constitutional courts, it is obvious that they have tried to ensure for 'their' constitutions certain formal priority in relation to the European law. The constitutional debate of the relations of the Member States to Community law however leads the constitutional courts to the revaluation of the importance of the constitution in the process of integration by the fact that they are making the statute of European law in their legal orders more precise, especially of the right, which is derived from primal treaties.

The relation between the constitutions and the Community law and so the position of constitutional courts depends on the position of monism or dualism; the first one is prioritising the international law in the relation to internal law; the second one prefers the constitution in relation to the international law. In the dualist system, the Treaties (EC/EU) are acting on the basis of law, which gives them such authority as the reception norm.

In the monist system, the treaties are gaining the supralegal level (Article 96 of the Spanish constitution, Article 55 of the French constitution). There is a crucial theoretical question in this system, which position is taken by the community law in relation to the constitutional norms (the so-called infraconstitutionality) and which in relation to common laws (the so-called supra legality).

The relation of the primal community law to the constitutional systems is generally one of respect. The European Union respects the historical, cultural and linguistic identity of the Member States and also their constitutional basis (compare with the Article 1, point 2 of the Union Treaty).

VII Heterogeneity of the Forms of Constitutional Models in the Member States of European Union

1 Introduction

Retaining statehood by the Member States of the European Union is naturally followed by retaining their constitutionality. It means one thing that the Union usually keeps the specifics of constitutional models, which not only means that the (novelized) constitutions of different periods of development of constitutionality stay in power, but that the constitutional basis of each of the Member States represents a special version of the form of state, form of government, form of ruling (model of democracy), constitutional control, judicial system, territorial autonomy and similar.

The superiority of the Community legal system is not only accepted by constitutions in different ways, but a model of horizontal and vertical separation of powers of the single states is tied in a wholly different way to the Community system, which can be shown by the relation of each of the constitutional 'powers' (law-giving, executive, judicial, banking, control and similar).

2 Variety of Forms of State and Forms of Government

The comparative study, which lists the single Member States of the EU, also shows that there are both federations and unitary states among these states, all of which have different stages of centralisation or decentralisation. In addition to the problem of the different forms of state is the diversity of systems from the viewpoint of the head of state, when the system of power of the EU is a complex of monarchies and republics. This fact does not significantly influence the vertical control in the European Union from the constitutional view, because the constitutionally 'weak' heads of states of all monarchies and the majority of republics are accentuating the position of prime ministers and so the main line of control, which is from the regular European Commission, unifies the executive power.

3 Variety of Modifications of the Technologies of Democracy

As is the natural condition for EC/EU membership the democratic order fixed in the constitution, the single constitutional systems differ in the use of the types of voting systems (proportional or majority). The constitutional systems are wholly independent in the view on the direct or indirect vote of the president, which again generally does not influence the type of European federalism. The use of a referendum in the inner state life is an extraordinary constitutional measure, on which the countries decide independently, and are gaining more importance for the democratic legitimacy, especially in the most important questions of the participation of the countries in the decision making of the EU. The Member States of the European Union are also so diverse in the structure of the parliamentary power itself, when the two chamber parliament is not typical only for federations (Germany, Austria), but also for some unitary states (Poland, France, the Czech Republic) and not for others (Slovakia, Hungary and so on).

4 Variants of Territorial Autonomy

The territorial composition is a basis for the execution of central power in the territories and for the organisation of territorial and local autonomy. However, the territorial administration is mainly dependent on the demographic localisation of its inhabitants and it is generally based on the basic elements of a legitimate power, which are cities, city agglomerations or villages and other localities, tourist season centres in the mountains or at the sea and similar entities. The vertical organisation of power depends also on the historical specialties of the original country parts (typical in Italy and France but also in the land order in Bohemia and Moravia), often also in the feudal medieval organisations (for example the original 'voivod' organisations in Poland).

The territorial organisation is also influenced by the original and existing church territorial organisation (for example the counties in England) and the original organisations of feudal territorial administration (the county system in Hungary).

The constitutional autonomy of Member States from the viewpoint of its own territorial organisation of the state is also wholly democratically original and inferior only to the international documents recommendation. The regional autonomy can however be an important factor for the receiving of supportive grants for developments from the single resources of the EC/EU.

5 The Special Position of Constitutional Judiciary

The establishment of the constitutional judiciary in the majority of states of continental Europe is an important phenomenon of the development of constitutionality after World War II in Europe, but it is also an important link, which influences the inner relations in the European Union of those states, which are its members and have established their constitutional courts. The phenomenon of the activity of those constitutional courts demonstrates itself in that they had to sort out separately the relationship of their own constitutional system to the system of Community law, to the organs of the EC/EU and to the case-law of the European Court of Justice. The constitutional courts have so decided about their role during the control of compatibility of their own laws with the constitution, but also about the character of the 'superiority' of Community law to their own constitutional order.

CHAPTER 6

The Interpretation Doctrine of the European Court of Human Rights

Viera Strážnická

The Convention with its Protocols established the most effective supervisory mechanism for the protection of human rights and fundamental freedoms in the European legal space. The evidence of the Conventions' impact is the legislative process in the new democracies of Central and Eastern Europe. The new Contracting States are an indication both of how far the influence of the Conventional system extends and of its vital quality. It is noteworthy that the European Convention has been the main source of inspiration for new constitutions and legislative acts on human rights guarantees in these countries. Soon after their accession to the Convention, more and more of their citizens turned to seek redress before the European Court of Human Rights (European Court or ECHR).

1 The Special Character of the European Convention

Reading the Convention may invoke questions concerning its nature, content and interpretation. At first glance, it is clear that the Convention is an international Treaty to which the rules of international law for interpreting international treaties should be applied.

The relationship of the Convention to the Vienna Convention on the Law of Treaties of 23 May 1969 (Vienna Convention) firstly and then its relationship to other international acts on human rights must be considered. Article 31 (1) states that a treaty shall be interpreted in good faith in accordance with the ordinary meaning to be given to the terms of the treaty in their context and in the light of its object and purpose. Of no less importance is Article 31 (2), which states that the Preamble to the Convention forms an integral part of the context for determination of the object and purpose of the Convention. According to Article 31 (3), account must be taken together with the context of any relevant rules of international law applicable between the parties, including the subsequent agreements and practice.

Considering the interpretation of the European Convention, the former Court expressly referred to Articles 31-33 of the Vienna Convention, which encompass generally accepted principles of international law in the Golder judgment. The Court also noted that *"account is to be taken of those Articles subject, where appropriate, to "any relevant rules of the organization" – the Council of Europe – within which it has been adopted (Article 5 of the Vienna Convention)".*[1]

Regarding the rules of interpretation of the provisions of a treaty, Article 32 of the Vienna Convention states that supplementary means of interpretation, such as the preparatory works of the treaty, are also relevant in certain circumstances. The rule reflects the historical background in the interpretation of the treaties.

* Prof. JUDr. Viera Strážnická, Ph.D. is Jean Monnet Professor on European Law and Vice-Rector at Bratislava Univercity of Law, Slovak Republic and the former Judge of the European Court of Human Rights.

1 *Golder v. the UK*, judgment of 21 February 1975, Series A-18, § 29-35.

Although the Court ruled in several cases on the basis of the *'travaux préparatoires'*, its role was limited by the dynamic interpretation prevailing in the Court case-law that the Convention is *"a living instrument, which should be interpreted according to present-day conditions".*[2]

In the case of *Tyrer*, a 15 year-old boy sentenced to corporal punishment, it was claimed that this type of judicial punishment constituted degrading treatment contrary to Article 3 of the Convention. The national authorities underlined the public opinion, which strongly supported the retention of corporal punishment and referred to Article 63 of the Convention. In its judgment, the Court held that:

> *'...there is no evidence before the Court to show that the law and order in the Isle of Man could not be maintained without recourse to that punishment. In this connection, it is noteworthy, that in the great majority of member States of the Council of Europe, judicial corporal punishment is not, it appears, used and, indeed, in some of them has never existed in modern times;... Likewise, in the Court's view, no local requirement relative to the maintenance of law and order would entitle any of those States, under Article 63 to make use of punishment contrary to Article 3'.* [3]

The Court's decision was a clear rejection of the concept, which considered the Convention as a static instrument protecting the rights at the level of 1950 when the Convention was adopted.

In the landmark judgment for extradition cases, in the *Soering* case, the Court recalled that the '*Convention is an instrument which...must be interpreted in the light of present-day conditions'* and considered that Article 3 contains an inherent obligation of the State not to extradite if there is a real risk that a person would face a treatment going beyond the threshold set by Article 3. [4] Since that time, the formula has been repeatedly used in many judgments and further developed in the *Loizidou* judgment, in which the Court held that the Convention '*cannot be interpreted solely in – accordance with the intentions of their authors as expressed more than forty years ago. Accordingly, even if it had been established ...that restrictions...were considered permissible...at a time when a minority of the present Contracting Parties adopted the Convention, such evidence could not be decisive'.*[5]

Nevertheless, the provisions of the Vienna Convention do not offer the explanation on the concept of the 'ordinary meaning' of the terms used in the European Convention.[6] Moreover, both authentic languages differ and their

---

[2] One of the first judgments was in the case *Tyrer v. the UK*, judgment of 25 April 1978, Series A-26, § 31. See also P.van Dijk, F.van Hoof, A. van Rijn, L. Zwaak (eds.), Theory and Practice of the European Convention on Human Rights, 2006, pp. 847, 852, 1080, 1113.

[3] *Tyrer v. the UK*, cit. above, § 38.

[4] *Soering* judgment of 7 July 1989, A-161, §§ 102, 111, 128.

[5] *Loizidou v. Turkey*, judgment of 23 March 1995 (Preliminary Objection), Series A-310, § 71.

[6] See Jacobs and White, The European Convention on Human Rights, Clare Ovey and Robin White, 2006, pp. 42-44.

reconciliation depends on the interpretation of the object and purpose of the Convention.

Sometimes vague provisions of the Convention have been interpreted and developed in the Court's practice by way of using several interpretation methods.[7] Among them, preference was given to the literal interpretation of the text combined with the comparison between the English and French versions and supported by a systematic, dynamic and progressive interpretation.

The Court created by its case-law the doctrine of the autonomous meaning of the terms, not always identical with their determination in the national laws. To avoid differences in the definition of the terms used in the Convention and in legal systems of the Contracting States, the Court has developed its own criteria for interpretation and application of the terms like 'civil rights and obligations', 'criminal charge', 'penalty', 'possession', 'tribunal', 'victim', 'prescribed by law', 'promptly', 'arguable claim', 'manifestly ill-founded', 'effective remedy', 'pressing social need', 'necessary in democratic society', 'public service', 'association', 'public order' etc.

The Court has always emphasized the common heritage in the traditional values and democratic principles of the European States. Its case-law proves that the Court attached decisive importance to the legal development in the Member States of the Council of Europe and would be willing to apply the 'consensus principle' based on the sufficient common ground in legislation or consistent practice of the Member States of the CE.[8] This approach has found its reflection in the doctrine of margin of appreciation and in the cautious increase of human rights protection in Europe.

The special nature of the Convention was underlined by the Court in the *Soering* judgment:

'In interpreting the Convention regard must be had to its special character as a treaty for the collective enforcement of human rights and fundamental freedoms (see the Ireland v. the United Kingdom, judgment of 18 January 1978, Series A-25, p. 90, § 239). Thus the object and purpose of the Convention as an instrument for the protection of individual human beings require that its provisions be interpreted and applied so as to make its safeguards practical and effective (see inter alia, the Artico judgment of 13 May 1980, Series A-37, p. 16, § 33). In addition, any interpretation of the rights and freedoms guaranteed has to be consistent with the 'general spirit of the Convention, an instrument designed to maintain and promote the ideals and values of a democratic society' (see the Kjeldsen, Busk Madsen and Pedersen judgment of 7 December 1976, Series A-23, p. 27, § 53)'.[9]

7 Among others R.A. Lawson & H.G. Schermers, Leading Cases of the European Court of Human Rights, 1999, pp. 15-22.

8 See Comments on *Handyside v. the UK*, judgment of 12 December 1976, Series A-24; *Dudgeon v. the UK*, judgment of 22 October 1981, Series A-45; *Sigurjonsson v. Iceland*, judgment of 30 June 1993, Series A-264; in: Leading cases of the European Court of Human Rights, cit. above, pp. 40, 133, 544; See also P. van Dijk, G.J.H van Hoof, Theory and Practice of the European Convention on Human Rights, 1998, p. 78.

9 *Soering v. the UK*, cit. above, § 87.

The Convention was for the first time characterised as a 'constitutional instrument of European public order' in the *Loizidou* judgment on the occasion when the Court considered the responsibility of the Contracting States and the supervisory role of the Court. Concerning the Articles 25 and 46 § 2 the Court held:

'If, as contended by the respondent Government, substantive or territorial restrictions were permissible under these provisions, Contracting Parties would be free to subscribe to separate regimes of enforcement of Convention obligations depending on the scope of their acceptances. Such a system, which would enable States to qualify their consent under the optional clauses, would not only seriously weaken the role of the Commission and the Court in the discharge of their functions, but would also diminish the effectiveness of the Convention as a constitutional instrument of the European public order (order public)'.

Bearing in mind the present state of incorporation of the European Convention into the national law of the Contracting States, under the concept of a 'European public order' all fundamental rules of law and principles which regulate to the behaviour of the Contracting States and reflect their common values and commitments under the Convention should be understood.

The Court's interpretation doctrine was influenced by the acts and practice of the international organizations like the United Nations, the International Labour Organisation, the Council of Europe and the European Communities.

In the case of *Pellegrin*, the Court established the interpretation of the term 'public service' based on the 'new functional criterion' and restrictive interpretation of the Convention. In its judgment, the Court referred to the public servants classification in the European Commission communication from 1988 and to the judgment of the Court of Justice of the European Communities from 1980.[10]

In other judgments, the Court used the references to the international human rights documents as the supplementary sources of interpretation, e.g. the 1966 International Covenant on Civil and Political Rights, the American Convention on Human Rights, the 1951 United Nations Convention relating to the Status of Refugees, the 1984 UN Convention against Torture and Other Cruel, Inhuman or Degrading Treatment or Punishment, the 1957 European Convention on Extradition, the 1961 European Social Charter. [11]

In the *Selmouni* judgment, the Court, sitting in the Grand Chamber, provided a more precise definition of 'torture' by referring to the United Nations Convention against Torture and Other Cruel, Inhuman and Degrading Treatment or Punishment:

---

10 *Pellegrin v. France*, judgment of 8 December 1999, Reports 1999-VIII, §§ 38, 66;

11 *Soering*, cit.above, § 88; *Niemetz v. Germany*, judgment of 16 December 1992, Series A-251-B, § 22; *Funke v. France*, judgment of 25 February 1993, Series A-256-A, § 42; *Chahal v. the UK*, judgment of 15 November 1996, Reports 1996-V, § 80; *Ahmed v. Austria*, judgment of 17 December 1996, Reports 1996-V, § 41; *Assanidze v. Geogia*, judgment of 8 April 2004, Reports 2004, § 139-143.

'In order to determine whether a particular form of ill-treatment should be qualified as torture, the Court must have regard to the distinction, embodied in Article 3, between this notion and that of inhuman or degrading treatment. As the European Court has previously found, it appears that it was the intention that the Convention should, by means of this distinction, attach a special stigma to deliberate inhuman treatment causing very serious and cruel suffering (see the Ireland v. the UK, judgment of 18 January 1978, pp. 66-67, § 167). The UN Convention against torture and Other Cruel, Inhuman or Degrading Treatment or Punishment, which came into force on 26 June 1987, also makes such a distinction, as can be seen from Articles 1 and 16...'[12]

Referring to the general principles of international law and other interpretative rules, the Court has often applied a combination of various interpretative techniques.

2 The Court's Interpretation Doctrine

The scope of the human rights protection in the European Convention is defined in Article 1:

'The High Contracting Parties shall secure to everyone within their jurisdiction the rights and freedoms defined in Section 1 of this Convention'.

Article 1 is the legal basis for the determination of the Contracting State's obligations and the scope of human rights guaranteed to all persons under the State's jurisdiction. The term 'jurisdiction' is rather wide concept that encompasses the jurisdiction of ratione temporis, ratione personae and ratione materiae. [13]

The notion 'within jurisdiction' invokes the question of the States' responsibility, which under the Convention includes its territorial and extra-territorial dimension. The question may arise whether a State is responsible for the international relations of a given territory (Article 56) in the situation when the application is lodged against it because of the acts of the authorities in those territories. The State is also responsible for the acts of its authorities, including its agents acting outside State territory as the State's representatives.

The Court has already developed the concept of 'jurisdiction' not strictly limited to the national territory of the Contracting State in its case-law.[14] In the case, *Loizidou v. Turkey*, the Court gave the following summary of the concept of 'jurisdiction':

---

12 *Selmouni v. France*, judgment of 28 July 1999, Reports 1999, §§ 96-106.

13 See P. van Dijk, F. van Hoof, A. van Rijn, L. Zvaak (eds.), Theory and Practice of the European Convention on Human Rights 2006, pp. 23-24, 184-192.

14 *Loizidou v. Turkey* (Preliminary obj.), cit. above.; *Loizidou v. Turkey*, (Merits), judgment of 18 December 1996, Reports 1996-VI; *Cyprus v. Turkey*, judgment of 10 May 2001, Reports 2001; *Asanidze v. Georgia*, cit. above.

'In this respect the Court recalls that, although Article 1 set limits on the reach of the Convention, the concept of "jurisdiction" under this provision is not restricted to the national territory of the High Contracting Parties. According to the established case-law, for example, the Court has held that the extradition or expulsion of a person by a Contracting State may give rise to an issue under Article 3 and hence engage the responsibility of that State under the Convention (see the case Soering v. the United Kingdom, judgment of 7 July 1989, Series A-161, pp. 35-36, § 91; the Cruz Varas and others v. Sweden, judgment of 20 March 1991, Series A-201, p. 28, § 69-70, and the Vilvarajah and Others v. the United Kingdom, judgment of 30 October 1991, Series A-215, p. 34, § 103). In addition, the responsibility of Contracting Parties can be involved because of acts of their authorities, whether performed within or outside national boundaries, which produce effects outside their own territory (see the case Drozd and Janousek v. France and Spain, judgment of 26 June 1992, Series A-240, p. 29, § 91).

Bearing in mind the object and purpose of the Convention, the responsibility of a Contracting Party may also arise when as a consequence of military action – whether lawful or unlawful – it exercises effective control of an area outside its national territory. The obligation to secure, in such an area, the rights and freedoms set out in the Convention derives from the fact of such control whether it be exercised directly, through its armed forces, or through a subordinate local administration.'[15]

In the case, *Bankovic and Others*, which concerned the consequences of the bombing carried out by 17 member States of NATO on the Radio-Television Serbia headquarters in Belgrade, the application was declared inadmissible. It was a typical case on the 'extra-territorial jurisdiction' of the States concerned. They disputed their jurisdiction *ratione loci* arguing that the applicants were not on their national territory and that it was the UN which had overall effective control of Kosovo. The respondent States submitted that the applicants were not resident in the legal space of the Convention.

The Court noted that the case was different from that of *Cyprus v. Turkey* in which Turkey exercised effective control of a substantial part of Cyprus territory by its military forces. In this case, the Court summarised the applicable rules of interpretation and its relevant case-law. It expressed its opinion on the 'ordinary meaning' of the term 'jurisdiction' in Article 1 of the Convention and held that, from the standpoint of public international law, Article 1 must be considered to reflect that the jurisdictional competence of a State was primarily territorial, other bases of jurisdiction being exceptional and requiring special justification in the particular circumstances of each case. The Court considered that it was its obligation:

'to have regard to the special character of the Convention as a constitutional instrument of European public order for the protection of individual human beings

[15] *Loizidou v. Turkey*, cit. above, § 62.

and its role as set out in Article 19 of the Convention, is to ensure the observance of the engagements undertaken by the Contracting Parties (the above-cited Loizidou judgment (preliminary objection), at § 93)...'

The Court further noted that:

'the Convention is a multi-lateral treaty operating, subject to Article 56 of the Convention, in an essentially regional context and notably in the legal space of the Contracting States. The FRY clearly does not fall within this legal space. The Convention was not designed to be applied throughout the world, even in respect of the conduct of Contracting States. ..

The Court is not therefore persuaded that there was any jurisdictional link between the persons who were victims of the act complained of and the respondent States. Accordingly, it is not satisfied that the applicants and their deceased relatives were capable of coming within the jurisdiction of the respondent States on account of the extra-territorial act in question .... The Court concludes that the impugned action does not engage the responsibility of the respondent States does not engage their Convention responsibility and that it is not therefore to consider the other admissibility issues raised by the parties.' [16]

In the case of *Ilascu and Others v. Moldova and Russia*, the applicants submitted that the Moldavian authorities were responsible for the violations of Articles 6, 1 of the Protocol No. 1, Articles 5, 2, 3, 8 and 34 of the Convention since they had not taken adequate measures to secure their human rights. Moreover, Russia shared that responsibility as the territory of Transdniestria was under Russia's de facto control supported by its troops. In the *Ilascu* judgment, the Court concluded:

'312...From the standpoint of public international law, the words 'within their jurisdiction' in Article 1 of the Convention must be understood to mean that a State's jurisdictional competence is primarily territorial..., but also that jurisdiction is presumed to be exercised normally throughout the State's territory.

This presumption may be limited in exceptional circumstances, particularly where a State is prevented from exercising its authority in part of its territory. That may be as a result of military occupation by the armed forces of another State which effectively controls the territory concerned..., acts of war or rebellion, or the acts of a foreign State supporting the installation of a separatist State within the territory of the state concerned.

313. In order to be able to conclude that such an exceptional situation exists, the Court must examine on the one hand all the objective facts capable of limiting the effective exercise of a State's authority over its territory, and on the other the State's own conduct. The undertaking given by a Contracting State under Article 1 of the

---

[16] Application *Bankovic and Others v. Belgium* and 16 other Contracting States was declared inadmissible, Decision on admissibility of 12 December 2001, §§ 59-61, 80, 82, 84, www. echr.coe.int.

Convention include, in addition to the duty to refrain from interfering with enjoyment of the rights and freedoms guaranteed, positive obligations to take appropriate steps to ensure respect for those rights and freedoms within the territory...

Those obligations remain even where the exercise of the State's authority is limited in part of its territory, so that it has a duty to take all appropriate measures, which it is still within its power to take.

314...According to the relevant principles of international law, a State responsibility may be engaged where, as a consequence of military action – whether lawful or unlawful- it in practice exercises effective control of an area situated outside its national territory. The obligation to secure in such area, the rights and freedoms set out in the Convention derives from the fact of such control, whether it be exercised directly, though its armed forces, or through a subordinate local administration...

316. Where a Contracting State exercise overall control over an area outside its national territory its responsibility is not confined to the acts of its soldiers or officials in that area but also to acts of the local administration which survives there by virtue of its military and other support '.[17]

Thus, the Court clearly stated that both Moldova and Russia were responsible for complying with the obligations under Article 1 of the Convention.

The obligations under the Convention may be considered in the Court's case-law as positive ones – to guarantee the protected rights to everybody under the jurisdiction and as negative ones – not to violate the protected rights and freedoms. The States are in general obliged to ensure that the domestic legislation is compatible with the Convention and that the acts of public authorities are in compliance with the rights and freedoms guaranteed by the Convention and its Protocols. The Court stated expressly that all legal rules, even constitutional provisions, come within the 'jurisdiction' of member States for the purposes of the Convention and may be reviewed by the Court for the purpose of compliance with the convention standard.

In the case of *The United Communist Party of Turkey and Others v. Turkey* concerning the dissolution of a political party ordered by the Constitutional Court of the respondent country on account of the statutes, which were held to be contrary to the Turkish Constitution, the Court stated:

'Article 1 requires the State Parties to 'secure to everybody within their jurisdiction the rights and freedoms defined in Section 1 of this Convention'. That provision, together with Articles 14, 2 and 13 and 63, demarcates the scope of the Convention, ratione personae, materiae and loci (see case Ireland v. the United Kingdom, judgment of 18 January 1978, Series A-25, pp. 90, § 238). It makes no distinction as to the type of rule or measure concerned and does not exclude any part of the Member States 'jurisdiction' from the scrutiny under the Convention. It is therefore with respect to their jurisdiction as a whole – which is often exercised in the first place

[17] *Ilascu v. Moldova and Russia*, judgment of 8 July 2004, cit. above, §§ 312-319.

through the Constitution – that the States Parties are called on to show compliance with the Convention.

The political and institutional organisation of the Member States must accordingly respect the rights and principles enshrined in the Convention. It matters little in this context whether the provisions in issue are constitutional (see for example, the case Gitonas and Others v. Greece, judgment of 1 July 1997, Reports 1997-IV) or merely legislative (see the Mathieu-Mohin and Clerfayt v. Belgium, judgment of 2 March 1987, Reports A-113). From the moment such provisions are the means by which the State concerned exercises its jurisdiction they are subject to review under the Convention.

Moreover, it may on occasion prove difficult, even artificial, in the proceedings before the Court, to attempt to distinguish between what forms part of a States institutional structures and what relates to fundamental rights in the strict sense. That is particularly true of an order for dissolution of the kind in issue in the present case. In view of the role played by political parties such measures affect both freedom of association and, consequently, democracy in the state concerned.' [18]

In general, a State is internationally responsible for all acts of its legislative, executive and judicial authorities. Under certain circumstances, the conclusion on the scope of State responsibility may be a rather complicated issue confronted with legal and political arguments.

The application will be declared inadmissible ratione personae if the alleged violation does not fall under the responsibility of the respondent State. The question may arise whether a particular organ or person can be considered as belonging to the governmental authority. The precise position of the State organ or so-called public enterprises or companies is important in answering the question of responsibility for the acts on behalf of the State.

The serious questions of extra-territorial 'jurisdiction' of the respondent States within the meaning of Article 1 of the Convention and the compatibility ratione personae and loci have arisen in the joint cases of *Behrami and Behrami v. France and Saramati v. France, Germany and Norway*. In the *Behrami* case, the applicant's father complained under Article 2 about the death of his son caused by a detonated cluster bomb, which remained from the bombardment by NATO in 1999 of Kosovo and the second applicant, his second son, about his serious injury caused by the detonated bomb. They submitted that the incident took place as the consequence of the failure of French troops and the KFOR mission to mark the un-detonated bomb. The applicant Saramati, an Albanian living in Kosovo, was arrested by the UN police on suspicion of attempted murder and illegal possession of a weapon. He complained under Articles 5, 6 and 13 about his extra-territorial detention by KFOR. The applicants maintained that the international mandate of UN/NATO, which the relevant States were executing,

18 *The United Communist Party of Turkey and Others v. Turkey*, judgment of 30 January 1998, Reports 1998-I, pp. 17-18, §§ 29-31.

would not absolve them from their Conventional responsibility. They submitted that there was a sufficient jurisdictional link within the meaning of Article 1 of the Convention, between them and the respondent States as the acts were carried out by the national contingents and as such involved the responsibility ratione personae of the respondent States.

The respondent States submitted that the case was inadmissible mainly because the applicants had not exhausted available remedies and the respondent States had no jurisdiction loci or personae because the territory of Kosovo was under the effective control of the United Nations. The Court recalled that:

'Article 1 requires Contracting States to guarantee Convention rights to individuals falling with their 'jurisdiction'. This jurisdictional competence is primarily territorial and, while the notion of compatibility ratione personae of complaints is distinct, the two concepts can be inter-dependent (Bankovic and Others, cited above, at § 75 and Bosphorus Airways v. Ireland, /GC/, no. 45036/98, §§ 136 and 137, ECHR 2005-VI)...

It also recalls that the principles underlying in the Convention cannot be interpreted and applied in vacuum. It must also take in account relevant rules of international law when examining questions concerning its jurisdiction and, consequently, determine State responsibility in conformity and harmony with the governing principles of international law of which it forms a part, although it must remain mindful of the Convention's special character as a human rights treaty (Article 31 §3c) of the Vienna Convention on the Law of Treaties of 23 May 1969; Al Adsani v. the United Kingdom /GC/no. 35763/97, § 55, ECHR 2001-XI; and the above-cited decision of Bankovic and Others, at § 75)...'.[19]

The Court examined its competence ratione personae and concluded that the impugned action and inaction were, in principle, attributable to the UN having a legal personality separate from that of its Member States and not being a Contracting Party to the Convention. The Court considered carefully the acts of the respondent States carried out on behalf of the UN and the relationship between the Convention and the UN acting under Chapter VII of its Charter. The Court concluded:

'...In the present case the impugned acts and omission of KFOR and UNMIK cannot be attributed to the respondent States and, moreover, did not take place on the territory of those States or by virtue of a decision of their authorities. The present cases are therefore clearly distinguishable from the Bosphorus case in terms both of the responsibility of the respondent States under Article 1 and of the Court's competence ratione personae.

---

[19] *Behrami and Behrami v. France and Saramati v. France, Germany and Norway*, Decision of 2 May 2007, /GC/, §§ 69, 122.

There exists, in any event, a fundamental distinction between the nature if the international organisation and of the international cooperation with which the Court was there concerned and those in the present case. As the Court has found above, UNMIK was a subsidiary organ of the UN created under Chapter VII and KFOR was exercising powers lawfully delegated under Chapter VII of the Charter by the UNSC. As such, their actions were directly attributable to the UN, an organisation of universal jurisdiction fulfilling its imperative collective security objective'.[20]

The Court declared the applicants complaints incompatible ratione personae with the provisions of the Convention.

The Contracting States cannot absolve themselves from the obligation to respect the human rights and fundamental freedoms guaranteed by the Convention as a consequence of transferring their sovereign powers to the international organisation. The Court examined the State's responsibility in this context in the case of *Matthews* and held that there had been a violation of Article 3 of Protocol No. 1 on the territorial application of the Protocol concerned by the UK on the ground that the UK had not organised an election to the European Parliament in Gibraltar. The Court stated that Article 3 of Protocol 1 applies in Gibraltar as the Convention was extended to this territory by the UK Declaration of 23 October 1953 and the Protocol has been applicable since 25 February 1988. The Court stated:

'The Convention does not exclude the transfer of the competences to the international organisations provided that Convention rights continue to be secured. Member States responsibility therefore continues even after such a transfer...

In determining to what extend the UK is responsible for 'securing' the rights in Article 3 of Protocol No. 1 in respect of the elections to the EP in Gibraltar, the Court recalls that the Convention is intended to guarantee the rights that are not theoretical or illusory, but practical and effective. It is uncontested that legislation emanating from the legislative process of the EC affects the population of Gibraltar in the same way as legislation, which enters the domestic legal order exclusively via the House of Assembly. To this extent there is no difference between European and domestic legislation and no reason why the UK should not be required to 'secure' the rights in Article 3 of Protocol No. 1 in respect of European legislation, in the same way as those rights are required to be 'secured' in respect of purely domestic legislation....

It follows that the UK is responsible for securing the rights guaranteed by Article 3 of Protocol No.1 in Gibraltar regardless of whether the elections were purely domestic or European.' [21]

Similarly, in the case *Prince Hans-Adam II of Lichtenstein* the Court recalled:

---

[20] Ibid, §§ 151-152.

[21] *Matthews v. the UK*, judgment of 18 February 1999, Reports 2000-I., §§ 32-35.

'Article 1 makes no distinction as to the type of rule or measure concerned and does not exclude any part of the Contracting States 'jurisdiction' from the scrutiny under the Convention (see above Judgment in case The United Communist Party...).

Thus the States' responsibility continues even after their having entered into treaty commitments subsequent to the entry into force of the Convention or its Protocols in respect of these States (see mutatis mutandis case Matthews v. the United Kingdom, 24833/94, §§ 29 and 32-34, Reports 2000 – I).

The Court recalls in this respect that where States establish international organisation in order to pursue or strengthen their co-operation in certain fields of activities, and where they attribute to these organizations certain competences and accord them immunities, there may be implications as to the protection of fundamental rights. It would be incompatible with the object and purposes of the Convention, however, if the Contracting States were thereby absolved from their responsibility under the Convention in relation to the field of activity covered by such an attribution'.[22]

In the case, *Bosphorus Airways,* the Court examined the seizure in Ireland of an aircraft leased from Yugoslav Airlines as a consequence of sanctions imposed against the Federal Republic of Yugoslavia (Serbia and Montenegro) in the European Communities Council Regulation 990/93. The applicant claimed the violation of his property rights under Article 1 of Protocol 1. The Court concluded:

'154...In establishing the extent to which the State can be justified by its compliance with the obligations flowing from its membership of an international organization to which it has transferred part of its sovereignty, the Court has recognised that absolving Contracting States completely from their Convention responsibility in the areas covered by such a transfer would be incompatible with the purpose and object of the Convention: the guarantees of the Convention could be limited or excluded at will thereby depriving it of its peremptory character and undermining the practical and effective nature of its safeguards... The State is considered to retain Convention liability in respect of treaty commitments subsequent to the entry into force of the Convention...'

The rights and freedoms guaranteed by the Convention and its Protocols were incorporated in the national systems of the Contracting States by way of their constitutional rules and must be enforced in their judicial systems. The States are obliged to ensure that their national legislation and the acts of all public authorities are compatible with the Convention. The effective implementation of the Convention includes also the States obligations to guarantee the enforcement of the Court's judgments in its territory.

[22] *Prince Hans-Adam II of Lichtenstein v. Germany*, judgment of 12 July 2001, Reports 2001, §§ 46-48.

3 The Key Principles of the Interpretation

The main function of the European Court of Human Rights is in the process of dealing with the applications to supervise whether the national systems of the Contracting States are compatible with the Convention standard.

Since its adoption, the Convention generated extensive jurisprudence in the Court's case-law. The importance of the Court's case-law may be seen at the spectrum of the subject matter of the judgments delivered in the past. Despite the prevailing applications about the administration of justice in civil, criminal and administrative proceedings, the variety of issues before the Court include cases concerning the alleged torture or inhuman treatment, a risk of such a treatment in case of expulsion and extradition of the nationals of non-contracting States, violations of human rights of the persons under arrest or in – detention, matters relating to the taking care of children, scope and respect of private and family rights, various aspects of freedom of expression, religion and freedom of association and also a wide scope of the property rights and restitutions issue.

The Court was consistently raising the minimum standard guaranteed by the Convention to the present level of human rights protection by interpretation of the Convention's provisions. Exercising its supervisory function as an international tribunal, the Court reviews the States compliance with their obligations according to the Convention in order to maintain the European standard in the protection of human rights.

Several leading principles relevant for interpretation of the Convention provisions emerged and were followed in similar cases. These principles create the present doctrine of the Court, which serves as guidelines for the application of the Convention and at the same time influence national courts' jurisprudence.

3.1 The Convention as 'a Living Legal Instrument'

The doctrine of dynamic evolutive interpretation is based on the Court's consideration of the Convention as 'a living legal instrument' which must be interpreted in the light of 'present-day conditions'.[23] Human rights are not invariable.. In the past, many situations such as apartheid, discrimination, intolerance against different sexual orientations, were considered acceptable in some areas of society and the law; however, nowadays those attitudes would be contrary to fundamental human rights.

The evolutive approach towards interpretation of the Convention implies that the Court takes into account contemporary realities and attitudes rather than the conditions and intentions at the time of drafting the Convention. Neverthe-

[23] *Tyrer v. the UK*, cit. above, § 32, *Marckx v. Belgium*, judgment of 13 June 1979, A-31, § 41; *Loizidou v. Turkey*, cit. above, § 71; *Soering v. the UK*, cit. above, § 102; *Cruz Varas v. Sweeden*, judgment of 20 March 1991, A-201, § 100; mutatis mutandis *F. v. Switzerland*, judgment of 18 December 1987, A-128, § 33.

less, in the case of *Johnsson*, the Court referred to the foregoing interpretation of Article 12 as consistent with its object and purpose as revealed by the *'travaux préparatoires'* and concluded: *'It is true that the Convention and its Protocols must be interpreted in the lights of present-day conditions (see, among several authorities, the above-mentioned Marckx judgment, Series A no. 31, p. 26, § 58). However, the Court cannot, by means of evolutive interpretation, derive from these instruments a right that was not included therein at the outset.'* [24]

In general the Court is rather cautious to follow a new standard in the legislation of some Contracting States until a clear European common ground or judicial practice will not prevail in the Contracting States.

On the other hand, the Court on various occasions, e.g. children born out of wedlock, death penalty abolition practice, common existence of interim measures, legal position of transsexuals etc. reflected the developed legislation or practice in the Contracting Parties on the interpretation of relevant provisions of the Convention. For example, the Court found no violation of Article 8 in the judgment of *X.Y. and Z. v. the UK* (1997) when it held:

'In conclusion, given that transsexuality raises complex scientific, legal, moral and social issues, in respect of which there is no generally shared approach among the Contracting States, the Court is of the opinion that Article 8 cannot in this context, be taken to imply an obligation for the respondent State formally to recognise as the father of a child a person who is not the biological father...'

And in the case of *Cossey* concerning the alleged violation of the right to respect for the private life of the applicant who wanted marry after a gender change, the Court stated that there is still little common ground between Contracting States on the issue in the area of which they enjoy a wide margin of appreciation. [25]

The judgments in the cases, *Salesi, Selmouni and Salman*, illustrate that evolutive interpretation is linked to a search for common European standards on the basis of national law and the practice of Contracting States, supported by the Court's case-law and other international or European instruments. This approach towards the Convention interpretation fully corresponds to the object and purpose of the Convention determined generally as protection of human rights and asserted in the Preamble to the Convention by the emphasis on the *'further realization of human rights and fundamental freedoms'. Moreover in accordance with the Article 32 of the Convention the Court's jurisdiction 'shall extend to all matters concerning the interpretation and application of the Convention and the protocols....'* [26]

---

[24] *Johnsson v. Ireland*, judgment of 18 December 1986, A-112, § 53.

[25] *X.Y. and Z. v. the UK*, judgment of 22 April 1997, Reports 1997-II; *Cossey v. the UK*, judgment of 27 September 1990, A-184.

[26] *Salesi v. Italy*, judgment of 26 February 1993, A-257; *Salman v. Turkey*, judgment of 27 June 2000, Reports 2000-I; *Selmouni v. France*, cit. above.

The Court examined the growing frequency of cases in which the violation of Article 6 §1 were found and draw attention to the *'important danger that exist for the rule of law'* within the legal orders when *'excessive delays in the administration of justice'* occur in respect of which litigants have no domestic remedy. [27] As a consequence, the Court reviewed its case-law concerning the national remedies in the relevant Contracting States and concluded that the correct interpretation of Article 13 was that it shall guarantee an effective remedy above all before a national authority for the alleged breach of the requirement to hear the case within a reasonable time.

The most persuasive argument for maintaining the dynamic evolutive interpretation among other means of interpretation is the flexibility of the doctrine enabling it to adapt to the existing Convention guarantees, to evolutions in the changing standard of the Contracting States and to raise the level of protection afforded by the Convention. Thus, the Court is vested with a special interpretation task to give contemporary meaning to relevant terms and expressions of the Convention taking into account the subsequent development in national and international standards. In order to fulfil its task the Court is continuing in the harmonisation of human rights protection and integration of Contracting States on the basis of the European public order. The relevance of the evolutive interpretation doctrine in conjunction with other interpretation principles may become pertinent, e.g. in specific cases of organised terrorism.

3.2 The Principle of Subsidiarity

One of the basic principles in the Court's interpretation technique is the principle of subsidiarity While the Court has generally been successful in developing the Convention standards by means of the interpretation methods, it has also recognized that the scope of its review may be limited in a situation where a delicate assessment is required for which national authorities are better placed than an international tribunal. In the light of the subsidiarity principle, the Court repeatedly stated that the primary responsibility for securing the protection of the rights and freedoms set forth in the Convention falls to the national authorities. Certainly, this is predicated on the assumption that the Contracting States are truly democratic and have an effectively functioning judicial system.

The subsidiarity applies within the framework of the Convention as a principle for the distribution of powers between the supervisory mechanism of the Convention and the national authorities. The system might function most effectively when the allegations of violation could be tested under the procedure before the national courts.

---

[27] *Kudla v. Poland*, judgment of 10 October 2000, Reports 2000; also Bottazzi v. Italy, judgment of 28 July 1999-V, § 22.

In its early *Belgian Linguistic* case, and later in other cases, the Court stated that it could not *'assume the role of the competent national authorities'* for to do so would be to *'lose sight of the subsidiary nature of the international machinery of collective enforcement established by the Convention. The national authorities remain free to choose the measures, which they consider appropriate in those matters governed by the Convention. Review by the Court concern only the conformity of those measures with the requirements of the Convention'.*[28]

As regards to the interpretation and application of national law, the Court reiterated in the context of the rule of exhaustion of domestic remedies that:

'the States are dispensed from answering before an international body for their acts before they have had an opportunity to put matters right through their own legal systems.... In this way, it is an important aspect of the principle (of exhaustion of domestic remedies) that the machinery of protection established by the Convention is subsidiary to the national systems safeguarding human rights (see the Akvidar and Others judgment cited in § 38 above, p. 15, § 65'.

and further stated:

'While the Courts duty, according to Article 19 of the Convention is to ensure the observance of the engagements undertaken by the Contracting Parties to the Convention, it is not its function to deal with errors of fact or law allegedly committed by a national court unless and in so far as they may have infringed rights and freedoms protected by the Convention (see among other authorities, the Schenk v. Switzerland judgment of 12 July 1988, Series A-140, p. 29, § 45).

Moreover, it is primarily for the national authorities, notably the courts, to interpret and apply domestic law. This also applies where domestic law refers to rules of general international law. The Courts role is confined to ascertaining whether the effects of such an interpretation are compatible with the Convention...'.[29]

The Court repeatedly stated that national courts are in a better position to make the most accurate assessment of the facts and law due to their local knowledge and expertise, and the relative rapidity with which they can intervene to guarantee the effective protection of the individual rights. In accordance with the principle of subsidiarity, the Court does not operate as an organ of the last instance, but of the last resort, when the national proceedings have failed to provide redress or when all domestic remedies have been exhausted.

---

[28] *Belgian Linguistic* case, judgment of 23 July 1968, A-6, § 35; *Handyside v. the UK*, judgment of 12 December 1976, A-24, § 48; *Edwards and Others v. the UK*, judgment of 16 December 1992, A-247-B, § 34; *Ilhan v. Turkey*, judgment of 27 June 2000, Reports 2000, § 61; *Horvat v. Croatia*, judgment of 26 July 2002, Reports 2002, § 37.

[29] *Aksoy v. Turkey*, judgment of 18 December 1996, Reports 1996-V, § 51; *Waite and Kennedy v. Germany*, judgment of 18 February 1999, Reports 1999; *Streletz,.Kessler and Krenz v. Germany*, judgment of 22 March 2001, Reports-2001, § 49.

Subsidiarity is a basic principle for implementing the Convention standard in Contracting States. The full effectiveness of the Convention shall be assumed in States where the competent authorities are empowered to apply the Convention directly.

3.3 The Margin of Appreciation Doctrine

In the context of the subsidiarity principle the margin of appreciation doctrine is applied. As the Convention lays down the minimum standard of conduct for Contracting States, the choice of means of its implementation is left to them. In many cases, the Court confirmed that the scope of the margin of appreciation of the national authorities may vary in respect of the restrictions on rights set forth in the Convention provisions and with regard to the facts of a concrete case. The position that national authorities enjoy a wide margin of appreciation if they use the restrictions on human rights in order to protect national security, public order, social and economic policy, private and family life, legal and cultural traditions etc. was confirmed in the Court's case-law. However, the Court noted that a wide margin of appreciation is not allowed automatically to the State authorities, especially in the scope where the State is obliged to fulfil the positive obligation to secure the particular guaranteed rights or freedoms, e.g. right to protect life or the right to respect the private life.

In the Court's interpretation, the concept of the right to respect for private life in Article 8 comprises rather broad components of the right to respect for private and family life, including the right to marry, e.g. respect for the home, for the physical and moral integrity of the person, including his or her sexual life,[30] the right to privacy often linked to the right to freedom of expression.[31] The cases concerning these rights are analysed from the aspect of the State's positive or negative obligation to take reasonable and appropriate measures within their margin to protect the rights of an individual against the interference of the public authorities and when necessary also against other persons.

At the same time, the Court carefully examined the restrictive measures applied by the national authorities in cases concerning the right to freedom of expression in which the national assessment went hand in hand with the international supervision. Bearing in mind the limits of the margin of appreciation, the Court required that the national authorities strike the right balance between the sometimes conflicting interests of the community and the protection of the fundamental rights of the individual.

---

[30] Concerning the content see e.g. *X. & Y v. the Netherlands*, judgment of 26 March 1985, A-91, §§ 23-27; *Gaskin v. the UK*, judgment of 7 July 1989, A-160, § 49; *Niemetz v. Germany*, cit. above, § 22; *Kronn and others v. Netherlands*, judgment of 27 October 1994, A-297-C, § 19; *Odiévre v. France*, judgment of 13 February 2003, Reports 2004, § 29.

[31] *Hatton and others v. the UK*, judgment of 8 July 2003, reports 2005, §§ 10-11; *Von Hunnover v. Germuny* judgment of 24 June 2004, Reports 2005, § 63.

The Court's jurisdiction is to review whether the States have used discretion allowed in a reasonable manner. In the light of a concrete case as a whole, the Court must examine whether the national power of appreciation was used in conformity with the principle of proportionality, according to the legitimate aim pursued and whether the reasons given by the national authorities to justify the restrictions are relevant and sufficient.[32]

The concept of the margin of appreciation as a natural product of the principle of subsidiarity was recognized as a technique developed to allocate decision-making authority to the proper body in the Convention system and determine in concrete cases the boundary between primary national discretion and the subsidiary international supervision.

In the light of International Human Rights Law and Article 53 of the European Convention, the subsidiarity principle enables the Contracting States to ensure even better protection of human rights under its law or under any other agreement.

The national authorities have the obligation and initial responsibility to safeguard the human rights of legal subjects at a European minimum standard. What is required is therefore the transformation of the Convention guarantees and the Court's case-law into the legal systems of the Contracting States. To what extent the national judiciary, particularly the Constitutional and Supreme courts play an active role in the process of implementation of the Convention into the national legal order might be influenced by the instruments of its transformation into the national legal order. Direct applicability, preference before national laws or the rank of the constitution, the Contracting States are free in the choice of the incorporation. They are responsible for the ultimate result of the implementation of their international obligations.

From the view of effectiveness of the Convention, the crucial question is the functioning of an effective national system for the protection of human rights with accessible and effective domestic remedies and application of criteria and principles of the Court's case-law in the proceedings before the national courts. In this process, the Constitutional Courts and Supreme Courts play the central role.

The substantial part of implementation of the Convention is enforcement of the Court's judgments, which are binding in respect of the States concerned. The proper execution of the Court's judgments entails removing the causes of the violation and prevents the grounds for future applications.

The States approach to this sensitive issue has been changed gradually. The majority of States have always faithfully, perhaps not very promptly, but consistently, executed the judgments. What is remarkable, under the influence of the Courts case-law, is that the States have been stipulated to take necessary legislative measures in order to avoid violations of a similar nature. The amendments

32 See *Handyside v. the UK*, cit. above, §§ 48-50.

in Italian and Slovakian legislation of the last few years are good examples of the impact of the Court's jurisprudence on national law.[33]

The European system is open to more than 800 million potential applicants from 47 Contracting States. Thus, the Court is facing an immense challenge indeed when making efforts to create a European legal space with a common standard in protection of human rights '*...based on human dignity and free of discrimination, on the premise of subsidiarity and the respect to different cultures and traditions in which member States live up to their primary obligations to take human rights seriously and to make of them a living reality.*'[34]

4 Resume

The Court's main role is to assist the national courts by interpretation of the Convention. There are differences in implementation of the Convention's standards in Contracting States. The Court's case-law is an element of the integration of the human rights law of European States and helps safeguard the equal standard of legal protection of individuals.

The core of the European human rights protection system is the European Convention. The way to make the system more effective is by strengthening the Convention's position in Contracting States by legislative measures and in practice by enforcement of the Court's judgments and implementation of its case-law principles in judicial practice. The functioning of the Convention system of effective protection of human rights requires the close co-operation of the Contracting States and all European institutions acting in the field.

33 Pinto Law of 18 April 2001 providing for awards of just satisfaction for failure to comply with reasonable time. Article 127 of the Constitution of the Slovak Republic as amended by the constitutional act of 23 February 2001 entered into force as of 1 January 2002.

34 Address by L. Wildhaber, Former President of the ECHR in the occasion of the opening of judicial year, 25 january 2001.

CHAPTER 7

Democracy in the EU: National Parliaments and the Quest for Legitimacy

Jiri Georgiev

Saying in general that the European Union suffers from a democratic deficit or that it is going through a crisis of legitimacy has nearly become an universal statement that we can find in most discourses exploring the current decision-making process in European institutions. However, these terms are not always based on clear concepts. Rather than providing an in- depth analysis describing the causes of the current situation, they often mean to criticise the 'creeping' increase in the Union's competences and/or the bureaucratic and technocratic forms of decision-making in such European institutions. The usually recommended solution is to implement a traditional system of political representation, i.e. parliamentary responsibility, on the European level.

The rationale for such reflections is usually that the European Union is seen as a body whose legitimacy is not derived from the status of an international organisation or a technocratic functional model but is based on the belief that the European Union can be subject to the liberal-democratic concept of legitimacy.[1] However, the promotion of the said theoretical postulate induces numerous contradictions in the reality of the EU's decision-making process. Transferring the traditional model of parliamentary democracy as applied on a national level to the environments of European institutions without changing the essence and nature of the European cooperation in an abstract form is difficult to imagine and not really feasible.

As the history of each EU country is different, the forms of parliamentary democracy existing in the respective Member States are very different, too. What kind of model would be most acceptable for the administration of public affairs in the EU? In his recently published discourse (also translated into Czech), the Oxford-based political scientist Larry Siedentop identifies the differences between the French, German and British ideas, each of which, quite obviously, reflects the particular domestic experience. Considering his 'insular' perspective, it is hardly surprising that Siedentop recommends getting inspired by the Anglo-Saxon format. [2] However, it is not clear to what extent such inspiration would be acceptable also for the other EU countries. Although transferring the specific formats of democratic structures developed historically on the national level to the European environment may be an attractive, and in some aspects, also applicable option in terms of the national prestige of the respective countries, it is probably an anachronic idea in the overall context. After all, it has been quite a long time since Peter Badura stressed the need to consider the institutional structure and format of the EU from a new, conceptually non-biased perspective, with respect to the changes in mutual relations on both the national and European decision-making levels.[3]

---

* JUDr. Jiří Georgiev is a Legal Adviser to the EU-Affairs Committee of the Czech Senate.

1 D. Beetham, Ch. Lord, Legitimacy and the European Union. London – New York 1998, p. 3.

2 L. Siedentop, Demokracie v. Evropě. Brno 2004, pp. 104 et seq.

3 Compare P. Badura, Bewahrung und Veränderung demokratischer und rechtsstaatlicher Verfassungstruktur in den internationalen Gemeinschaften. In: Veröffentlichungen der Vereinigung der deutschen Staatsrechtslehrer 23/1966, pp. 34 et seq. Similarly, B. Thalmaier (Die zukünftige Gestalt der

What have been the answers to the question of the legitimacy of the Union's decision-making over the past decades? As the Union's jurisdiction is derived from the Member States by means of delegated authority, the legitimacy of decision-making has been based on the Member States' authority since the beginning of the Community's existence.[4] However, as the initial, primarily economic union was gradually converted to a political one, the belief that it was necessary to extend the indirect and mediated legitimacy with elements of direct justification of European-level standard setting was becoming increasingly strong.[5] With direct elections to the European Parliament and the concept of European citizenship, the supranational character of decision-making was gradually getting stronger and stronger. After all, as the degree of legal regulation was growing, the Union's actions increasingly and directly affected citizens, who acknowledged the legitimacy of the European legislation. The strengthening of the European Parliament's authority was therefore a logical reaction to the requirement of direct representation of citizens in the decision-making concerning such legislation. Other ways, such as implementing elements of direct democracy, are not considered feasible in a situation where there is no European civil society[6] and the European Parliament represents the 'peoples of the States brought together in the Community'.[7]

It is certainly remarkable but not surprising that the academic community and political representation in Great Britain, the Member State that has the most distinct tradition of parliamentary democracy on the European continent, was loudest in objecting to the ideas promoting the need to establish a specific, liberal democratic format for the EU's political arrangement. Obviously, this corresponds with the history of the British Empire and the specific progress of integrating the United Kingdom into the Community.[8] After all, the way the

---

Europäischen Union. Baden-Baden 2005) considers the EU as *neuartig strukturiertes politisches System* (a newly structured political system) that, in terms of the relation to its Member States, can be characterised as a "supranational union".

4 The latest items of domestic literature concerning legitimacy in connection with the process of European integration: V. Belling, Federální model a evropská realita. Krize legitimity a její překonání. In: Mezinárodní vztahy 3/2006, pp. 5-18, here p. 7.

5 J.H.H. Weiler, 'After Maastricht: Community legitimacy in post-1992 Europe'. In: W.J. Adams (ed.), Singular Europe: Economy and Polity of the European Community after 1992. University of Michigan Press 1992, pp. 11-41, especially pp. 19-20.

6 In connection with the absence of citizens' identification with the European integration project, W. Gellner and A. Glatzmeier talk about the "missing public" (Die Suche nach der europäischen Zivilgesellschaft. In: Aus Politik und Zeitgeschichte 36/2005, pp. 8-15, here p. 13).

7 Article 189 of the Treaty establishing the EC.

8 Compare e.g. the stances of one of the key pioneers of the idea of European integration, R. Coudenhove-Kalergi, Pan-Europa. Prague 1993, p. 29. Also in the post-war period, it took Coudenhove some time to accept the idea of British membership in the EC; see R. Coudenhove-Kalergi, Weltmacht Europa. Stuttgart 1972, p. 23. Let us add that Coudenhove was no exception among the philosophers and schol-

public in Great Britain perceives the EU is still significantly different from the attitudes in, e.g. France or Germany. The defence of the intergovernmental nature of cooperation among European countries is therefore accepted much better in the UK than in many countries of continental Europe.[9]

However, the implementation of elements of liberal democracy in the EU involving the establishment of direct parliamentary representation is also subject to reservations on the part of both key players in the area of European cooperation. During the discussions of the European Convention on the new Constitutional Treaty, France disagreed upon the concept of establishing the traditional instrument of parliamentary control, i.e., the direct responsibility of the European Commission to the European Parliament, in the text of the future document. The reason for its stance is a fear of excessive politicisation of decision making in the EU.[10] In its already "classic" awards on Maastricht and Solange, the Federal Constitutional Court in Germany acknowledged the position of the Member States as the 'Masters of the Treaty' who delegate the performance of selected powers to the European level, without forgetting about the emphasis with which the Member States pursue compliance with human rights in the context of the development and application of European law. The belief that European integration takes a dual form (Europe of citizens and states) and the corresponding concept of the EU as a consociational federation[11] are not sporadic in German jurisprudence.

The generally shared belief that the EU will need to be based on both direct and indirect legitimisation in a predictable future is based on a number of theses. The first thesis is that the sense of European identity and loyalty is 'embryonic' at best among the European electorate.[12] According to Ernst–Wolfgang Böckenförde, former judge of the Federal Constitutional Court in Germany and a leading law philosopher, the strengthening of the position of the European Parliament can make sense in terms of reforming the EU institutions

---

ars of that time as far as the position of Great Britain's integration to a union of European countries was concerned. Responding to the Briand Plan of 1930, Great Britain's comments on the idea of European integration were reserved, as the country preferred to address the problems of its own empire in the first place. Also V. Goněc, Evropská idea. Part I.: Idea mírové, kooperující a sjednocující se Evropy do roku 1938. Brno 2000, p. 123.

9 In the Anglo-Saxon world, one of those who polemicise against the existence of a serious democratic deficit in the Union, completely unknown in the Member States' situation, is the popular professor of politics Andrew Moravcsik – compare his polemics The EU ain't broke published in the Prospect magazine in March 2003, pp. 38-45.

10 J. Georgiev, Nad institucionální reformou EU. In: Právní rozhledy 9/2003, Annex Evropské právo.

11 M. Nettesheim, Die konsoziative Föderation von EU und Mitgliedsstaaten. Zeitschrift für europarechtliche Studien 4/2002, pp. 507 et seq.

12 D. Beetham, Ch. Lord, Legitimacy..., p. 29: "Most commentators are agreed that a sense of European identity and loyalty is embryonic at best among the European electorate."

but will not solve the problem of democratic responsibility.[13] If we accept this perspective, even the considered integration of the European Parliament election methods, where the parallel elections in the Member States would be replaced with an integrated pan-European election ticket,[14] it would be a technical change rather than a major step towards changing the Community's democratic legitimisation. Considering the doubts about the existence of a European political nation (European *demos*), it is more adequate – as stated by C. Skach – to talk about a deficit of legitimacy rather than a democratic deficit in the European context, at least as far as the objective of such reflections is to eliminate the claimed deficit.[15]

What method should we employ for such remediation? It is certainly worth noticing that the feeling of the need for an appropriate complementary existence of the European Parliament on one side and national parliaments on the other side, very popular in academic environments, has been appearing also in political discussions on the future of Europe over the past few years. However, this trend has not been relevantly reflected in terms of changing the establishing Treaties so far. We can only see a significant change in terms of reinforcing the position of the European Parliament which, for that matter, is getting stronger also through inter-institutional agreements – the last case was the supervision over comitology in July 2006.[16] National parliaments have been rather reserved so far, the reasons being the emphasis on the supranational character of the Community, a fear of protracting and complicating the legislative process and the understandable reluctance to intervene from above in the (often different) parliamentary routines in the respective countries.

As a result, the national parliaments have become subject to a paradox identified by German political scientist Klaus von Beyme: the democratisation of the EU has contributed to the weakening of the role of the national parliaments.[17] While the EU is getting more responsible over time as a result of the increasing power of the European Parliament, the opposite is happening on the national level. With many items of legislation adopted on the national level, the national

---

13 E.-W. Böckenförde, Welchen Weg geht Europa? In: E.-W. Böckenförde, Staat, Nation, Europa. Studien zur Staatslehre, Verfassungstheorie und Rechtsphilosophie. Frankfurt am Main 2000, pp. 68-102, here p. 92.

14 On this aspect: M. Zralá, Š. Pecháček, Suverenita Evropského parlamentu. In: Politologický časopis 2/2003, pp. 149 et seq.

15 C. Skach, 'We, the Peoples? Constitutionalizing the European Union.' in: Journal of Common Market Studies 1/2005, pp. 149-170, here p. 153.

16 For the position of the European Parliament, with special emphasis on the area of comitology, see Ch. Neuhold, Das Europäische Parlament im Rechtsetzungsprozeß der Europäischen Union. Demokratische Kontrollmöglichkeiten im Hinblick auf die Durchführungsbefugnisse der Europäischen Kommission. Frankfurt am Main 2001, especially pp. 127 et seq.

17 K. von Beyme, Die parlamentarische Demokratie. Entstehung und Funktionsweise 1789-1999. Dritte Auflage. Opladen-Wiesbaden 1999. p. 541.

parliaments are obliged to implement the European bills into their law in the development of which they were not able to participate (sui juris).[18] Yet, as the co-decision-making procedure is getting increasingly common, the parliamentary dimension in the dialogue with the Council of Ministers is represented by the European Parliament, and the national parliaments, according to Beyme, often act as 'lobbyists' in the communication with their governments.[19] In the context of the increasing volume of legislation adopted on the European level, the hitherto position of the national parliaments in terms of controlling European affairs has not had an ideal outcome.

This trend is certainly worth noticing in the post-communist countries of Central and Eastern Europe where the process of reinforcing parliamentary mechanisms as a result of the fall of totalitarian regimes was a certain counterbalance to the 'deparliamentarisation' of the political life that many countries of Western Europe had gone through in the 1990's.[20] However, considering the political stabilisation and the convergence of standards of parliamentary decision-making in European countries, we can hardly expect the countries in Central and Eastern Europe to resist to the de-parliamentarisation trend more efficiently than the other European countries do. Generally, we can see a number of common symptoms, including transferring some powers to unelected bodies, reinforcing the position of the executive branch and emphasising the importance of parliaments' articulation functions as compared with the traditional and basic legislative function.[21]

However, not all the national parliaments have stayed defenceless to this process. In connection with the European integration, some of them are considering new forms of the relation between the responsibility of the executive branch and that of the legislature.[22] Sharing information and experience through inter-parliamentary cooperation, they are creating sort of a minimum pan-European standard for parliamentary control of European affairs.[23] The

---

[18] See reflections of Roman Herzog in Die Welt 13.1.2007 on this issue.

[19] Ibidem. Also to this discussion: J. Dieringer, Nationale Parlamente im Integrationsprozess. In: J. Dieringer, A. Maurer, E. Györi (Hg.), Europäische Entscheidungen kontrollieren. Nationale Parlamente im Ost-West-Vergleich. Dresden 2005, pp. 11 et seq.

[20] A. Ágh, Parliamentarization as a Regionally Specific Way of Democratization in East Central Europe. In: E. Bos, M. Mommsen, P. von Steinsdorff (Hrsg.), Das russische Parlament. Schule der Demokratie? Opladen 2003, pp. 47 et seq.

[21] To the roles of parliaments: K. von Beyme, l.c., pp. 253 et seq.

[22] The respective models of parliamentary control are described by L. Pítrová et al., Úloha národních parlamentů v legislativním procesu v Evropské unii. In: Právník 10/2002, pp. 1013-1070. For an up-to-date typology of parliaments in terms of their involvement in the control of Union-level decision making see A. Maurer, Post-2004 elements for comparative analysis of national parliamentary participation in EU affairs. In: J. Düringer et al. (Hg.), Europäische Entscheidungen..., pp. 49 et seq.

[23] The Copenhagen Parliamentary Guidelines, an attempt to formulate a minimum common standard for parliamentary control of European affairs, are certainly worth mentioning in this connection. Also J.

two protocols annexed to the Amsterdam Treaty of 1997, the Protocol on the Role of National Parliaments in the EU and the Protocol on the Application of the Principles of Subsidiarity and Proportionality, were also significant in terms of the self-awareness of the national parliaments. In particular, we should be interested in the latter as far as the legitimisation of the Union's decision-making is concerned, because it includes substantive criteria for reviewing compliance with two principles that are central to the Union's decision-making procedures – the principles of proportionality and subsidiarity. However, the protocol did not address the procedural aspects, i.e., who should be made responsible for supervising the compliance with the said principles and how should that occur. To some extent, this deficiency was eliminated through the Protocol on the Application of the Principles of Subsidiarity and Proportionality annexed to the draft European Constitutional Treaty. Nevertheless, even this latest document – that can be implemented to some extent, regardless of the overall fate of the Constitutional Treaty (considering the procedural character of the so-called early warning system) – is not perfect. As pointed out by Christian Calliess of the University of Göttingen, the most serious deficiency is that the document does not include the material criteria for reviewing the compliance of the proposed EU legal act with the subsidiarity principle, i.e., the criteria that are part of the applicable wording of the Amsterdam Protocol.[24]

Referred to above many times, the nature of the principles of subsidiarity and proportionality is becoming constitutional in European law,[25] regardless of the dispute over the legitimacy of using the term constitution and constitutionality in the EU's legal environment[26]. For this reason, it is also interesting whom the draft Constitutional Treaty 'appoints' as the arbiter over the compliance with the two principles. On one hand, the responsibility for this role lies with the European Court of Justice, in compliance with Article 230 of the Treaty

---

Georgiev, Jakou roli přisoudil Konvent EU národním parlamentům? In: EMP 2/2003, pp. 3-10, here p. 4.

24 Besides his special monograph (Ch. Callies, Subsidiaritäts- und Solidaritätsprinzip in der Europäischen Union. Baden-Baden 1999), compare the speech delivered at the subsidiarity principle conference organised under the Austrian EU presidency on 18.-19.4.2006 in St. Pöllten, Austria: http://www.eu2006.at/de/News/Speeches_Interviews/1804Calliep.html.

25 M. W. Schröter, Das Subsidiaritätsprinzip als verfassungsgenerierender Modus. Arbeitspapiere – Mannheimer Zentrum für europäische Sozialforschung, 54/2002, pp. 8-9.

26 Arthur Dyèvre states quite rightly that the use of the term constitution alone does not really help in building a shared understanding of the European political identity – the word means only as much as the respective languages of the European nations can envisage behind it or gets meanings the Member States' governments attach to it. See A. Dyèvre, 'The constitutionalisation of the European Union: discourse, present, future and facts,' in European Law Review, April 2005, pp. 165-189, here pp. 166-167. After all, the term constitution has a number of meanings and meaning nuances even in the classical constitutional law theory. Compare C. Schmitt, Verfassungslehre. Neunte Auflage. Berlin 2003, pp. 4 et seq. For an interesting comparison in the context of the Euro-Atlantic area see G. Nolte (ed.) European and US constitutionalism. Cambridge University Press 2005.

establishing the EC. According to prevailing opinions, the European Court of Justice should have the role of the institution that performs a European-level parallel to national constitutional judicatures. Obviously, this status of the Court of Justice is not absolutely exclusive, because we need to consider the judicature of national constitutional courts that have their own roles in protecting the constitutional systems and powers of the Member States.[27] Also involved is the European Commission that, under Articles 211 and 226, has the role of 'Guardian of the Treaties'. As pointed out by Franz C. Mayer, the status of the European Court of Justice is based on the model of the Federal Constitutional Court in Germany, while the position of the Commission reflects the French tradition under which the representative of the executive branch has the function of 'Guardian of the Constitution'.[28]

A similar duality is also apparent on the vertical level, in terms of guarding the split of authority between the Member States and the EU. Besides the said national constitutional courts, the national parliaments are involved, too. It is the national parliaments to which the aforesaid Protocol on the Application of the Principles of Subsidiarity and Proportionality annexed to the draft European Treaty gave the role of the guardian of compliance with the subsidiarity principle. Some of the national parliaments have become inspired by the Protocol wording in the meantime and, in compliance with the European Council's conclusions of June 2006, a new mechanism was established for the communication between the European Commission and the national parliaments under which the Commission should act with due respect to the national parliaments' positions, especially with regard to compliance with the principles of subsidiarity and proportionality in draft EU legal acts.

However, the European Court of Justice does not need to be afraid of competition from the national parliaments. Considering the principle of subsidiarity under the applicable establishing Treaties as well as under the draft EU Constitutional Treaty, the position of the national parliaments remains rather modest, even significantly more modest than what many constitutions and rules of procedure applicable in the respective Member States guarantee for governments' national control in decision-making on European affairs. Nevertheless, in connection with the principle of subsidiarity, it seems that the position of the national parliaments should be changed some more to meet the requirements of the establishing treaties more effectively and ensure *better regulation*. The

---

[27] On the situation in the Czech Republic, compare the commentary by Jiří Zemánek for the Jurisprudence magazine 5/2006 regarding the Constitutional Court award Pl. ÚS 50/04 (No. 154/2006 Coll.). On the latent conflict between the European Court of Justice and the Federal Constitutional Court in Germany that has arisen over the definition of the force of the national constitution and European law, compare H.P. Folz, Demokratie und Integration. Der Konflikt zwischen Bundesverfassungsgericht und Europäischem Gerichtshof über die Kontrolle der Gemeinschaftskompetenzen. Heidelberg 1999.

[28] Compare Article 5 of the Constitution of France; also F.C. Mayer, Wer soll Hüter der europäischen Verfassung sein? Walter Hallstein-Institut für europäisches Verfassungsrecht. Paper 20/04, p. 4.

principle of subsidiarity has a political dimension that goes beyond the nature of a strictly legal rule in many cases, and the application of the principle by a court institution might therefore pose the risk of politicising the justice system.[29] In addition, although the hitherto cautiousness of the European Court of Justice in using the concept of subsidiarity may also arise from some other reasons, it fully corresponds with the above statement.[30] We can therefore expect that it is not the European Court of Justice that has got the supervisory authority under the aforesaid protocol, but the national parliaments that can play the crucial part. The only precondition for the assertion of this authority is the existence of political will.

We cannot currently and seriously predict any further development of the role of the national parliaments in controlling the principles of subsidiarity and proportionality and in preliminary supervision of compliance with the split of authority between the EU and the Member States with regard to the legal base of legislation adopted by EU bodies[31]. A number of interesting and inspiring stimuli aimed at stronger legitimisation of the decision-making process in the Union were discussed by the national parliaments' working group that met during the discussions on the new basic EU treaty at the Convention on the Future of Europe. However, some of the items that appeared in the final draft Treaty (flexibility clause in Article I-18 and the generally formulated bridge clause in Article IV-444) did not respect the position of the national parliaments as the 'Masters of the Treaty' and, paradoxically, weakened the institutional legitimacy of the European Union.[32]

Nevertheless, strengthening the role of the national parliaments in legitimising the EU decision-making by following up the actions that have been taken so far seems to be a logical answer to the current search for a solution to the situation that arose once the process of ratifying the European Constitutional Treaty was blocked. The specific role of the national parliaments in supervising the specification of the jurisdiction of European law cannot be principally rejected

---

[29] This risk was stressed out already by Carl Schmitt, a leading person of German law theory, who, however, is generally sceptical to the possibility of abstract control of constitutionality by court bodies: "(...) mit einer Expansion der Justiz auf eine vielleicht nicht mehr justiziable Materie die Justiz nur geschädigt werden kann. Denn die Folge wäre, wie ich öfters, sowohl für das Verfassungsrecht wie für das Völkerrecht, gezeigt habe, nicht etwa eine Juridifizierung der Politik, sondern eine Politisierung der Justiz." Conf. C. Schmitt, Der Hüter der Verfassung. Vierte Auflage. Berlin 1996, p. 22.

[30] According to Trevor Hartley, the principle of subsidiarity associating certain reservations in the legislative process on EC level does not fit to the philosophy of the European Court of Justice as a body promoting the European integration. Compare T. C. Hartley, Constitutional problems of the European Union. Oxford-Portland 1999, p. 87.

[31] It is logical that confirming the existence of a sufficient legal base that makes it possible to adopt a Union act of secondary law has to precede a review of the act's harmony with the principles of subsidiarity and proportionality.

[32] V. Belling, Federální model..., p. 14.

as completely inappropriate, one of the reasons being the existing historical parallels. We do not have to refer to the Roman Senate – referring to the long tradition of the French Senate that has been performing some of the functions of the 'Guardian of the Constitution' in the country's institutional system is enough.[33] If the EU's legitimacy deficit is to be eliminated, the formulation of the Community's 'constitutional doctrine'[34] also has to reflect the role that should be played by the Member States' legislatures as the institutions performing the important mediating role towards the public.

[33] C. Schmitt, Der Hüter der Verfassung, p. 9.

[34] As stated by J.H.H. Weiler (The constitution of Europe: "Do the new clothes have an emperor?" and other essays on European integration. Cambridge University Press 2005, p. 8), the problem of the European Union is that it does have a "constitutional system", but lacks an adequate constitutional doctrine.

CHAPTER 8

Some Consideration about the Application of the Principle of Subsidiarity upon Execution of Public Power

Aleš Gerloch

1 Introduction

I would like to present several notes on the principle of subsidiarity and how it operates in legal spheres within society, in operation of a state and in organised systems in general. Obviously, the relationship of the Member states or regions of the European Union and the Union itself is one of those cases. The principle of subsidiarity is a principle under which each activity of the state and society, or of supranational institutions and organisations, should be only ancillary, supportive, and, i.e. subsidiary. In other words, it should only be applied upon a tasks solution which is beyond the capability of the lower unit.

Where is such an attitude applied? First, it is in the sphere of organised systems. Its theory and practice is well worked out in churches, not only the Catholic Church, and those institutions may be even more decentralised in the system of their organisation. Another typical example of the application of the principle of subsidiarity is self-government, both territorial and professional. Other typical examples originating from the application of this idea are autonomy or federalism.

2 Immanency of the Principle of Subsidiarity and its Aspects

There is a question if the principle of subsidiarity is in organised systems immanent and in a way also necessary. Of course, this is an issue for further discussion, and I would not support this opinion since there are examples of organisations that are strongly centralised and that do not operate with this principle. The issue is that the establishment of lower units does not necessarily mean that those units perform functional tasks only on their level, and everything else is then solved on a higher level, i.e. that such an organisation meets the criteria of the principle of a structured hierarchy.

Examples of the opposite attitude are, of course, the structure of the army, police, or some other institutions. Typical is the prison system where the centralised system prevails. It has already been mentioned here that totalitarian regimes always tend to centralisation. Historically, we can find those features in the systems of absolutistic monarchy or, even earlier, in theocratic regimes, etc.

However, the system where there is an effort to subordinate lower units to the higher ones should always be differentiated from the principle of subsidiarity. In this sense, we can place this principle inside an organisation as a system, or in a relationship between the state and supranational units, or also between regions – state, regions – supranational units, as opposed to subordination, in which we do not expect for such units to have an independent scope of competence, or to be permanently interfered with in respect to reaching uniform objectives that are defined from the centre.

* Prof. JUDr. Aleš Gerloch, CSc., Head of the Department of Constitutional Law and Department of Legal Theory, and Dean of the Faculty of Law, Charles University in Prague, Czech Republic.

Other examples of the application of the principle of subsidiarity concern the functioning of legal systems within the system of social relationships. First is the application of directory legal provisions, where a directory rule usually has two dispositions. One disposition is at the addressee's discretion, so that they define their rights and obligations by themselves, or lay down their legal relationships, there is certain autonomy, namely contractual discretion of contractual parties. In fact, the second standard is subsidiary, supportive, reserved for the event when the addressees will not use this option, and therefore it represents the other, alternative solution, of course, of a mandatory nature.

It should be noted that the directory range of legal provision or the form as such creates a certain space for individual units to make independent decisions within the existing legal order. Typically, this will lead to the sphere of private law, i.e. to the sphere of a family of business relationships or the like, though not exclusively. Obviously, there is a question as to how far to go upon application of the directory form of legal provisions, since currently there is hardly any legal order based primarily on directory standards and functioning prevailingly on the principle of subsidiarity, i.e. a legal order that prefers autonomy of the parties and that sets alternative solutions only in a limited range, if the parties concerned are unable to reach consensus. It is the other way round – most legal standards are peremptory, namely in public law, and even here the principle of subsidiarity does not have to be used as an exclusive rule of legal regulation, as will be discussed later.

3 Subsidiarity of Sources of Law

Similarly, though at a different level, is the relation of the principle of subsidiarity functions within the system of legal standards as concerns relationships between single acts or other sources of law. It is one of the structuring criterions of legal order, deliberately chosen by legislators, not given automatically, where a certain provision is a special one and is superior to general provisions. This general provision then has a subsidiary character in relation to the special provision. A typical example in the Czech private law is the relationship between the Commercial Code and Civil Code. It is noteworthy that effective from January 1, 2007, such shifting applies also to the Labour Code, which was in the past strictly separated from civil law, and currently it uses, though in a limited scope as appears in a detailed analysis, the principle of subsidiary in respect to the Civil Code. In many provisions, it refers to the Civil Code, stating that its provisions shall be used in a subsidiary manner.

This method is relatively frequent and practically enables mutual interlinking of particular legal regulations while respecting special features of certain branches or sub-branches of law in their relations to more general provisions. Another typical example could be legal regulations on residential leases or the lease of non-residential spaces in relation to general regulations on rent and in relation to the general regulation of legal acts in civil law.

Is it obvious that legislators themselves judge to what extent the specific differences should be preferred and what is common for them; the common then could be the subsidiary for certain cases. It should be noted that the preparatory works on the new Civil Code, in addition to many other issues, have to solve a problem that originated the way that a certain internal consistence was affected by the fact that a special law, the Labour Code, was adopted earlier and refers to the current Civil Code. From the purely formal point of view, they will not correspond, since the Civil Code will refer to different provisions; the same applies to conceptual backgrounds, which vary in the concerned codes. Apparently, if not aforethought thoroughly, the chosen procedure may lead to certain questionable consequences.

4 Interpretation of Law and the Principle of Subsidiarity

Another field in which to employ the principle of subsidiarity is the interpretation of normative legal texts. In general, we can speak about subsidiary methods of interpretation, which complement the basic or standard methods of interpretation, while the subsidiary methods are used still more frequently. It is noteworthy that standard methods of interpretation are based mainly upon linguistic, logic and systematic interpretation, and interpretation of a normative legal text should in general be completed by the use thereof.

In recent years, or rather decades, if we consider the wider European context and not only the narrower national viewpoint, still more frequent are so-called difficult cases, wherein the authorities that execute the application of laws or other sources of law reach for super-standard methods of interpretation. Teleological interpretation plays a key role, complemented by historical and comparative ones, and it is apparent that a strict distinction between basic and subsidiary methods of interpretation is of high importance for keeping a borderline between the making and interpretation of law as well as application of law, since interpretation is usually performed in connection with application.

Should we consider subsidiary methods – namely teleological interpretation – as primary ones, i.e. if we try to interpret a normative text through above-standard arguments, i.e. legal principles, purposes, values and other so-called extralegal standards, then we would strikingly reduce the options of the legislator to define his own balance of legal principles, the way he highlights certain principles or prefers special purposes, and which ones he considers relatively less important.

The one, who would consequently apply the rules, would actually be able to reinterpret the text rather freely, or to even misinterpret the text, and for many reasons we may think that the current development follows this direction. However, the role of those having the power then gains in importance both at the national level, usually constitutional courts, and at the European level, i.e. the European Court of Justice EC/EU or within the Council of Europe the European Court for Human Rights.

Another example would be the application of the principle of subsidiarity within the EC/EU, i.e. the principle of subsidiarity highlighted in the Maastricht Treaty, solving the issue on the specific level of relationships between Member states and the European Union, or regions and the European Union.

There is a question of what is unifying for those cases, what is the linking point. The linking point could be the idea that decision making activities should not be excessively shifted towards particular centres and that we should preserve a certain autonomy for those who perform either application activities upon solving actual cases or upon the creation of legal regulation at the respective local level, or upon decision making as concerns specific issues within specific local units. This is to respect the complexity of the internal organisation of the human society, either at the level of individual states or in a wider European scope.

This a very important issue for the future, because we must remember that all higher units always tend towards a certain centralisation or to acquiring a number of powers higher than they have originally been entitled to, may it be either the traditionally federative system or the hybrid one, which are European Communities or the European Union as a non-typical federation.

5 Concurring Principles

Let us confront the principle of subsidiarity with another principle, which is the principle of sovereignty of the people. The idea, that activities performed functionally and effectively at an adequate level should not be transposed onto a higher level, is undoubtedly correct. We may however ask if this principle could be self-standing, without any further support. It is not always like that in organised systems, and we must say that in democratic societies it is namely the principle of the sovereignty of the people, which will always be in a certain contradiction to the principle of subsidiarity.

Why? Because the principle of sovereignty of the people assumes that, the people are a general entity in a certain territory, historically in the territory of a state who is the sovereign, and whose sovereignty is not limited in any way. In other words, it must be pursued within the whole entity; the question is if the principle should be applied to its full extent and lower units should not enjoy any autonomy, or if those two principles may be combined.

It is a classical expression of the principle of sovereignty or exclusiveness of law, known also in the Czech legislation, embedded both in the Constitution and in the Charter of fundamental rights and freedoms, stating that many issues may be regulated solely by law, and therefore set uniformly within the entire territory of the state. *Nullum crimen, nulla poena sine lege* is probably historically one of the oldest rules upon forming a modern state, saying that it is not the self-governing units who should define crimes, penalties and punishments. As you may have noticed, today it is also being shifted to the European level within the third pillar, though widely discussed, but these are only the first sprouts of the European criminal law or of its shaping.

Further, there is a rule stating that every body of public power may only act as prescribed by law, in other words, its establishment, powers, competences or procedures are defined by law. This rule is strongly centralising as opposed to the principle of subsidiarity, where each body of public power could define its own scope of decision making and acquire competences not primarily performed by the state administration.

Another important rule states that fundamental rights may only be restricted by law. This is a most important issue from the viewpoint of the addressees of everyday practice of legal standards, even though the two previous rules should not be underestimated. Frequent are conflicts concerning the definition of powers of municipalities and regions, when they often have to face the exclusiveness of law upon issuance of their own local bylaws and regulations.

Of course, there is the issue of a division of competences, and first of all the key question of the functionality of the system. Classification of certain principles as prevailing will depend on their functionality and effectiveness. We may state that what is not possible to perform efficiently on a lower level should definitely be delegated to a higher one, or vice versa, issues that can be effectively managed on a lower level should not be delegated to the higher one.

6 Summary

To summarise, modern society (perhaps with certain postmodern features) is a society rather decentralised, with so many ongoing complex processes that society is almost impossible to control from a single centre. On the other hand, there are a number of real pressures pushing against this decentralisation, or traditional liberalism, based on the idea stating that public power should be strictly limited. These phenomena are collectively referred to as globalisation trends, or that a number of objective, economic and probably also technologic and other options and requirements create a pressure to introduce standards which should be uniform within Europe (European Union), prospectively worldwide. This issue may not be on today's agenda, but while talking about the European Union and us as a part of it, the issue will soon become very important as concerns development or organisation of the European structures.

In my opinion, it is impossible to find a criterion given once for all in respect of determination of what can effectively be decided upon, managed etc. on lower or higher levels, including the European level. This is probably a dynamic issue and should be assessed with respect to those two fundamental attitudes. First, there is a premise that decision making is always more effective at a lower (local, regional, national) level, unless the issues of respective technology, cultural background or differences between concerned entities could be disregarded. On the other hand, the trend of standardisation of living conditions within

Europe or worldwide will probably go stronger together with the option of its application, which is in direct opposition to this rule or attitude, or philosophical concept.

In certain cases, the solution is apparently more effective on local or regional levels, maximally at the level of EU Member States. In other cases, it would be disputable, and possible solutions will become subject of discussions, of course, arising from different opinions based on different interests, views, experience, etc. For example, before regions were established as self-governing units, many issues were undoubtedly over centralised, and the principle of subsidiarity was not applied. For example, the issue of regional transportation or medical facilities networks, etc., controlled from the centre, should undoubtedly fall within the competence of regional authorities. Regional authorities are more likely to be able to judge if a particular railway should remain, to which extent it should be subsidised, what a certain hospital network should look like, etc. On the other hand, it is apparent that all issues cannot be left in the regions' hands; the situation might become rather diversified and could eventually lead to a crisis with a wide social impact, e.g. if a particular region underestimated the issue of health care and the people consequently relied upon the state to arrange and ensure a remedy somehow.

The same applies on the European level. The situation here is rather different in the aspect that individual states still are the decision-making subjects having the power to grant an exclusive or joint competence to the EC/EU and to determine how to proceed. However, the process of Europeanisation seems to be irreversible and in this sense, we should consider the situation as was in the past decades and as will be in the future.

Very important and already mentioned here is the principle of proportionality. Should we agree that certain issues are necessary to be solved on a supranational, i.e. European, level, then we must strictly follow the principle of proportionality, i.e. to give good reasons for the particular purpose and not vice versa, where it should be reasoned that a certain activity is more effective at a national level than at the level of the EU, taking into account the proportionality between the purpose and chosen means.

To conclude, in my opinion, the changes discussed here, where the Agreement on European Constitution is a first form or an attempt to solve these issues, should be considered on three levels – in discussions whether the European Court of Justice should stay either the exclusive or dominant authority, or if the power should be delegated to national parliaments, or the European parliament, or another body. The first level is the making of political decisions. This is a role for governments, represented in the Council, i.e. the executive power. It is necessary to discuss the particular decisions or drafts that will result in legal acts, from the viewpoint of the principle of subsidiarity and proportionality, already on that level. In legislative processes, it is the undoubtedly desired strengthening of the role of national parliaments, and finally, the European

Court of Justice must take its part upon the application of those legal acts of the European Union.

In my opinion, the control over observance of the principle of subsidiarity in relation to the principle of proportionality should not be limited only to the level of the decision-making of the European Court of Justice, but it is necessary that it proceeds at all stages of the preparation of legal acts of the European Union and application thereof.

CHAPTER 9

Citizenship in International and European law

Ján Klučka & Peter Pecho

I Nationality in International Law

Traditionally, nationality constitutes a notion that is closely intertwined with the existence of a State, and in the broader context, with the concept of international community *(societas maxima)*. From a historical perspective, nationality emerged at a certain stage of society's development when it displaced subordination of individuals (vassalage), which was prevalent in the feudal system. The feudal subordination presupposed a sovereign-vassal relationship based on land possession where the inhabitants represented an 'integral part' of the land. Creation of nationality as a particular legal bond between the State and the individual residing on its territory emerged with the democratic revolutions in the Western Europe in the 18th and 19th century that replaced the mastery of nobility and sovereign families with the bourgeoisie. However, this concept does not incorporate the patrimonial aspect concerning the possession of land and its inhabitants anymore. Nowadays, the legal regulation of nationality as a distinctive State-national legal bond constitutes a traditional part of *public law* of every country and provides basic tools for application of not only the fundamental rights and freedoms conferred to nationals, but also obligations.

Nationality represents a legal institution that falls within the scope of the exclusive competence of States. Accordingly, the contribution of international law to its regulation has not been very significant, since nationality concerns national and not international law. Nevertheless, it would be incorrect to consider that countries are free from all obligations under international law, although it must be stated that international law fully upholds the State's right to settle the conditions of the acquisition, change and loss of nationality. This fact is, *inter alia,* explicitly confirmed by Article 3 of the 1997 European Convention on Nationality, which provides that each State shall have the right to determine under its own national law who are its citizens. At the same time, it clearly states that this law shall be recognised by other States in so far as it is 'consistent with applicable international conventions, customary international law and the principles of law generally recognised with regard to nationality'.

The principle of state sovereignty and non-interference with other States' internal affairs introduced by international law represents the first *delimitation* on the concept of nationality. In other words, internal regulation of nationality must respect the same right of other States and cannot affect citizens of other States. Even though citizens of another State can represent a national minority within the territory of the host state, and the regulation of nationality can become a complicated matter in case of cession of a State's territory, or where a new State is created (e. g. whose frontiers are not yet securely defined), none of these difficulties could justify disrespect of the State's sovereignty in defining of its citizenship.

The second outlining principle on the scope of nationality imposed by international law is the need to respect the principle of *effectiveness* or the close relationship between the individual and the State where the individual applied for citizenship. In 1956 with the *Nottebohm* case, frequently referred to for embodying the relevant international law doctrine, the International Court of Justice stated that a national cannot successfully seek the protection of his State and his nationality cannot be considered genuine if it was granted by a State with whom the individual did not have any close or intensive bond.[1] Consequently, the evidence of a close or effective relationship between the State and the national in both original and derived modes of a nationality acquisition (e.g., birth, naturalisation, marriage, etc.) has been tested on the international scene.

States can determine their own modes of nationality acquisition. These vary from one State to another, which can result in conflicts between the provisions of various national legal systems,[2] and these negative circumstances have direct effect on the existence and/or non-existence of nationality.

These conflicts between national regulations can result in a situation where an individual becomes *stateless*, without any State-national bond. The opposite case is the status of *double* or *multiple nationalities*, where the State-citizen bond exists with two or more countries. Indeed, none of the abovementioned situations is ideal. For example, a stateless person does not have the right of protection by the diplomatic authorities of any State and a person with double or multiple nationalities can face problems relating to taxation or military service.

If the negative consequences of these situations are not eliminated by internal regulations, then the problems concerning the status of 'non-nationality' that results from the differences in national regulations are mainly left to be solved by international law via bilateral or multilateral treaties. However, in this context we cannot talk about any 'targeted' routing of international law, since the international community usually only responds to 'pathological' situations directly affecting the question of nationality and which can not be solved without close international cooperation, that is subsequently reflected in the content of international treaties.

In order to avoid these problematic situations, Article 4 of the 1997 European Convention on Nationality provides the principles that form the basis of rules on nationality in each Contracting State. According to this article (a) everyone has the right to a nationality; (b) every Contracting Party shall avoid the statelessness on its territory; (c) no one shall be arbitrarily deprived of his or her nation-

---

* Prof. JUDr. Ján Klučka, CSc. is a judge at the European Court of Justice in Luxembourg, Peter Pecho, LL.M is his 'référendaire' (legal clerk to the judge). This article represents the personal point of view of the authors and does not bind the institution, of which they are members. The authors would like to express their acknowledgement to Mgr. Juliana Pogáčová, DEA, assistant at the ECJ for her cooperation in the preparation and editing of this contribution.

1 Case *Nottenbohm*, ICJ Reports 1455 [1955], p. 24.

2 Most common differences appear in the acquisition of nationality at birth. In this context, either the principle of *ius sanguinis* (determining criteria is the nationality of both or one of the parents regardless of the place of birth) or the principle of *ius soli* (following the criteria of the place of birth regardless of the parents' nationality) applies.

ality; (d) neither marriage nor the dissolution of marriage between a national of a Contracting State and an alien, nor the change of nationality by one of the spouses during marriage, shall automatically affect the nationality of the other spouse.

The second main direction in the area of international rules concerning nationality is related to international protection of human rights, that grants to nationals certain tangible privileges. From this perspective, nationality can be considered as a 'pathway' to the acquisition of specific privileges under international law.

After all, it should be emphasised that the issue of nationality also appears in the *domain of conflicts of laws*, where it belongs (at least in the continental legal system) within the scope of *personal status*.

As has already been noted, the situation of *statelessness* is inconvenient for the individuals, as well as for the States. One can become *stateless* by birth (so-called original stateless status), as a result of a particular life situation (marriage with a foreign national, loss of nationality as a form of sanction) or for political reasons (dissolution of State or cession of part of the State's territory, so-called derived stateless status).

The problem of statelessness was initially addressed at the 1930 League of Nations Conference for the Codification of International Law at The Hague. This conference adopted the *Convention on certain questions relating to the conflict of nationality laws* that prescribes measures to be implemented in order to decrease the number of stateless individuals. Certain of these measures relate to the nationality of married women (Arts. 8 and 9) as well as children and their adoption process (Arts. 13-14 and 17). The Final Act of the Hague conference calls on the States 'to attempt, within the exercise of their powers in the area of nationality, to reduce (as far as possible) the occurrence of statelessness'.

The first convention that specifically focused on the exclusion of the loss of nationality with regard to a particular category of individuals was the 1957 *New York Convention on the Nationality of Married Women* (hereinafter the Nationality Convention). The primary objective of the Nationality Convention was the right to maintain nationality for women marrying citizens of States other than their home countries. The Nationality Convention reflected the reaction of the international community to domestic laws and practices in a number of countries (mostly from the Arabic part of the world), where women (foreigners) by marriage to their nationals automatically lost their nationality without obtaining the nationality of their husband. Consequently, they ended up living their lives with no nationality in an unknown environment with a new lifestyle. They were also denied the access to consular assistance and prevented from seeking diplomatic protection from their home State.

Another effort of the international community to resolve the problem of stateless persons was materialized in the adoption of the Convention on the Reduction of Statelessness in 1961 (hereinafter the Statelessness Convention). Its preamble emphasizes that it is desirable 'to reduce statelessness by means of an international agreement'. Without engaging in a detailed analysis, one can conclude that the Statelessness Convention binds the contracting States in two ways. On the one hand, every contracting State shall refrain from the exercise of powers that affect adversely the nationality of its citizens (e.g., by depriving an individual from the nationality against her or his will). On the other hand, the contracting States shall avoid the situation where an individual (born or found on its territory) remains without nationality as a result of their 'home country' internal laws or for any other reason.

The cases that affect the nationality of large groups of people, such as a *cession of the State territory or creation of a new State,* are of particular importance. The international law practice shows that the nationality of persons residing in a territory that is being subjected to a cession is generally part of a relevant cession agreement. Residents of the concerned territory are usually granted the right to choose (option) between the original nationality and the nationality of the State, which is acquiring the territory. This mechanism has been designed to prevent the situation that results in the statelessness of the residents in such territory.

The question of nationality and its impact on the millions of people also plays a significant role in the process of State-creation either by division or disintegration of existing States (Czechoslovakia, Yugoslavia or USSR). The experience has shown that the newly established States in the 1990's followed in principle the rule under which no one's nationality shall be prejudiced by territorial changes. However, it does not mean that somebody could retain the nationality of a no-longer existing State (this possibility ceases to be available with the cessation of that State). Such a person will acquire or will have the possibility to acquire (without any discrimination) the nationality of the newly established State.

In adopting rules regarding its nationality, newly created States have to avoid two extreme situations. The individuals having a genuine link to such a new State should not be deprived from nationality granted by this State and on the contrary, nationality should not be granted to anyone whose relationship to the State is just temporary or purely random (even though at the moment of the new State creation they reside on its territory). The experience from the 1990's demonstrates that several newly established States chose as a criterion for granting their nationality, the nationality of the precedent federated State, within the federative State, that ceased to exist. That was *inter alia* the case in the situation of the Slovak Republic. Likewise, the European Convention on the Nationality in its Article 18[3] (State succession and nationality) underlines that 'in particular in order to avoid statelessness' in cases of succession, every State shall take account particularly of the genuine and effective link of the person concerned with the State, habitual residence of the person at the time of the State succession as well as the will and origin of the person.

[3] Id.

As already stated, the situation of *double nationality*, although its negative consequences are less notable than the consequences of statelessness, is not ideal for both the State and its residents. States attempt to address the detrimental effects in bilateral agreements that either prevent the creation of double nationality or resolve the conflict between two nationalities by the choice (option) of one of them as decisive for the specific relationship. Concerning military obligations in cases of multiple nationalities, Article 21 of the European Convention states that persons possessing the nationality of two or more States are required to fulfil their military obligations only in relation to one of those States. The modalities of its application are settled by a mutual agreement of the concerned States and in the case of absence of such an agreement, the state where the person resides determines the military duties. Under international law (and personal status), this special rule is used, for example by employing the law of the State of the last acquired nationality or the person's last permanent residence, etc.

In conclusion, it is at this stage when the European Union interferes in the issue of nationality.

II Citizenship in the European Union Legal System

1 Way to the 'European Citizenship'

None of the historical attempts to unite Europe (Roman Empire, Turkish Empire, Napoleon, Hitler, Vatican) we successful, mainly because they were enforced by the military. It should be stated that Pierre Dubois[4] in his work 'De recuperatione terre sancte' from 1306 had already suggested the creation of a State-community of European catholic sovereigns whose members would voluntarily give up a part of their sovereignty, providing that the remaining part of their sovereignty would be guaranteed by the community itself. It is only after the Second World War that a *voluntary process* of unification of Europe began and progressively developed through various stages, gradually increasing in intensity and scope.

With the adoption of the Treaty of Rome in 1957, the generation of Robert Schumann, Jean Monet and many other European idealists unveiled the revolutionary idea of a new concept of Europe, 'alive and organized' union of constantly converging European nations, which would be based on rules and common institutions with profound respect of fundamental rights and freedoms.

The Community, initially created as an economic group of States, naturally involved not only its member States but also individuals and legal entities on

---

4 Dubois, P. (Dominican monk from Normandy); *De recuperatione Terre Sancte*. Traité de politique générale. Published in conformity with the manuscript from Vatican, Ch.-V. Langlois, Paris, Picard [1891].

their territories that became subjects of European law[5]. However, at a first stage, the treaty and the European legislator did not consider the citizens of member States as citizens of the Community, but focused on their social and economic status, and referred to them as to 'employees',[6] 'self-employers',[7] 'service providers',[8] 'unemployed',[9] 'retirees',[10] 'students,'[11] etc. The citizens in the 'pure sense' enter only on the international scene at this particular level of the Community integration.

Almost forty years after the ratification of the Treaty of Rome, it became necessary to examine whether the citizen of the Union as a human being, aside from the economic aspect, is entitled, without discrimination, to his freedom to move and reside within the Community and to the protection of his fundamental rights. The Maastricht Treaty signed in 1992[12] amended and completed the Treaty of Rome with Articles 17 to 22 EC introducing the citizenship of the Union.

Under Article 17 EC, every person holding the nationality of a Member state is a citizen of the Union. The citizenship of the Union shall complement and not replace the national citizenship. This provision helped to eliminate the tight connection between fundamental rights and the exercise of an economic activity within the Community, which has served to facilitate the development of the internal market. In this respect, the Commission's report on the Union citizenship provides that the Maastricht Treaty established a direct political link between the citizens of the Member States and the European Union. Previously, such a relation within the Community did not exist. Its current objective is to form an affiliation of citizens to the Union.[13] For this reason, the Treaty establishing the European Community lays down particular rights and obligations for the citizens of the Union.

The rights conferred on EU citizens are specified in Articles 18 to 21 EC. The most important among them is the right of all citizens to move and reside freely within the territory of the Member States [Article 18(1) EC], which represents a cornerstone of European integration. The other political rights granted to the citizens of the Union are the right to vote and to stand as a candidate at municipal and European Parliament elections (Article 19 EC) and the right to

---

5 See, *inter alia*, Case 26/62 *Van Gend en Loos* [1963] ECR 3.

6 See, e.g. Art. 39 EC.

7 See, e.g. Art. 43 EC.

8 See, e.g. Art. 49 EC.

9 See, *inter alia*, Regulation No 1408/71 of the Council of 14 June 1971 on the application of social security schemes to employed persons and their families moving within the Community, Art. 4(1)(g).

10 See, e.g. Council Directive 90/365/EEC of 28 June 1990 on the right of residence for employees and self-employed persons who have ceased their occupational activity.

11 See, inter alia, Council Directive 93/96/EEC of 29 October 1993 on the right of residence for students.

12 Entered into force on the 1st of January 1993.

13 Doc. COM (93) 702.

protection by diplomatic or consular authorities of any Member state in the territory of a third country in which the Member state of which he is the national is not represented (Article 20 EC). In accordance with Article 194 EC and 195 EC, every citizen of the Union has the right to petition the European Parliament [Art. 21(1) EC], to apply to the Ombudsman [Art. 21(2) EC] and to address himself to any of the institutions or bodies in his or her mother tongue and request an answer in the same language [Art. 21(3) EC].

Another important principle related to the nationality of Member States is enshrined in Article 12 EC, which explicitly states that within the scope of application of the Treaty '*any discrimination on grounds of nationality shall be prohibited*'. In this context, the European legislator treats all nationalities as equivalent and equal, and therefore, prohibits any discriminatory treatment of their 'holders' based on the nationality.[14]

However, it is more difficult to identify the duties imposed on the citizens of the Union on the grounds of the European citizenship. Among them can be mentioned, according to C. Blumann, the general obligation to respect the Community legal order, to contribute to the expenses of the Community within the scope of the prescribed procedures, to participate in the realisation of the principle of solidarity, etc.[15]

2 Application *Ratione Personae* of the European Citizenship

The interplay of the Union citizenship with the nationality of the Member States indicates that there is no real Community legal basis, but only national legal rules of different Member States. Therefore, a part of the doctrine points out the weakness of the European citizenship that is entirely dependent on the nationalities of the Member States, since the decision of who its citizens are is not taken by the European Union, but rests with the Member States applying their internal rules. Thus, the harmonisation of the Member States national rules could serve as a basis for a more or less uniform European citizenship. With regard to the historical and ideological differences coupled with the issue of sovereignty and matters falling into the exclusive competence of the Member States, this harmonisation is, in our opinion, not likely to be achieved in the near future.

Despite the abovementioned historical and ideological differences linked with sovereignty and the fact that these affairs (e.g. rules related to the attribu-

---

[14] In addition, the question of discrimination was analysed at the 10th Autumn School of Law in Modra-Harmónia, Slovakia, in November 2005, which included two lectures on the principles of equity and non-discrimination in the European Union. See Klučka, J.: *Rovnosť a rovnoprávnosť v európskom a medzinárodnom práve.* Právny obzor, 89, 2006, No 2, p. 123-138; Pecho, P. – Michel, F.: *Zásada rovnosti v. práve EÚ a v judikatúre Súdneho dvora Európskych spoločenstiev* Právny obzor, 89, 2006, No 2, p. 139-162.

[15] C. Blumann: *Citoyenneté européenne et champ d'appplication personnel du droit communautaire.* R.A.E.-L.E.A. 2003/2004/I, p. 79.

tion of nationality) will remain for some more time in the scope of Member States' exclusive competences, it would be incorrect to think that these competences are unlimited. *The European Convention on nationality* from 1997 delimits such competences since it outlines the values of international law that bind the Member States; however, it does not identify tangible conditions for the national practices conferring nationality. That is why we can conclude that the governing systems for nationality of different Member States respect in principle the international rules on nationality, as they all are contracting parties to the convention.

Nonetheless, concerning the principle of effectiveness of citizenship[16] followed by international law, the European Court of Justice (ECJ) adopted in the case, *Micheletti,*[17] a strict legalistic interpretation of the institution of nationality. Mr. Micheletti was at the same time a national of a Member State, Italy, and of a third country, Argentina. However, his link to the latter country was more intensive then his liaison to Italy. The question was whether this person can claim the rights conferred by the Treaty to the citizens of Member States. The ECJ, without analysing the effectiveness, quality or how profound the State-national links were, stated that even the less intensive link of Mr. Micheletti to the Member State in comparison with the link he had to that third country, in which he had the habitual residence, is sufficient for the exercise of his rights as European citizen.[18] In this way, the ECJ conferred the rights granted by the Treaty to every person that can prove the holding of the nationality of one of the Member States of the Union. The ECJ considers that the acquisition and the loss of nationality are a part of the exclusive competence of Member States and the ECJ is bound to the recognition of such a relationship.

This approach of the ECJ can be explained by its willingness to allow the nationals of the Member States the maximum benefit from the rights conferred upon them by the Treaty, and above all the right to move and reside freely within the Community. Equally, the conference of the government representatives of the Member States that adopted the Treaty on the European Union proclaimed in its declaration no. 2 (annexed to the final acts of this Treaty) that, in so far as the Treaty refers to nationals of Member States, the question of whether a person holds the nationality of one of them is to be analysed exclusively under the Member State's internal rules. For this reason, Member States are permitted to make public unilateral declarations specifying which persons are considered to be their nationals.

In this regard, the ECJ maintained this interpretation in the cases *Manjit Kaur*[19] and *Zhu and Chen.*[20] The former case (characteristic for nationality rules

---

[16] See *Nottebohm.*

[17] Case C-369/90 *Micheletti* [1992] ECR 4239.

[18] See *Micheletti.*

[19] Case C-192/99 *Manjit Kaur* [2001] ECR I-1237.

[20] Case C-200/02 *Zhu and Chen* [2004] ECR I-9925.

of countries with imperial or colonial past) was about Ms Manjit Kaur, born in Kenya, who under the 1948 British Nationality Act[21] became a citizen of the United Kingdom and of British Colonies. On the other hand, Ms Kaur did not belong to any of the categories of persons who were conferred the right of residence in the United Kingdom by the amended Immigration Act from 1971. The 1981 British Nationality Act granted her the status of a British 'Overseas Citizen'. As such, she had, in the absence of special authorisation, no right under national law to reside in the UK. Both of these laws were *inter alia* the subject-matter of a Declaration of the UK adopted in order to delineate who should be considered as a UK national in regard of the Community law. After several unsuccessful attempts to obtain the right to reside on the British territory, Ms Kaur applied to the referring court and claimed that she wished to reside permanently in the UK in order to benefit from the advantages conferred on the Union citizens by the Community law. The national court referred to the ECJ a question for a preliminary ruling in which it sought to ascertain the relevant criteria for determining whether a person has the nationality of a Member State and, thus, falls under the scope of application of the Community law. The ECJ, referring to the Micheletti case, concluded that the conditions for acquisition and loss of nationality are to be determined by each Member State with due regard to Community law.[22] The ECJ also recognised that in this context, the UK government's declaration must be taken into consideration as an instrument relating to the Treaty for the purpose of its interpretation and, more particularly, for determining the *ratione personae* scope of the Treaty.[23] Therefore, the ECJ will refer to these legal instruments in order to define to whom Community law would apply.

The *Zhu and Chen* case concerned the recognition and the effectiveness of the nationality of a Member State for the purposes of the Community law application. The ECJ stated that despite the fact that the nationality of a Member State was acquired without any genuine link between the concerned person and the Member State, it is not permissible for any Member State to withhold such an individual from the exercise of fundamental rights provided for in the Treaty.[24]

Another question was raised in respect of the relationship between the EU citizenship and the nationalities of different Member States. From what age on is an EU citizen allowed to claim the benefit of rights conferred upon him by the Treaty? In this context, the ECJ stated that it does not follow either from the terms of or from the aims pursued by Article 18 EC that these rights could be made conditional upon the attainment of a certain age, which is regulated by internal legal regimes in different ways (e.g., attainment of the age prescribed

---

[21] British Nationality Act 1948.

[22] *Manjit Kaur*, paragraph 19.

[23] *Manjit Kaur*, paragraph 24.

[24] *Zhu and Chen*, paragraph 39.

for the acquisition of legal capacity). Therefore, even a minor can take advantage of the rights guaranteed on the basis of his or her 'euro-citizenship'.[25]

3 Specific Rules of Application of the Union Citizenship Provisions

As the citizenship of the Union does not replace national citizenships, but only complements them,[26] the rights thereby granted only complement or broaden already existing individual rights conferred by the Community law to certain categories of persons, but do not replace them. In other words, respecting the principle of priority of specific legal rules over general rules, the general 'Union citizenship rights' do not affect the rights enjoyed by various 'specialized' categories of the Union citizens, *e.g.*, employees, self-employers, service providers, etc.

Although the ECJ recognised the direct effect[27] of Articles 12 and 18 EC, which provide for certain fundamental rights of the persons that fall within the scope of application of the Treaty,[28] it results from the terms and the position of these provisions in the Treaty as well as from the ECJ case-law, that the rights guaranteed are neither absolute nor unconditional. The application of these rights is delimited by the scope of the Community law[29] and its various provisions.[30] In the light of the principle *'lex specialis derogat legi generali'*, this limitation leads to the fact that the application of Articles 12 and 18 EC became in the ECJ jurisprudence subsidiary.

It is settled case-law that these articles apply independently only to situations governed by Community law, which were not the subject of special provisions of the Treaty or the secondary legislation prohibiting discrimination in a specific domain.[31] If any of the specific prohibitions rules apply, it is not necessary to make use any longer of Articles 12[32] or 18 EC.[33] Therefore, any discrimination or obstacle in respect to the right of the Union citizens to move or to reside freely are examined in the first place from the perspective of specific provisions and

---

[25] *Zhu and Chen*, paragraph 20.

[26] Art. 17(1) EC.

[27] See, e.g. Case 36/74 *Walrave and Koch* [1974] ECR 1405 and Case C-482/01 *Baumbast* [2002] ECR I-7091.

[28] Principle of non-discrimination on the grounds of nationality.

[29] Case C-85/96 *Martínez Sala* [1998] ECR I-2691.

[30] See, in particular, Case C-378/97 *Wijsenbeek* [1999] ECR 6207; Case C-356/98 *Kaba* [2000] C-356/98, ECR I-2623; Case C-413/99 *Baumbast* [2002], ECR I-7091; Case C-482/01 *Orfanopoulos* [2004] ECR I-5257.

[31] Cases C-131/96 *Carlos Mora Romero* [1997] ECR I-3659 and *Baumbast*.

[32] Case 59/85 *Ann Florence Reed* [1986] ECR 1283.

[33] Case C-92/01 *Stylianakis* [2003] ECR I-1291. See also Case C-456/02 *Trojani* [2004] ECR I-7573, and Case C-470/04 *N* [2006] ECR I-7409.

only afterwards, if these do not apply on the specific case, in the view of the two 'general' articles.[34]

Article 19 EC grants to all Union citizens, irrespective of their nationality, an active and passive voting right at the municipal[35] and European Parliament elections[36] in the Member State of their residence. Under the Treaty, the exercise of this right is subject to arrangements adopted by the Council acting unanimously on a proposal from the Commission and after consulting the European Parliament. This was settled in two Council directives – 93/109/EC and 94/80/EC – which the Member States were bound to transpose into their internal legal orders. Following subsequent implementation, the rights enshrined therein became directly enforceable at the domestic level.[37] Nonetheless, likewise in internal electoral right regulations, there is no automatic link between the statute of 'European citizen' and an unconditional right to vote in the elections to the European Parliament. On the one hand, this right was granted to a number of persons without the nationality of an EU Member State[38] (*e.g.*, residents of Gibraltar, which is a British dependency). On the other hand, the ECJ case-law established that Member States can limit the right to vote in the European Parliament elections to the nationals with permanent residence on the territory of such States.[39] Finally, we can conclude that the abovementioned voting rights are indeed guaranteed and respected by the Member States. This is corroborated by the evidence that the municipal elections and the elections to the European Parliament in the presence of candidates and electors, nationals of other Member States, proceed generally without major problems.

The exercise of the right provided in Article 20 EC is considerably more difficult. In principle, this Article confers on every Union citizen in the territory of a third country, where the Member State of which he is a national is not represented, the right of diplomatic or consular protection from the authorities of any other Member State in the same conditions as its own nationals. Due to the fact that the second sentence of this Article asks the Member States to establish necessary rules among them and to initiate the necessary international negotiations to secure the exercise of this right, the effective diplomatic and consular protection of the Union citizens in a third country, in which the Member State of their nationality is not represented, depends on the intergovernmental cooperation of Member States. This cooperation was demonstrated by the adoption of the Decision 95/553/EC concerning protection of citizens of the European Union by diplomatic and consular representations. Articles 1 and

34 See also Pecho, P. – Michel. F.; Op. cit.

35 Article 19(1) EC.

36 Article 19(2) EC.

37 See, e.g. Case C-300/04 *Eman and Sevinger* [2006] ECR I-8055 and C-145/04 *Spain/United Kingdom* [2006] ECR I-7917.

38 See *Spain/United Kingdom*.

39 Case C-300/04 *Eman and Sevinger* [2006] ECR I-8055.

2 thereof determine the conditions under which the representative authority of a Member State is due to provide diplomatic or consular assistance to the nationals of other Member States. Articles 5 and 6 settle detailed rules for the minimal diplomatic or consular protection. Under Article 8, the decision will enter into force when all the Member States have notified to the General Secretariat of the Council that the procedures required by their legal systems for the Decision to apply have been completed. This requirement has still not been accomplished, since the Decision 95/553 has yet to become effective and the protection of the Union citizens in third countries remains dependent on bilateral agreements between the Member States.

Concerning the rights laid down in Article 21 EC, their application in practice appears to be the least problematic, because they represent the fundamental rights of citizens in relation to the EU administration and do not interfere, unlike the abovementioned rights with any internal regulations of the EU Member States. Article 21 EC simply refers to Articles 194 EC, 195 EC and 314 EC that specify the application of rights provided in the former Article. Therefore, possible conflicts with regard to the rights specified in Article 21 fall under the responsibility of the ECJ and particularly of the Court of first instance of the European Communities.

4 Right of EU Citizens to Move and Reside Within the Territory of other Member States

Based on the previous discussion, it can be concluded that the Union citizenship relates to specific rights. It concerns political rights[40] as well as the right of the Union citizens to move and reside in the territory of any Member State. Originally, the latter right concerned the socio-economic situation of workers or other subjects of the common market. The aim of the application of such right was to allow these persons the exercise of their economic functions. The rights were subject to a considerable evolution, mainly due to the ECJ case-law, that broadened their scope and were afterwards 'codified' in the European Parliament and Council directive on the right of citizens of the Union and their family members to move and reside freely within the territory of the Member States.[41] Another category of rights described below can be considered as complementary to the right to move and reside freely. This is due to the fact that these rights result from the economic consequences of the exercise of the right to move and reside freely within the territory of the EU Member States.

---

40 See Articles 19 EC to 21 EC.

41 Directive 2004/38/EC of the European Parliament and of the Council of 29 April 2004 on the right of citizens of the Union and their family members to move and reside freely within the territory of the Member States.

a) Evolution of the exercise of the Union citizens' right to move and reside freely

Initially, the right of nationals of the Member States to move and reside freely within the territory of the European community granted by the Community primary law was conditional on the exercise of an economic activity.[42] Likewise, secondary law at first conferred this right only to certain socio-economic groups.[43] The three Council directives from the beginning of the 1990's represent the first exception to the economic meaning of the abovementioned right. The directives conferred this right also to some economically non-active persons. Concerned were the employees[44], self-employed persons that ceased their economic activity[45] and students.[46] However, the right of persons belonging to those three categories was not absolute and was subject to obligation to prove sufficient financial resources and a complete health insurance so that the national of a Member State does not cause inadequate financial cost to the hosting Member State.

It is obvious that such a complex and incomprehensible regulation of the right to move and to reside freely became too complicated for the individuals. Hence, the advocates general of the ECJ began to analyse the possibility of the

---

42 See Articles 39 EC to 55 EC.

43 See, in particular, Regulation (EEC) No 1612/68 of the Council of 15 October 1968 on freedom of movement for workers within the Community; Regulation (EEC) No 1251/70 of the Commission of 29 June 1970 on the right of workers to remain in the territory of a Member State after having been employed in that State; Council Directive 68/360/EEC of 15 October 1968 on the abolition of restrictions on movement and residence within the Community for workers of Member States and their families; Council Directive of 17 December 1974 concerning the right of nationals of a Member State to remain in the territory of another Member State after having pursued therein an activity in a self-employed capacity; Council Directive 73/148/EEC of 21 May 1973 on the abolition of restrictions on movement and residence within the Community for nationals of Member States with regard to establishment and the provision of services; Council Directive 64/221/EEC of 25 February 1964 on the co-ordination of special measures concerning the movement and residence of foreign nationals which are justified on grounds of public policy, public security or public health; Council Directive of 18 May 1972 extending to workers exercising the right to remain in the territory of a Member State after having been employed in that State the scope of the Directive of 25 February 1964 on coordination of special measures concerning the movement and residence of foreign nationals which are justified on grounds of public policy, public security or public health; Council Directive of 17 December 1974 extending the scope of Directive No 64/221/EEC on the coordination of special measures concerning the movement and residence of foreign nationals which are justified on grounds of public policy, public security or public health to include nationals of a Member State who exercise the right to remain in the territory of another Member State after having pursued therein an activity in a self-employed capacity.

44 Council Directive 90/364/EEC of 28 June 1990 on the right of residence (OJ L 180, 13.7.1990, p. 26-27).

45 Council Directive 90/365/EEC of 28 June 1990 on the right of residence for employees and self-employed persons who have ceased their occupational activity (OJ L 180, 13.7.1990, p. 28-29).

46 Council Directive 93/96/EEC of 29 October 1993 on the right of residence for students (OJ L 317, 18.12.1993, p. 59-60).

application of Article 18 EC as a subsidiary legal basis in order to include all the different categories of persons that showed the interest to relocate and reside freely but did not fall within the scope of any particular primary or secondary rule.[47]

Despite some early reluctance, the ECJ judges took these innovative opinions into consideration. In the *Wijsenbeek* case,[48] the question raised concerned identity controls of the EU citizens at the internal frontiers of the Community. The ECJ stated that indeed Article 18 EC confers on the Union citizens the right to move and reside freely in all the Member States.[49] However, the Court reiterated that the exercise of this right is subject to limitations and conditions laid down in the Treaty establishing the EC.[50] Thus, by the measures adopted to give it effect, the Council may adopt provisions to facilitate the exercise of those rights. Therefore, as long as Community provisions on controls at the external borders of the Community, which also include common or harmonised rules on, in particular, conditions of access, visas and asylum, have not been adopted, the exercise of those rights presupposes that the person concerned is able to establish that he or she has the nationality of a Member State. Thereby, the ECJ refused the unconditional character of rights laid down in Article 18 EC and the direct effect of this article.[51]

A similar judgment to the *Wijsenbeek* case was rendered shortly after, in the *Kaba*[52] case. The ECJ indirectly[53] expressed its opinion on the compliance of the immigration law of a Member State with the Community law. The internal legislation in question provided that the nationals of a third country residing in the Member State and who are spouses of persons settled in that territory, can apply for indefinite leave to remain after 12 months of legal residence in this State. However, the condition of four years of legal residence is required for the spouses of migrant workers who are nationals of other Member States settled in

---

47 Opinion of Advocate General Léger in case C-214/94 *Boukhalfa*; Opinion of Advocate General La Pergola in Joined cases C-4/95 and C-5/95 *Stöber and Pereira*; Opinion of Advocate General Cosmas in Case C-378/97 *Wijsenbeek*.

48 Case C-378/97 *Wijsenbeek* [1999] ECR I-6207.

49 Id., paragraph 41.

50 For example restrictions on grounds of public policy, public security or public health.

51 *Wijsenbeek*, paragraphs 42 and 43.

52 See *Kaba*.

53 Since it concerns the reference for a preliminary ruling (Article 234 EC) and not the failure to fulfill an obligation under the Treaty (Article 226 EC), the ECJ does not give its opinion on the conformity of internal legislation with Community law. The ECJ provides only an interpretation of Community law with regard to the facts of the case brought before a national court and with regard to national law. Therefore, conformity of national legal rule with Community law is reviewed indirectly. See, in particular, Klučka, J.: '*Charakteristika právnej úpravy konania pred Súdnym dvorom ES*', Bulletin advokácie, 8/2005, p. 25; Pecho, P. – Pogáčová, J.: '*Miesto a úloha advokátov v. prejudiciálnom konaní pred Súdnym dvorom ES*', Bulletin advokácie, 9/2005, p. 46 and 10/2005, p. 45.

the territory of the former one. Analysing the conformity of this legislation with Article 18 EC, the ECJ stressed that the exercise of the right to move and reside freely within the EU is subject to the limitations and conditions laid down in the Treaty and in the measures adopted giving it effect. Accordingly, the Member States are entitled to rely on any potential objective difference between their own nationals and those of other Member States when they establish the conditions under which the leave to remain indefinitely in their territory is to be granted to the spouses of such persons.[54] In this context, the ECJ underlined that the nationals of third countries that derive their right to reside from the right of their spouses cannot be granted more rights than those to which their spouses are entitled.

The substantial qualitative change in the Article 18 EC application followed from the *Baumbast* case.[55] Mr. Baumbast is a German national; his spouse and her natural daughter have Colombian nationality, while their common younger daughter has dual German and Colombian nationality. Mr. Baumbast pursued from 1990 on an economic activity in the United Kingdom. Consequently, the members of the Baumbast family were granted the right of residence in the UK for five years. Meanwhile, Mr. Baumbast lost his job and when his 5-year long right of residence expired, he applied for the indefinite leave in this Member State, without having been re-employed yet. The question was whether Mr. Baumbast, despite the fact that he did not fall under any 'specific' category of persons entitled to claim the right to move freely on the basis of a particular provision, had, as a Union citizen, the right to indefinite residence in the UK, and if so, whether his family was able to derive the right to indefinite leave from his own one.

The ECJ acknowledged that Mr. Baumbast pursued during several years an economic activity in the UK. Consequently, the Court agreed to confer on his children the right to reside in that Member State in order to attend general educational courses pursuant to Article 12 of Regulation No 1612/68 despite the fact that the father ceased to be a migrant worker. The ECJ held that the refusal of the right of residence could discourage this EU citizen from the exercise of the freedom of residence and cause therefore barriers to the exercise of the rights conferred by the Treaty.[56] Equally, the ECJ affirmed that under Regulation 1612/68, Mr. Baumbast's wife, a third country national, who after her divorce from Mr. Baumbast became the primary caretaker for both children, was authorized to remain on British territory so that her children could attend general educational courses.[57]

---

54 *Kaba*, paragraphs 30 and 31.

55 See *Baumbast*.

56 *Baumbast*, paragraphs 47 to 63.

57 *Baumbast*, paragraphs 68 to 75 Although the argumentation of the ECJ was marked by an extensive interpretation of the Regulation 1612/68, it is consistent with its progressive case-law in the field of free movement of workers within the Community Member States.

The Baumbast case is exceptional because of the new approach in the application of Article 18 EC on the freedom of movement of those EU citizens who cannot rely on a Community law specific provision. The Court recalled that, before the Maastricht Treaty entered into force, the right to move and to reside freely within the territory of the Member States was subject to the condition that the person concerned was carrying on an economic activity in the meaning of Articles 39, 43 and 49 EC. At the same time, the ECJ admitted that, since then, Article 18(1) EC, which has been introduced into the Treaty, confers clearly and unambiguously on every citizen the right of free movement and residence. Although this right is subject to limitations and conditions laid down by the EC Treaty and by the measures adopted to give it effect, the right of residence in any Member State can be considered unconditional, and any limitations and conditions are subject to judicial review. Specifically, Article 1(1) of the Directive 90/364 provides that migrants-nationals should be covered by health insurance in respect of all risks in the host Member State and have sufficient resources to avoid becoming an unreasonable burden for the social assistance system of the host Member State during their residence.[58]

In respect of the principle of proportionality and strict interpretation of exceptions to the general rule, the ECJ confirmed that the host Member States are not entitled to require the health insurance to cover every possible risk that may occur during the residence of the Union citizen in the territory of concerned Member State.[59] As to the condition relating to the sufficient resources, the ECJ held in the *Commission/Belgium* case[60] that the host Member States cannot require that a Union citizen must have sufficient personal resources. For that purpose, it is possible that a third person can stand as guarantor for these citizens. If the national of one Member State resides in the territory of another Member State without adequate resources and seeks to receive a social assistance benefit, the ECJ, considered in *Trojani* that a citizen of the Union cannot claim on the basis of the Article 18 EC the right to reside in the territory of a Member State of which he is not a national,[61] without fulfilling the conditions specified by the Community law.

It results from the ECJ case-law that, on the basis of rules defined in the Treaty or in the secondary legislation, which confer the right to move and reside within the Member States of the Union, the EU citizens are entitled to base a right of claim under Article 18(1) EC. In fact, this provision meets all the requirements for direct effect laid down in the *Van Duyn* case.[62] It means that it is clear, precise, unconditional and does not require intervention of any act on the part either of the institution of the Community or of Member States or a decision falling into the discretional power of the national authorities. The ECJ

---

58 *Baumbast*, paragraphs 84 to 90.

59 *Baumbast*, paragraphs 89 to 93.

60 Case C-408/03 *Commission/Belgium* [2006] ECR I-2647.

61 Case C-456/02 *Trojani* [2004] ECR I-2647, paragraph 36.

62 Case 41/74 *Van Duyn* [1974] ECR 1337.

admitted that the parties of the national proceedings can invoke directly Article 18(1) EC in order to protect their rights conferred on them on the basis of their EU citizenship.

The ECJ judgment in the *Baumbast* case softened to a certain extent the existing case-law (cases *Wijsenbeek* and *Kaba)* and laid down other basic rules for the application of Article 18 EC. It concerns the rule of wide interpretation of the principle of free movement of the Union citizens in the territory of Member States and restrictive interpretation of any exception to this principle. Direct or indirect restrictions to the exercise of the freedom to move and to reside in another Member State can be justified, with regard to Community law, only if they are based on objective considerations of public interest independent of the nationality of the persons concerned and proportionate to the legitimate objective of the national provisions,[63] or if they are founded on a particular Community rule.

In the *Orfanopoulos* case,[64] the ECJ specified the exceptions to the freedom of the Union citizens to move and to reside in Member States other than the ones of their origin. In a case concerning a national of a Member State who suffered from toxicomany and had been several times convicted of such offences, the ECJ affirmed its interpretation of Article 18(1) EC and added that the rights provided therein can be restricted not only by the requirements laid down in Article 1(1) of the Directive 90/364, but also by the Directive 64/221/EEC on the co-ordination of special measures concerning the movement and residence of foreign nationals which are justified on the grounds of public policy, public security or public health.[65]

b) Harmonisation of the right of EU citizens to move and to reside freely within the territory of Member States

Reflecting the ECJ case-law, Article 18(1) EC has become the legal basis for the free movement of the Union citizens on the territory of Member States. Nevertheless, because of the conditional and subsidiary application[66] of this provision, it merely complements, and does not replace national legislation. Moreover, the Member States were not happy with the fact that the conditions and limits of the right to move and reside freely in the territory of Member States had been determined rather by the Court of Justice and not by the Community legislator.

By adopting the Directive 2004/38/EC[67] on the right of citizens of the Union and their family members to move and reside freely within the territory of the Member States, the Community legislator sought to unify the miscellaneous

---

63 Case C-406/04 *De Cuyper* [2006] ECR I-6947, paragraph 40.

64 See *Orfanopoulos*.

65 Council Directive 64/221/EEC of 25 February 1964 (OJ 56, 4.4.1964, p. 850-857).

66 See Part C in this Chapter.

67 Directive 2004/38/EC of the European Parliament and of the Council of 29 April 2004 on the right of citizens of the Union and their family members to move and reside freely within the territory of the

rules governing European citizenship. The directive implemented to a large extent the principles and rules established by the ECJ, amended the Regulation 1612/68, and repealed several directives that became obsolete after its adoption.

It resulted from the preamble of the Directive 2004/38 that due to recent Community law developments, it appeared necessary to codify and review the existing legislation on the free movement and residence of citizens dealing separately with workers, students, other inactive persons, etc. The unification aimed to simplify and to strengthen the right of free movement and residence of all Union citizens regardless of their socio-economic situation within different Member States. From the *ratione personae* aspect, the directive specifies the scope of persons that enjoy the right to move and reside freely within the territory of the Member States. Beside the Union citizens, meaning the nationals of all the Member States, the right of free movement and residence is also granted to their family members (spouses, registered partners[68] of the opposite or the same sex, descendents, natural children or stepchildren) for the purpose of family merging, irrespective of their nationality.[69] Accordingly, the right to move and to reside within the Union encompasses a wider spectrum of individuals residing in the territory of Member States.

This definition created the basis for protection of fundamental rights and freedoms laid down in the Treaty. The right of the Union citizens to leave the territory of a Member State and to move to another Member State corresponds to the obligation of other Member States to grant Union citizens and their family members (even if they are not Union citizens) leave to enter their territory with a valid identity card or passport (Articles 4 and 5 of the directive). The directive itself distinguishes the right of residence for a period up to three months (Article 6), for a period longer than three months (Article 7) and the right of permanent residence (Article 16 et seq.).

A residence not exceeding three months is not subject to any conditions or formalities other than the requirement to hold a valid identity card or passport. This also applies to family members of the Union citizen who are not nationals of any Member State.

A residence longer than three months requires certain formalities with a view to avoid the situation that the EU citizens or the members of their family become an excessive burden for the social security system of the Member State in the territory of which they reside. In this context, Article 7 of the directive states that this right is granted to the workers employed in the host Member State or the Union citizens and their family members who have sufficient

---

Member States amending Regulation (EEC) No 1612/68 and repealing Directives 64/221/EEC, 68/360/EEC, 72/194/EEC, 73/148/EEC, 75/34/EEC, 75/35/EEC, 90/364/EEC, 90/365/EEC and 93/96/EEC.

68 The provision no. 5 of the preamble of the Directive states that the definition of 'family member' should also include the registered partner if the National legislation treats registered partnership as equivalent to marriage.

69 Same solution was adopted in the case *Baumbast*, supra, paragraph 63.

resources allowing them to reside without the need to claim the social assistance services and comprehensive health insurance cover in the host Member State. According to Article 8(1) of the directive, for periods of residence longer than three months, the host Member State may require Union citizens and their family members to register at the relevant authorities. As regards the permanent residence, under Article 16(1) and 16(2), this right is granted to the Union citizens and their family members who have resided legally in another Member State than the one of which they are nationals for a continuous period of five years.

Although since the adoption of the directive the right to move and to reside freely is conferred on the citizens and their family members by homogenous legal rule, it can be restrained under certain conditions. Such an obstacle may be justified by the interest to maintain or install public order, public security or public health. However, all the restraints of this right have to respect the principle of proportionality. Under this principle, it is necessary to take into account the stage and the intensity of the integration of the person to the new society, the duration of the residence in the country, the age, family status, economic background and the existing link to the home country. The appreciation must be based exclusively on the personal conduct of the individual concerned, and has to answer the question whether he or she represents a real danger or a sufficiently serious threat to the requirements of public policy affecting one of the fundamental interests of the host State[70]. In order to avoid the misapplication of these provisions, Article 31 of the directive confers on the persons concerned the access to judicial and, where appropriate, administrative redress procedures in the host Member State to appeal against or seek review of any decision taken against them on the grounds of public policy, public security or public health that can lead to expulsion from the territory of the host State.

5 Economic Consequences of the Free Movement and Residence of the Union Citizens Within the Territory of Member States

The objective of Article 18 EC is not only to generalise the right of the Union citizens and their family members to move and reside freely within the Member States, but it has also broader social and economic consequences. In fact, the ECJ considers as a violation of the right to enter or to reside in a Member States' territory not only those rules that physically prevent these persons to enter or to reside in the territory of a Member State, but also rules that introduce social or economic discrimination based on the nationality.

According to the ECJ's wide interpretation of Article 18(1) EC, citizenship of the Union is destined to be the 'fundamental status of nationals of the Member

[70] Same solution was adopted for example in the case *Orfanopoulos*, paragraphs 62 to 71.

States' that entitles them, in principle, to the same treatment irrespective of their nationality.[71] According to settled case-law, a citizen of the European Union, lawfully resident in the territory of the host Member State can rely on Article 12 EC in all situations which fall within the *ratione materiae* scope of Community law.[72] This includes situations involving the exercise of fundamental freedoms guaranteed by the Treaty and those involving the exercise of the right to move and to reside within the territory of the Member States, as conferred by Article 18 EC.[73] Therefore, the nationals who decided to exercise their right to move and to reside freely cannot be treated less favourably than those who do not exercise this right.

Such an expression of the general principle of equality applies not only in the relationships between the Union citizens and the host Member States (restrictions to enter the territory of a Member State[74]), but also in the relations between the EU Member States and their nationals that can be treated unfavourably on the exit from their country (restriction to exit from the home country[75]), or on the return to their home country (restrictions on the return[76]). By consequence, this can discourage them from the exercise of the rights granted to them by the Treaty on the basis of the European citizenship.

The following cases illustrate the wide and meticulous application of Article 18(1) EC by the ECJ. In the *Martinez Salà* case,[77] the ECJ explained that on the basis of Articles 12 and 18 EC a Member state national, who resides legally in another Member State, is entitled to apply for the scholarship from the host Member State under the same conditions that apply to nationals of this State. In the *Grzelczyk* case,[78] the ECJ granted to a student coming from a Member State the right to obtain from the Member State in the territory of which he resides legally, the so-called minimal social assistance granted to students and nationals of the host Member State. Furthermore, the ECJ stated that a student's application for the social assistance cannot be considered as a reason to lift his residence permit in the host Member State as this minimal social assistance cannot be qualified as an 'unreasonable' burden on the public finances of this State. Nonetheless, to avoid the abuse of the social security systems, the ECJ recognised in the *Collins* case[79] the right of Member States to restrain the number of

[71] Case C-184/99 *Grzelczyk* [2001] ECR I-6193, paragraphs 30 and 31; Case C-148/02 *Garcia Avello* [2003] ECR I-11613, paragraphs 22 and 23, and Case C-209/03 *Bidar* [2005] ECR I-2119, paragraph 31.

[72] Case C-85/96 *Martínez Sala* [1998] ECR I-2691, paragraph 63; *Grzelczyk*, paragraph 32, and *Bidar*, paragraph 32.

[73] Case C-274/96 *Bickel and Franz* [1998] ECR I-7637, paragraphs 15 and 16, *Grzelczyk*, paragraph 33; Garcia Avello, paragraph 24, and *Bidar*, paragraph 33.

[74] See, inter alia, *Bidar*.

[75] See, e.g. Case C-224/02 *Pusa* [2004] ECR 5763.

[76] See, e.g. Case C-224/98 *D'Hoop* [2002] ECR 6191.

[77] *Martínez Sala*, supra, paragraphs 59 to 65.

[78] *Grzelczyk*.

[79] Case C-138/02 *Collins* [2004] ECR I-2703.

the other Member States' citizens seeking social security assistance during their job search in the host Member State, to those who have an effective link to the employment market of that host Member State.[80] The existence of this link can be proven by the fact that the applicant has resided for a sufficiently long time in the territory of the Member State where he applies for the social assistance.

In the *D'Hoop* case,[81] the ECJ was faced with the issue of whether a Member State can refuse to grant to one of its nationals an unemployment allowance normally allocated to high school graduates (tideover allowance) on the sole ground that she completed her secondary education in another Member State. If the applicant had completed secondary education in her own State, she would have been granted the allowance. However, the ECJ confirmed that a national of a Member State cannot be discriminated on the sole ground that he or she exercised the rights conferred to him by the Treaty, meaning here the right to reside in another Member State in order to pursue secondary school studies. If these nationals were treated less favourably after their return to their own State, it would be incompatible with the right of freedom of movement and residence conferred on them by the Treaty. Similar conclusion was adopted in the case *Pusa,*[82] which concerned the execution rules of a Member State that settled less favourable conditions for debtors residing in other Member States compared to the debtors residing in the territory of their own State, Finland.

Furthermore, what would be the ECJ's attitude towards a national legislation under which the students can only be awarded an education or training grant for their studies in another EU Member State, if they have accomplished at least one year of the same studies in an establishment in their Member State of origin? This question was raised in the case *Morgan and Bucher.*[83] Two German nationals who studied in other Member States subjects not available in Germany applied for a scholarship from Germany. Their application was rejected *inter alia* for the reason that they did not pursue the abovementioned obligatory one year of studies in that Member State. Firstly, the ECJ stated that Mss Morgan and Bucher were German nationals and therefore the 'Union citizens'. As such, they had the right to refer to the Article 18 EC including against their Member State of origin.[84] Secondly, the ECJ confirmed that although the Member States are competent, under Article 149(1) EC, as regards the content of teaching and the organisation of their respective education systems, that competence must be exercised in compliance with Community law,[85] what means that they could not treat less favourably their own nationals who exercised a certain number of the rights conferred to them by the Treaty, e. g. the freedom to move within the territory of EU Member States. Consequently, where a Member State provides

80 *De Cuyper.*

81 *D'Hoop*, supra, paragraph 31.

82 Id.

83 Case C-11/06 *Morgan and Bucher* [2007] ECR I 0000.

84 Id., paragraph 22.

85 Id., paragraph 24.

for a system of education or training grants for students if they pursue their studies in another Member State, it must ensure that the detailed rules for the award of those grants do not create an unjustified restriction of the right to move and reside within the territory of the Member States.[86] Considering that this condition of scholarship award could discourage German nationals from studying in another Member State and from exercising their right to move and reside in other EU Member States, the ECJ stated that Germany did not have a legitimate reason to maintain such a condition and the German legislation in question was *de facto* contrary to the Article 18 EC.

The case *Morgan and Bucher*, where two students could not fulfil the legal requirement of spending at least one year at an educational institution in Germany, deserves certain comments despite the fact that the ECJ in its decision strictly followed the question referred for the preliminary ruling and did not engage in any discussion of general concepts. First of all, neither Article 149 EC nor any other provision of the Treaty establishing the European community obliges Member States to promote the mobility of its students by awarding them scholarships. Furthermore, this provision excludes any harmonisation of the laws and regulations of the Member States.[87] Therefore, on the basis of this Treaty or the secondary legislation of the Community, Germany obviously was not bound to establish any system of the grants for students studying in another Member State. Even though, with regard to its sovereign policy in the field of promoting higher education, this Member State decided to grant scholarships to certain students intending to pursue their studies abroad. On this account, Germany voluntarily and within its capacity contributed to the achievement of the objectives referred to in Article 149(1) EC.

Secondly, contrary to the measures mentioned in the cases cited above, this provision did not result in discrimination based on nationality, State of residence or graduation. Nonetheless, the ECJ did not consider these arguments relevant and pointed at the rule, on the basis of which Member States in their normative actions have to respect the fundamental freedoms provided for by Community law and this even in the fields where the Community legislator has no power and Member States are not obliged to grant any special rights to individuals falling within the scope of its jurisdiction.[88]

III Conclusion

In conclusion, the conditions of citizenship in international and European law do not have a lot in common. When the nationality *ex lege* became the basis of the Union citizenship, it was empowered later by several

[86] Idem, paragraph 28.

[87] Article 149(4) EC.

[88] See, for example in the field of assessed taxes Case C-279/93 *Schumacker* [1995] ECR I-225.

fundamental rights and freedoms. This feature represents its commonality with the citizenship in international law. However, the exercise of these rights and freedoms is subject to the control of Member States, which can require the fulfilment of various conditions. Contrary to the double citizenship in international law, the 'coexistence' of nationality and citizenship does not cause any problems in practice, since these two cannot compete. (also with regard to Article 17 EC).

In addition, the traditional international law institutions of diplomatic and consular protection can be based on the Union citizenship. While under international law this protection can be sought only by the nationals of State, which the representation belongs to, in the scope of Union citizenship this protection can be granted to any Member Sate national. The application of this institution is not inhibited by a double nationality of Member States, whereas the plurality of nationalities can cause problems in international law.

In this context, citizenship represents the 'right to have rights', that means all fundamental rights guaranteed by Community law without discrimination on the basis of nationality by the Member States.

Civis europeae sum...

CHAPTER 10

The Current Issues of Competition Law and its Human Rights Dimension

Michal Petr

The EC competition policy ranks among the clear successes of the Common Policies of the Community. The legal provisions thereof have been redrafted recently, creating a system in which the EC competition law is applied not only by the Commission, but also by the Member States; by them, it might even be applied in parallel with their national competition law. The EC competition law itself will most probably remain intact by the further development of the EU, including its possible future constitutionalisation. However, it will be argued in this Chapter that the increasing emphasis being laid on the protection of Human Rights, which would without doubt be expanded by the constitutionalisation or any other further changes made to the Founding Treaties, could change the way in which EC competition law is applied.

I Introduction to EC Competition Law

By the term *competition law,* we understand in this text the regulation of certain coordinated conduct of the undertakings, the so-called *cartel agreements*, and of their unilateral conduct, i.e. the questions of the *abuse of a dominant position*; it is also called *antitrust law.* Apart from antitrust law, the EC competition law is concerned also with *merger review*; this regulation nonetheless constitutes a relatively independent (and recent)[1] area and will not be discussed in depth here.

The legal basis for the competition law constitutes the Treaty establishing the European Community (hereinafter referred to as the 'Treaty') itself, which among the activities of the Community specifically mentions the maintaining of the '*system ensuring that competition in the internal market is not distorted*'.[2] The concept of *agreements* is then defined in Article 81 and the *dominant position* in Article 82 of the Treaty. The rules of application of these provisions are set by a Council regulation (hereinafter referred to as the 'Implementing regulation').

The Treaty identifies the concepts of agreements and dominance only in general terms and they therefore had to be defined by the jurisprudence of the ECJ. The agreements are described as any direct or indirect contacts between undertakings, '*the object or effect whereof is either to influence the conduct on the market of an actual or potential competitor or to disclose to such a competitor the course of conduct which they themselves have decided to adopt or contemplate adopting on the market*'.[3] As far as these 'contacts' are concerned, the Treaty mentions three forms thereof: the agreements between undertakings *stricto sensu*, the

* JUDr. Michal Petr, Ph.D. is the Director of Legislative Departement of the Czech Office for the protection of the competition.

1 The regulation of the merger control was introduced in 1990 by Council Regulation (EEC) No 4064/89 of 21 December 1989 on the control of concentrations between undertakings, OJ L 257, 21.9.1990, p. 13; unlike the antitrust, it is not mentioned in the Treaty itself.

2 Art. 3 (1) (g) of the Treaty.

3 ECJ judgment 40/73 *Suiker Unie* [1975] ECR 1663, 174.

decisions by associations of undertakings and the concerted practices. This distinction is nonetheless not decisive, because the Treaty '*is intended to apply to all collusion between undertakings, whatever the form it takes. There is continuity between the cases listed. The only essential thing is the distinction between independent conduct, which is allowed, and collusion, which is not, regardless of any distinction between types of collusion*'.[4]

Not every collusion between undertakings is prohibited, only those agreements, which have '*as their object or effect the prevention, restriction or distortion of competition within the common market*', e.g. agreements which directly or indirectly fix purchase or selling prices, share markets or sources of supply, apply dissimilar conditions to equivalent transactions with other trading parties, thereby placing them at a competitive disadvantage, etc.[5]

The dominant position is described in the case-law as '*a position of economic strength enjoyed by an undertaking which enables it to prevent effective competition being maintained on the relevant market by giving it the power to behave to an appreciable extent independently of its competitors, customers and ultimately of its customers*'.[6] The competition law prohibits not the dominant position as such, but its abuse; according to the ECJ, '*the concept of abuse is an objective concept relating to the behaviour of an undertaking in a dominant position which is such as to influence the structure of a market where, as a result of the very presence of the undertaking in question, the degree of competition is weakened and which, through recourse to methods different from those which condition normal competition in products or services on the basis of the transactions of commercial operators, has the effect of hindering the maintenance of the degree of competition still existing in the market or the growth of that competition*'.[7] The conduct perceived as abusive includes imposing unfair purchase or selling prices, limiting production, markets or technical development to the prejudice of consumers, making the conclusion of contracts subject to acceptance by the other parties of supplementary obligations which, by their nature or according to commercial usage, have no connection with the subject of such contracts, etc.[8]

It is noteworthy that when the competition law was first introduced by the Treaty,[9] the Member States did not have national legislation corresponding to the competition law, as we understand it now,[10] while nowadays, all the Member States apply national competition laws broadly similar to the EC one.

---

4 ECJ judgment C-49/92 P *Anic Partecipazoni* [1999] ECRI-4125, point 108.

5 Art. 81 (1) of the Treaty.

6 ECJ judgment 27/76 *United Brands* [1978] ECR 207, point 65.

7 ECJ judgment 85/76 *Hoffmann-La Roche* [1979] ECR 461, point 91.

8 Art. 82 of the Treaty.

9 Competition law was firstly enacted on the Community level in the Treaty Establishing the European Coal and Steel Community; it might be interesting that this treaty mentioned the merger review as well.

10 For more details on the history and development of competition law, see Gerber, D. J. *Law and Competition in the Twentieth Century Europe* (Oxford, 1998).

II The Modernization of EC Competition Law

As already mentioned above, the rules for application of Articles 81 and 82 of the Treaty are laid down by the Implementing regulation. The original Implementing regulation (the 'Regulation No. 17')[11] was adopted already in 1962; it remained in force for more then 40 years and although it had been four times amended,[12] its basic principles remained intact.

Similarly to numerous other instruments of EC law, Regulation No. 17 had been drafted for the Community of six Member States, whose experience with competition law had been, at the most, limited. All the powers were therefore concentrated with the Commission and the role of the Member States was marginal; some of them did not establish any National Competition Authority (hereinafter referred to as the 'NCA') for decades.[13] Application of the EC competition law according to the Regulation No. 17 was thus confronted with severe systemic problems[14] and there was a general agreement that a new Implementing regulation was necessary.

Coming into force on the 1st May 2004, the new Implementing regulation (hereinafter referred to as the 'Regulation 1/2003')[15] was adopted by the Council; adoption of this regulation and a few related notices and guidelines is commonly named the 'Modernization' of the EC competition law. The Modernization had two principal goals: to *decentralize* the application of antitrust law, i.e. to shift the burden from the Commission to the NCAs, and to stimulate the *private enforcement*, i.e. to motivate the undertakings and consumers effected by violation of antitrust rules to file actions against those undertakings who had broken these rules to civil courts, claiming especially the recovery of damages sustained by that anticompetitive behaviour.

While the first goal was successfully achieved, the second one still remains to be accomplished. The Commission's work is currently focused on problems related to the private enforcement. In 2005, it issued a Green Paper[16] and the White Paper was published this year. Nonetheless, it is generally believed that the modifications to the EC competition law that are about to be proposed will be rather limited, incomparable to the profound changes brought by the Regulation 1/2003.

---

[11] EEC Council: Regulation No. 17: First Regulation implementing Articles 85 and 86 of the Treaty, OJ L 13, 21.2.1962, p. 204.

[12] By the Regulation No. 59, OJ L 58, 10.7.1962, p. 1655, Regulation No. 118/63/EEC, OJ L 162, 7.11.1963, p. 2696, Regulation No. 2822/71, OJ L 285, 29.12.1971, p. 49, and Regulation No. 1216/1999, OJ L 148, 15.6.1999, p. 5.

[13] For example in Italy, the competition authority was not established until 1990.

[14] For their brief overview, see e.g. the White Paper on modernization of the rules implementing Articles 85 and 86 of the EC Treaty, OJ C 132, 12.5.1999, p. 1.

[15] Council Regulation (EC) No. 1/2003 on the implementation of the rules on competition laid down in Articles 81 and 82 of the Treaty, OJ L 1, 4.1.2003, p. 1.

[16] Green Paper – Damages actions for breach of the EC antitrust rules, COM(2005) 672 final.

Thus it seems that the 'modernized' competition law is not about to be further modified in the foreseeable future. Even in the Constitution for Europe (hereinafter referred to as the 'Constitution') the articles concerned wit the agreements (Article III-161) and with the abuse of dominant position (Article III-162) are virtually identical with the Articles 81 and 82 of the Treaty. Since the Implementing regulation would remain in force,[17] even the Constitution would not bring about any changes to the EC competition law as such. This is even more true with regard to the Reform Treaty, which is about to be drafted upon the recently approved IGC 2007 Mandate (hereinafter referred to as the 'Mandate'),[18] since the Mandate does not propose any changes to Articles 81 and 82 of the Treaty.

However, the way in which the competition law is applied could be significantly affected by the ever-growing emphasis laid on the protection of Human Rights within the European Union. In this chapter, I will focus on the relationship between National and EC competition law, which would in my opinion be radically changed should the Charter of Fundamental Rights of the Union (hereinafter referred to as the 'Charter') become a legally binding instrument and (or) should the European Union (or the European Community) access to the European Convention of Human Rights (hereinafter referred to as the 'Convention'), both of which is proposed by the Constitution[19] as well as the Mandate.[20] Moreover, I am going to suggest that these changes are already taking place, though they are unlikely to materialize in the foreseeable future without these instruments.

III Competition Law and the Protection of Human Rights

Since my further considerations are to a large extent concerned with the possible effects of the Charter and the Convention becoming binding on the EC institutions, this section will focus on interconnections between these instruments and on their possible influence on competition law.

1 Human Rights in EC Law

It is now well established case-law that '*by virtue of Article 6 EU, the Union is founded on the principle of the rule of law and it respects fundamental rights, as guaranteed by the European Convention for the Protection of Human Rights and Fundamental Freedoms, signed in Rome on 4 November 1950, and as*

[17] Art. IV-438 (3) of the Constitution.

[18] The Mandate is accessible at http://register.consilium.europa.eu/pdf/en/07/st11/st11218.en07.pdf.

[19] In Art. I-9 of the Constitution it is stated that '*(1) The Union shall recognise the rights, freedoms and principles set out in the Charter of Fundamental Rights which constitutes Part II*' and that '*(2) The Union shall accede to the European Convention for the Protection of Human Rights and Fundamental Freedoms*'.

[20] Annex 1, paragraph 5) of the Mandate.

they result from the constitutional provisions common to the Member States, as general principles of Community law. It follows that the institutions are subject to review of the conformity of their acts with the Treaties and the general principles of law, just like the Member States when they implement the law of the Union'.[21]

As far as the Convention is concerned, it was not until 1975, in the *Rutilli* judgment,[22] that the ECJ explicitly identified the Convention as another source (i.e. apart from constitution laws of the Member States) it would use to identify the general principles of Community law; it nevertheless took the ECJ another 30 years to decide that the institutions of the Community were in breach of the Human Rights, as defined by the Convention.[23]

As already mentioned, not only the Community's institutions, but also the Member States, when implementing the EC law, are bound by the general principles of Community law;[24] the ECJ thus retains jurisdiction over the Human Rights protection in the Member States, including indirect supervision over their observance of the Convention, since the general principles of Community law stem from it. Its jurisdiction could therefore possibly conflict with that of the European Court of Human Rights (hereinafter referred to as 'the ECHR'), in particular because the ECHR is empowered to review even the activities of the Member States mandated by their international obligations, including implementation of the EC law.[25] Accordingly, even though the institutions of the Community are excluded from the jurisdiction of the ECHR,[26] the conflict of jurisdictions cannot be ruled out in cases where the EC competition law is applied (or implemented) by the NCAs. Some possible areas of concern have already been identified by the legal theory.[27]

2 The ECJ and the ECHR

The basic approach of the ECHR towards reviewing activities of the Member States implementing the EC law can be deduced from its recent *Bosphorus* judgment.[28] Generally, '*the Convention does not prohibit a Member State*

---

[21] ECJ judgment C-303/05 *'European Arrest Warrant'*, not yet published, point 45.

[22] ECJ judgment 36/75 *Rutili* [1975] ECR 1219, point 32.

[23] ECJ judgment C-185/95 *Baustahlgewerbe* [1998] ECR I-8417, concerned with the inadequate length of the antitrust proceedings before the Commission; in this judgment, the ECJ also, as an analogy, referred to decisions of the ECHR (see point 29 of the judgment).

[24] ECJ judgment 5/88 *Wachauf* [1989] ECR 2609, point 19.

[25] ECHR decision *X v. Germany*, application No. 42/57; in details e.g. Douglas-Scott, S. *'A Tale of two Courts: Luxemburg, Strasbourg and the Growing European Human Rights acquis.'* Common Market Law Review, 2006, No. 3, p. 636 et seq.

[26] ECHR decision *Dufay v. EC*, application No. 13539/88.

[27] Ameye, E. *'The Interplay between Human Rights and competition law in the EU.'* European Competition Law Review, 2004, No. 6, p. 332.

[28] ECHR judgment *Bosphorus v. Ireland*, application No. 45036/98. In detail e.g. Costello, C. *'The Bosphorus Ruling of the European Court of Human Rights: Fundamental Rights and Blurred Boundaries in Europe.'*

from transferring powers to international organisations'; nonetheless, this '*transfer of powers does not necessarily exclude a State's responsibility under the Convention with regard to the exercise of the transferred powers*'. Therefore, it can be concluded that, '*the transfer of powers to an international organisation is not incompatible with the Convention provided that within that organisation fundamental rights will receive an equivalent protection*'.[29] As far as the EU is concerned, it has so far been the case.

In the *Bosphorus* judgment, the ECHR clarified its jurisprudence by stating that the Member State remains fully responsible under the Convention '*for all acts falling outside its strict international legal obligations*' imposed by an international organization to which it has transformed a part of its sovereignty,[30] i.e. for the purposes of this Chapter and for all cases of application or implementation of the EC competition law, where the Member State retains any discretion. On the other hand, when the Member State has no discretion, its actions are '*justified as long as the relevant organisation is considered to protect fundamental rights, as regards both the substantive guarantees offered and the mechanisms controlling their observance, in a manner which can be considered at least equivalent to that for which the Convention provides*'.[31]

It is therefore possible to summarize that the Member State is fully responsible for its obligations stemming from the Convention (and hence under full jurisdiction of the ECHR) in case it is acting in order to implement measures of EC law which leave it some discretion as to how to do it, whereas in case it has no discretion at all, the Member State would not be in breach of the Convention as long as the Community protects Fundamental Rights in a way equivalent to the Convention, which has so far been the case. In both cases, the Member State would also be under the jurisdiction of the ECJ.

Although there has so far been no overt conflict of interpretation between the two Courts, it is not improbable that such a conflict will arise in the future, and a few areas of concern have been identified by legal scholars.[32] These cannot be examined here in detail and we will therefore further focus only on one specific problem – is the system of parallel application of the EC and national competition law consistent with the *ne bis in idem* principle, guaranteed by the general principles of Community law, the Charter and the Convention?

Human Rights Law Review, 2006, No. 1, p. 87.

[29] ECHR decision *M & Co v. Germany*, application No. 13258/87.

[30] *Bosphorus*, op. cit., point 157.

[31] *Bosphorus*, op. cit., point 155.

[32] *Ameye, E.*, op. cit.

IV Parallel Application of EC and National Competition Law

1 When does EC Competition Law Apply?

The EC competition law applies only to the conduct that *may affect trade between Member States*,[33] hereinafter referred to as the 'conduct with Community dimension'. This *effect on trade* concept is clarified by the Commission in a notice, based on extensive jurisprudence of the ECJ.[34]

With regard to every behaviour relevant from the point of view of the competition law, it is thus necessary to conduct a three step analysis, ascertaining (1) whether it can be regarded as *trade between Member States* and (2) whether it is susceptible to *affect* the pattern of this trade (3) in an *appreciable way*. If all these conditions are fulfilled, it is considered to be conduct with a Community dimension and it is governed by the EC competition law. Otherwise, it is the conduct without Community dimension, to which the EC competition law does not apply, but which can be subject to one (or more) national competition laws.

The fact that conduct with Community dimension is governed by the EC competition law does not preclude national competition law (or even laws) being applied *in parallel*. One and the same conduct may thus be subject to more than one legal regime and in case the competition law was breached, it can be subject to more than one sanction. This raises the question of whether this system is compatible with the *ne bis in idem* principle.

2 Parallel Application of Competition Law

It might be useful to consider separately the cases when the national competition law being applied in parallel with the EC one is on the one hand the law of the Member State and on the other hand the law of a non-Member State.

As described above, the EC competition law may, after the Modernisation, be applied in full extent by the Commission as well as by the NCAs. The Commission has in this respect a privileged position and initiation of a proceeding by the Commission relieves the NCAs from their power to apply the EC competition law (but not their national ones) in this matter.[35] The Commission is empowered to apply only the EC competition law, never the national one.

When the proceeding is being conducted by the NCAs, Regulation 1/2003 states that when they are about to apply their national competition law to a conduct with a Community dimension, they must *also* apply the EC competition law.[36] Parallel application is thus explicitly acknowledged by the Implementing regulation.

---

33 Art. 81 (1) and Art. 82 of the Treaty.

34 Commission Notice – Guidelines on the effect on trade concept contained in Articles 81 and 82 of the Treaty, OJ C 101, 27.4.2004, p. 81.

35 Art. 11 (6) of the Regulation 1/2003.

36 Art. 3 (1) of the Regulation 1/2003.

It is worth mentioning that the original proposal of the current Implementing regulation provided for exclusive application of the EC competition law, i.e. the conduct with Community dimension was to be governed exclusively by the EC competition law.[37] When in the course of the legislative process the principle of exclusive application was abandoned, it was necessary to set specific rules guaranteeing that even the parallel application would have consistent results.

These rules require in every case with a Community dimension EC competition law to be applied; the NCAs are free to chose whether they will also apply their national law, but in case they do, the effectiveness of the EC law cannot be endangered. This means that the national law cannot prohibit the behaviour allowed by the EC one and *vice versa*, it cannot authorise a behaviour prohibited by the EC law.[38]

It is therefore possible to utilize the jurisprudence of the ECJ, based on the classical *Walt Wilhelm* judgment,[39] where the question of parallel application was addressed for the first time. The ECJ declared that '*one and the same agreement may, in principle, be the object of two parallel proceedings, one before the Community authorities under Article* [81] *of the* [EC] *Treaty, the other before the national authorities under national law*',[40] basically because of different objectives pursued by these legal systems: '*Community and national law on cartels consider cartels from different points of view. Whereas Article* [81] *regards them in the light of obstacles which may result for trade between Member States, each body of national legislation proceeds on the basis of the considerations peculiar to it and considers cartels only in that context*'.[41]

As far as the parallel application of the EC competition law and the competition law of a non-Member State is concerned, it is not governed by the EC law. This question is only addressed by the ECJ (or the CFI) when the objection of *ne bis in idem* is raised before it.

3 The *Ne Bis In Idem* Principle

As discussed above, the fundamental rights rank among the general principles of the EC law, which are to be observed both by the Community and by the Member States while applying the EC competition law; the jurisprudence of the ECJ ascertains that the *ne bis in idem* principle belongs to them. As regards observance of this principle, the ECJ clarified that it is '*subject to the threefold condition of identity of the facts, unity of offender and unity of the*

[37] The proposal of the Implementing regulation, published in OJ C 365 E, 19.12.2000, p. 284, stated that '*Community competition law shall apply to the exclusion of national competition laws*'.

[38] Art. 3 of the Regulation 1/2003; the specific regime set for the *unilateral conduct*, allowing the national law to prohibit a behaviour which is not an abuse of dominant position according to Artcle 82 of the Treaty is not relevant for this Chapter.

[39] ECJ judgment 14/68 *Walt Wilhelm* [1969] ECR 1.

[40] *Walt Wilhelm*, op. cit., point 3.

[41] *Walt Wilhelm*, op. cit., point 3.

legal interest protected. Under that principle, therefore, the same person cannot be sanctioned more than once for a single unlawful course of conduct designed to protect the same legal asset'.[42] This approach of the ECJ is in line with the general legal theory.

The jurisprudence of the ECJ is rather limited with respect to *ne bis in idem* within the Community. It is based on the above-mentioned *Walt Wilhelm* judgment, accepting the possibility of parallel application (and indeed sanctioning), with the only limitation of *general principles of natural justice* demanding that *'any previous punitive decision must be taken into account in determining any sanction which is to be imposed'*;[43] this latter requirement was later explained by the fact that the same undertaking is punished again for the same action *'committed on Community territory'*.[44] The possible implications of this conclusion stressing the territory affected by an offence will be discussed later.

Most of the ECJ's judgments have been concerned with cases in which the Commission imposed a fine on an undertaking after another fine had previously been imposed on it by a jurisdiction outside the EU for the same anticompetitive behaviour, typically an international cartel; characteristically, the same cartel has been prosecuted (and punished) in the USA and by the Commission.

We may consider the recent *Graphite electrodes*[45] judgment as an example. A few undertakings, essentially the only producers of the graphite electrodes (which is a technology used primarily in the production of steel in electric arc furnaces), concluded and kept in force for a number of years a global (worldwide) price fixing and market sharing agreement, thus distorting worldwide competition on the market of graphite electrodes. For this 'single' behaviour (i.e. for this international cartel), they were sanctioned in the USA, Canada and the EU.

The decision of the Commission was brought before the CFI and later the ECJ by an action for annulment based among other claims on an allegation that the *ne bis in idem* principle was breached by imposing a sanction on undertakings that had already been punished for the identical behaviour in other jurisdictions. The CFI stressed in this connection that the principle of *ne bis in idem* cannot *ex definitionem* apply in this case, because *'the procedures conducted and penalties imposed by the Commission on the one hand and the United States and Canadian authorities on the other clearly did not pursue the same ends. The aim of the first was to preserve undistorted competition within the European Union or the EEA, whereas the aim of the second was to protect the United States or the Canadian*

---

42 ECJ judgment C-204/00 P, C-205/00 P, C-211/00 P, C-213/00 P, C-217/00 P and C-219/00 P *Aalborg Portland* [2004] ECR I-123, point 338.

43 *Walt Wilhelm*, op. cit., point 11.

44 ECJ judgment 7/72 *Boehringer* [1972] ECR 1281, point 3.

45 CFI judgment T-236/01, T-239/01, T-244/01 to T-246/01, T-251/01 and T 252/01 *Tokai Carbon, SGL Carbon, Nippon Carbon, Showa Denko, GrafTech, SEC and The Carbite/Graphite Group* [2004] ECR II-1181, hereinafter referred to as the '*Graphite electrodes*', approved by the ECJ judgments C-289/04 P *Showa Denko* [2006] ECR I-5859, and C-308/04 P *SGL Carbon* [2006] ECR I-5977.

market... The application of the principle ne bis in idem is subject not only to the infringements and the persons sanctioned being the same, but also to the unity of the legal right being protected'.[46] The ECJ confirmed this judgment, emphasizing that the *ne bis in idem* principle cannot apply to sanctions imposed on the one hand by the institutions of the Community and on the other hand by the institutions of non-Member States, stressing their different, non-overlapping territorial jurisdiction, as will be discussed in detail later.[47]

The complainants also claimed that at the least there is an obligation to take into account, while setting a fine to an undertaking that has already been punished for the same offence by another competition authority, the sanction imposed by the former authority, and therefore, that there is a duty to reduce the fine; this is the case within the EU, as described in the *Walt Wilhelm* judgment above. The CFI concluded that such an obligation exists only with regard to '*the particular situation which arises from the close interdependence between the national markets of the Member States and the common market and from the special system for the division of jurisdiction between the Community and the Member States with regard to cartels on the same territory, namely the common market, that the Court, having acknowledged the possibility of dual sets of proceedings and having regard to the possibility of double sanctions flowing from them, held it to be necessary, in accordance with a requirement of natural justice, for account to be taken of the first decision imposing a penalty*'; therefore, such an obligation does not exist with regard to decisions of the non-EU jurisdictions.[48] The ECJ confirmed this reasoning, stressing that there is no Community nor international law principle '*that prevents the public authorities, including the courts, of different States from trying and convicting the same natural or legal person on the basis of the same facts as those for which that person has already been tried in another State. In addition, there is no public international law convention under which the Commission could be obliged, upon setting a fine ..., to take account of fines imposed by the authorities of non-member States pursuant to their competition law powers*', although it remains in its discretion to do so.[49]

It is nevertheless noteworthy that while the CFI, and even more the Advocate General,[50] founded their argumentation to a large extent on a claim that the *ne bis in idem* principle cannot by its very nature apply because due to different objectives pursued by competition legislation of different jurisdictions, the different competition authorities do not deal with the '*idem*', the ECJ did not discuss the question of identity of the facts at all. It supported its conclusions primarily by different (territorial) jurisdiction of competition authorities of different states, emphasizing that since these different authorities protect 'their' markets, the sanctions imposed by them must necessarily take into account different criteria

---

46 *Graphite electrodes*, op. cit., point 134, emphasis added.

47 *Showa Denko*, op. cit., points 55 and 56, and *SGL Carbon*, op. cit., points 32 a 33.

48 *Graphite electrodes*, op. cit., points 141 and 142.

49 *Showa Denko*, op. cit., points 57, 58 and 60, and *SGL Carbon*, op. cit., points 33, 34 a 36.

50 Opinion of Advocate General Geelhoed to case *SGL Carbon*, op. cit., points 46 to 50.

and in particular, that the *ne bis in idem* principle prohibits only double punishment within the same jurisdiction.[51]

This difference in reasoning is in my opinion a manifestation of a continuous shift of interpretation as to what constitutes the *identity in the facts*. In the *Aalborg Portland* judgment, it was stated that because different competition authorities pursue different objectives, there was no identity in the facts in the case when a single behaviour was repeatedly punished by different competition authorities, and therefore, '*there was no breach of the principle ne bis in idem*'.[52] In the later *Archer Daniels Midland* judgment, it was pronounced that '*where the sanction imposed in a non-member country covers only the applications or effects of the cartel on the market of that State and the Community sanction covers only the applications or effects of the cartel on the Community market, the facts are not identical*',[53] hence stressing the territoriality criterion. In the *Graphite Electrodes* case, the ECJ did not mention the identity of facts at all and emphasis the differences of territorial jurisdiction, the different objectives pursued by different competition authorities being the consequence of it.

The argument based on the assertion that the *ne bis in idem* principle is by its very nature bound to each and every jurisdiction and does not apply internationally is in my opinion unambiguous and persuasive. As far as the relations between the EU and non-EU institutions are concerned, I fully agree that the *ne bis in idem* principle does not apply at all, since the international law confines it only to proceedings within one jurisdiction. Any further development of the EC law cannot in my opinion alter this approach, for it stems from the international, not the EC law.

On the other hand, as far as the relations of different jurisdictions within the EU are concerned, I believe that this 'jurisdictional' reasoning might in the future lead the ECJ to reconsidering its approach as far as parallel application of competition law within the EU is concerned. It should be observed that the Advocate General Tizzano declared in its Opinion in the *Archer Daniels Midland* judgment that '*it should be pointed out that since the Court delivered its judgment in Walt Wilhelm (more than 30 years ago) the degree of interdependence and integration of Community and national systems for safeguarding competition on which that judgment was based has significantly increased, in particular with the decentralisation of the application of Community antitrust law introduced by the recent Regulation No 1/2003. A very original system has thus been created, in which the Commis-*

51 For an in-depth of international law, case-law of international tribunals and case-law of the constitution courts of a few Member States, see the Opinion of Advocate General Tizzano to case C 397/03 P *Archer Daniels Midland*, points 93 et seq.

52 *Aalborg Portland*, op. cit., points 339 and 340. This was due to the fact that decisions of different competition authorities pursue different objects.

53 ECJ judgment C 397/03 P *Archer Daniels Midland* [2006] ECR I-4429, states in point 69, that '*where the sanction imposed in a non-member country covers only the applications or effects of the cartel on the market of that State and the Community sanction covers only the applications or effects of the cartel on the Community market, the facts are not identical*'.

sion and the authorities of the Member States, acting according to the extent and limits of their respective powers, in practice jointly safeguard freedom of competition within the Community'.[54] Nonetheless, the *Walt Wilhelm* case-law was confirmed recently by the *Manfredi* judgment,[55] even though in my opinion, the reasoning in *Walt Wilhelm* is different from (tough not inconsistent with) the jurisprudence of the current *ne bis in idem* cases, as described above.

The parallel application on the EC and national competition law *stricto sensu*, i.e. the situation when a single anticompetitive conduct with Community dimension is assessed and penalized by a single NCA, does not pose any *ne bis in idem* problems; no objection has so far been raised to this effect and consequently, there is in this respect no ECJ case-law. On the other hand, problems with the *ne bis in idem* principle might arise when a NCA applies its national competition law to conduct with a Community dimension that has already been subject to a decision of the Commission, or *vice versa*, when the Commission decides about a conduct with a Community dimension which has already been dealt with by the NCA. The latter case should be rather hypothetical, because the Commission, if it would consider taking over the proceedings conducted by a NCA, would normally do so before the NCA comes to a decision; we will therefore further discuss only the former case. Nonetheless, as the ECJ mentioned in the *Masterfoods* judgment, the Commission '*is entitled to adopt at any time individual decisions under Articles 85 and 86 of the Treaty, even where an agreement or practice has already been the subject of a decision by a national court and the decision contemplated by the Commission conflicts with that national court's decision*';[56] even the second possibility therefore cannot be outright excluded.

The problem of *ne bis in idem* within the EU has so far been considered only from the point of view of the general principles of the EC law; the perspectives can in my opinion change if we take into account the Convention and the Charter.

As far as the Convention is concerned, it associates the *ne bis in idem* principle, enshrined in the Article 4 (1) of the Protocol Number 7 to the Convention,[57] only with double penalties being imposed by the same state,[58] and therefore it does not apply even between the Member States, as the ECHR proclaimed in the *Graf* decision.[59] Thus, nowadays, the Convention does not alter the abovementioned conclusions about the possibility of parallel application. This situation

[54] Opinion of Advocte General Tizzano to Case C-397/03 P *Archer Daniels Midland*, point 107.

[55] ECJ judgment C-295/04 to C-298/04 *Manfredi* [2006] ECR I-6619, point 38.

[56] ECJ judgment C-344/98 *Masterfoods* [2000] ECR I-11369, point 48.

[57] This provision is not yet in force in all the Member States; for the chart of signatures and ratifications, see http://conventions.coe.int/Treaty/Commun/ChercheSig.asp?NT=117&CM=7&DF=5/17/2007&CL=ENG.

[58] This Article provides: *'No one shall be liable to be tried or punished again in criminal proceedings under the jurisdiction of the same State for an offence for which he has already been finally acquitted or convicted in accordance with the law and penal procedure of that State'*.

[59] ECHR decision *Graf v. Austria*, application No. 72954/01, point 2.

might in my opinion change in case the Community (or the EU) became itself a party to the Convention. Then the jurisdiction of the Community and the Member States would overlap and the *ne bis in idem* principle could become applicable even within the EU.

Even if the ECJ would not be willing to change its approach, the Member States would be scrutinized by the ECHR, and since the parallel application is not their duty, but depends on their discretion, they would be under its full jurisdiction, as described in the *Bosphorus* judgment.

The same effect would be achieved should the Charter become legally binding, because it states explicitly that '*no one shall be liable to be tried or punished again in criminal proceedings for an offence for which he or she has already been finally acquitted or convicted* within the Union *in accordance with the law*'.[60] It therefore seems that in the case of the Charter, the scope for manoeuvring is even less limited for the Member States. Nonetheless, as long as the Charter is not legally binding, the ECJ recourses to it only occasionally[61] and it has not yet been mentioned in any judgments dealing with parallel applications within the EU.

V Conclusions

We have seen that after Modernization, the EC competition law became an effective instrument and it is not probable that it is about to be changed to any significant extent in the foreseeable future. One of its characteristics today, its application by the NCAs in parallel with their national competition law, would nonetheless have to be abandoned should the Convention and (or) the Charter become binding for the institutions of the Community and the Member States. In my opinion, the current practice when a single anticompetitive behaviour is prosecuted by the Commission with regard to the EC competition law and subsequently by NCAs with regard to their national competition laws would then no longer be consistent with the *ne bis in idem* principle, as understood by those legal instruments.

Even though it was stated by the Member States that the constitutional concept of the Founding Treaties is abandoned,[62] the growing emphasis on Human Rights and thus the accession to the Convention and the legal nature of the Charter in my opinion is inevitable, which is confirmed by the Mandate itself. I therefore believe that the above-mentioned opinions should be valid with regard to whatever possible changes of the Founding Treaties are about to come.

---

60 Art. 50 of the Charter, Art. II-110 of the Constitution; emphasis added.

61 The *European Arrest* Warrant, op. cit.

62 Paragraph 1 of the Mandate.

CHAPTER II

Constitutionalisation of Private Law in Europe

Anna Lytvynyuk

The present section will bring about the academic discussion on the degree of influence of fundamental rights on private law. The effect of fundamental rights on private law will be explored on the level of national law through the examples of the decisions of the German Federal Constitutional Court. The concept of 'constitutionalisation' of private law will, thus, be introduced. The mechanism, through which the process of 'constitutionalisation' of private law takes place, will be further followed onto the supranational legal order – the EU legal order where the impact of fundamental freedoms of the EU on private law relationships will be examined, in particular, in relevance to the questions of 'State sphere' and third-party effect in equal treatment cases. The doctrine of 'State's duty to protect' will thus be compared on the national and supranational levels.

I Constitutionalisation of Private Law

A) 'Indirect Horizontal Effect' of Fundamental Rights: Solutions Found by National Constitutional Courts

The debate over 'constitutionalisation' of private law received its first impulse in 1950's when after the famous decision of the German Federal Constitutional Court in the *Lüth* case the lawyers and academics in law began a discussion on the scope and scale of the application of constitutional rights in the pure private law litigations, i.e. in the claims of private individuals against one another.

Let us take a look at the facts in the *Lüth* case.[1] The dispute in this case arose between Erich Lüth, a Hamburg press official acting in his private capacity and Veit Harlan, an anti-Semite film director (his first film 'Jud Süß'). Mr. Lüth was sensitive to the fact that the film director Harlan was a film director from the Nazi times. Lüth, thus, urged the distributors, cinema owners and the public to boycott Harlan's new film 'Immortal Beloved'.[2]

Veit Harlan sought an injunction within the regional court (*Landgericht*) that would prohibit Lüth boycotting his film. In his legal action, Harlan fell back on section 826 of the German Civil Code (BGB) that provided a remedy against a person who 'intentionally causes injury to another person in a manner contrary to good morals'. Read together with section 1004 of the Civil Code of Germany, it granted Harlan a right to seek an injunction that would prohibit Lüth (a

---

* Anna Lytvynyuk, LL.M, MA, researcher at the Univerzity of Regensburg, Germany, Kiev National University of Taras Schevchenko, Kiev, Ukraine; MA College of Europe, Warsaw, Poland; PhD Candidate at the University of Regensburg, Germany.

1 BVerfGE 7, 198 (Lüth) (1958). BVerfGE =*Bundesverfassungsgericht* (Federal Constitututional Court of Germany).

2 'Unsterbliche Geliebte'.

tortfeasor) the further boycotting of Harlan's film. The regional court did, indeed, issue such an injunction. The way in which Lüth responded was to file a constitutional complaint with the German Federal Constitutional Court (FCC). He claimed that the injunction issued by the regional court violated his constitutional right – freedom of expression provided for by Article 5 (1), first sentence, of the Basic Law. The FCC did not uphold the injunction of the regional court. In overturning such an injunction the FCC held that Lüth enjoyed a constitutionally protected right of freedom of speech (protected by Article 5 (1)) and that the regional court had violated the Basic Law by prohibiting the complainant (Lüth) to freely express himself by means of issuing the statements that would lead others to boycott Harlan's film.

Why the *Lüth* case is so important for German constitutional law is because it restates a number of constitutional law positions and establishes its view on the concept of the effect of fundamental rights on private law. In particular, the FCC states:

1) constitutional rights are regarded not only as defensive rights of the individuals against the state, but they also form '*an objective system of values*';[3]
2) because fundamental rights form 'an objective system of values' they '*...must be valid as a constitutional disposition for all the branches of law; legislation, administration and jurisprudence receive guidelines and impulses from it* [from this system of values];[4]
3) hence, the fundamental rights, as they form the 'objective system of values' and are valid for all the branches of law, also '*...influence civil law; no civil law rule can be in contradiction with it, each one of it must be interpreted in its spirit*';[5]
4) '*In order to determine what is required by social norms* [such as 'good morals'], *one has to consider first the ensemble of value concepts that a nation had developed at a certain point in its intellectual and cultural history and laid down in its constitution. That is why the general clauses [of the Civil Code] have rightfully been described as* 'points of entry' *of basic rights into private law.*'[6]

---

3 BVerfGE 7, 198 (Lüth) [205]: 'Ebenso richtig ist aber, daß Grundgesetz, das keine wertneutrale Ordnung sien will [...], in sinem Grundrectsabschnitt auch eine *objective Wertordnung* aufgerichtet hat und daß gerade hierin eine prinzipielle Verstärkung der Geltungskraft der Grundrechte zum Ausdruck kommt [...]'.

4 Ibid.: 'Dieses Wertsystem, das seinen Mittelpunkt in der innerhalb der sozialen Gemeinschaft sich frei entfaltenden menschlichen Persönlichkeit und ihrer Würde findet, muß *als verfassungsrechtliche Grundentscheidung für alle Beriche des Rechts gelten*; Gesetzgebung, Verwaltung und Rechtsprechung empfangen von ihm Richtlinien und Impulse.'

5 Ibid.: 'So beeinflußt es selbstverständlich auch *das bürgerliche Recht; keine bürgelich-rechtliche Vorschrift darf in Widerspruch zu ihm stehen, jede muß in seinem Geiste ausgelegt werden.*'

6 BVerfGE 7, 198 (Lüth) [205]: 'Der Rechtsprechung bieten sich zur Realisierung dieses Einflusses vor allem die 'Generalklauseln', die, wie § 826 BGB, zur Beurteilung menschlichen Verhaltens auf außerzivilrechliche, ja zunächtst überhaupt außerrechtliche Maßstäbe, wie die 'guten Sitten', verweisen.

What the FCC did was to have cited Günter Dürig's theory of *Mittelbare Drittwirkung* – theory of 'indirect effect on third parties', a concept which was meant to counterpart Nipperdey's theory of the direct effect of fundamental rights on private law. Before outlining the difference between indirect horizontal effect and direct horizontal effect of fundamental rights on private law, let us first understand the so-called *vertical* and *horizontal* approaches to fundamental rights.

Constitutional jurisdictions of some countries vigorously defend the orthodox *vertical approach* to fundamental rights (for example, the United States). Such a stand has as its ground the axiom that constitutional rights impose duties only on the state, and not private parties. Such rights regulate only the actions of government and governmental bodies and not relations among private individuals.[7] Other jurisdictions, such, for example, as Germany, Ireland, South Africa, Canada and even the EU, as we shall see further, favour a diametrically different, *horizontal approach* to constitutional rights – constitutional rights impose duties not only on a state, but also on private individuals in their interpersonal relations. The vertical and horizontal approaches are considered to be the two polar positions of the scope of constitutional rights.

There is a third position too, known as *indirect horizontal effect*. The essence of this position lies in the assumption that although constitutional rights bind directly only the state (government and governmental bodies), they may also be, to a certain extent, indirectly applied to private individuals.[8] 'Indirectly applied' means that private law courts can 'indirectly' apply fundamental rights provisions when deciding on the private law cases. They can do so through the 'open-ended' clauses of the civil code (commercial code). We have seen this already in the *Lüth* decision.

Denn bei der Entscheidung darüber, was diese sozialen Gebote jeweils im Einzelfall fordern, muß in erster Linie von der Gesamtheit der Wertvorstellungen ausgegangen warden, die das Volk in einem bestimmten Zeitpunkt seiner geistig-kulturellen Entwicklung erreicht und in seiner Verfassung fixiert hat. Deshalb sind mit Recht die Generalklauseln asl die '*Einbruchstellen' der Grundrechte in das bürgerliche Recht* bezeichnet worden (Dürig in Neumann-Nipperdey-Scheuner, Die Grundrechte, Band II S. 525)'. Translation into English taken from Stephen Gardbaum '*The "'Horizontal Effect"' of Constitutional Rights,*' Michigan Law Review Vol.102:387 [December 2003] at note 76.

7 Gardbaum389. See also Murray Hunt '*The "'Horizontal Effect"' of the Human Rights Act,*" 1998 Public Law 423, 427.

8 Gardbaum 398. See also on indirect horizontal effect: Greg Taylor, '*The Horizontal Effect of Human Rights, the German Model and its Applicability to Common Law Jurisdictions*', King's College Law Journal 187 (2002); K.M.Lewan, '*The Significance of Constitutional Rights for Private Law: Theory and Practice in West Germany,*' International and Comparative Law Quarterly 571 (1968); Ralf Brinktrine, '*The Horizontal Effect of Human Rights in German Constitutional Law,*' European Human Rights Law Review 421 (2001); Olha Cherednychenko, '*EU Fundamental Rights, EC Fundamental Freedoms and Private Law,*' European Review of Private Law 1-2006 [23-61], 30-32.

Nipperdey and Leisner supported direct application of fundamental rights to the relations governed by the norms of private law. They suggested that the only case when direct application of the fundamental rights is appropriate is when the judge is in a situation to do so, because private legislation fails to provide for the necessary tools (private law norms are inadequate) and the relevant appropriate new laws cannot be passed on time.[9]

As we have seen, the FCC in the *Lüth* decision, as well as in the subsequent decisions,[10] followed Dürig's theory of indirect horizontal effect, or, the 'radiation effect of fundamental rights on private law'. However, over the years, the Federal Constitutional Court of Germany has transformed; the doctrine of 'radiation effect of fundamental rights on private law' (or, 'indirect effect of fundamental rights') into the well developed doctrine of '*state duties to protect constitutional rights*' *('Grundrechtilche Schutzpflichten')* – a concept, traditionally applied in the sphere of public law.

The *Handelsvertreter* case is an illustrative example of such a new concept of the Federal Constitutional Court of Germany.[11] The stimulus for such a conceptual novelty was urged by the fact that the infringement of the fundamental rights in the *Handelsvertreter* case occurred in a purely *contract law setting:* when the two parties exercised their private autonomy right binding each other with the mutually agreed contractual obligations.

The controversy in this case occurred between a commercial agent and his employer – the wine company.[12] Part of the contractual agreement between the two was the so-called 'non-competition clause' which was meant to preclude the agent from selling wines of his employer's competitors even for two years after the termination of the contract. Such a clause was governed by Section 90 (a) of the German Commercial Code.[13] In their contract, the parties have also agreed that should the contract be violated due to the agent's culpable behaviour, the wine company would terminate the contract without paying the agent any compensation.

Having learned that the agent, indeed, was selling wines of the competitor, the wine company terminated the contract with the agent with an immediate effect and requested from the German Supreme Court in private matters (*Bundesgerichtshof*) an injunction restraining the agent from further working for a competitor. Such an injunction was granted by the Supreme Court on the ground that the contractual clause on non-discrimination, indeed, was valid. It held that being a self-employed, professionally and economically independent

---

9 Leisner, *Grundrecht und Privatrecht* (1960), 317, 368.

10 BVerfGE 30, 173 [*Mephisto*] (188), BVerfGE 35, 79 [Hochschulurteil] (114), BVerfGE 39, 1 [Schwanerschaftsabbruch I] (41) etc.

11 BVerfGE 81, 242 [*Handelsvertreter*].

12 Ibid. (243).

13 Handelsgesetzbuch (HGB).

merchant, the agent was free to weigh the advantages and disadvantages of the contract with his employer.

Having lost his appellate claim in the State Court of Appeal (*Oberlandesgericht*), the agent filed a constitutional complaint with the Federal Constitutional Court of Germany. The FCC overturned the decision of the Supreme Court. It ruled that the agent's fundamental right of *freedom of profession* was violated by the Supreme Court granting the injunction prohibiting the agent from working for the competitor. However, the FCC reasoned, such a limitation of the basic right of the agent does not primarily stem from the act of the State – the agent had voluntarily agreed to the non-competition clause and thus exercised his personal freedom. The Court reasoned that such an autonomous contractual agreement should, in principle, be respected by the State.[14] Such private autonomy, the Court continued, is granted by private law. However, and here the Court retrieves the reasoning in the *Lüth* case, private law itself cannot be contrary to the principles enshrined in basic rights. In situations where there is an inequality of bargaining power and an economically more powerful party dictates to the other the terms of the contract, contract law alone cannot guarantee the balance of interests. It is the *legislator's* obligation, then, to restore the parity in order to 'ensure the protection of basic rights'.[15]

In cases when the legislator fails to do so, the *courts* take over the duty to protect fundamental rights by restoring the contractual parity using the means available within private law (usually those are the open-ended general clauses of private law and general principles of private law). Thus, weighing the two equally legitimate interests (an employer's economic interest to prevent competition from his former agents and the fundamental right of the agent to freedom of profession), the FCC needed to evaluate the constitutionality of the mandatory provisions of Section 90 (a) of the Commercial Code of Germany (HGB). The FCC found that the legislator failed, in the mandatory provision of Section 90a (2) (which entitled the employer to refuse to pay compensation) to counter balance the two competing interests, both deriving from the fundamental rights. The FCC stated that a solution of Section 90a (2) was disproportional and that such a severe sanction was unnecessary. The Constitutional Court declared that Section 90a (2) (second sentence) was incompatible with Article 12(1) of the Constitution.

The FCC further stated that following the reasoning of the agent, the private law courts should have availed themselves of Article 100 (1) of the Constitution and filed an inquiry to the FCC, asking them to provide for a decision on the question of the constitutionality of Section 90a (2) of HGB. We see that in the *Handelsvertreter* case, the Federal Constitutional Court of Germany introduced the concept of *the State's duty to protect constitutional rights*. The classical function of constitutional rights is, of course, one of the *defensive rights* against

---

14 Supra note 12 [254].

15 Ibid.

the State (*'Eingriffsverbotsfunktion der Grundrechte'*), which, by prohibiting any intrusion of the State into constitutional rights, imposes *negative obligations* on the State. The FCC interpreted constitutional rights as having also the *protective function (Schutzgebotsfunktion der Grundrechte'*) by which the State acquires *positive obligations*, or, in other words, the duty to protect constitutional rights. Said differently, such positive obligations of the State presuppose its duty to *act* should the constitutional rights of one natural person be violated by another natural person. Thus, reaching over the traditional duty of the State to protect fundamental rights of the individuals against a State, the protective function has as its purpose a duty to protect individuals from each other.

In the relatively recent *Bürgschaft* case, the FCC of Germany reinstated the duty of the private law courts (as being part of public power) to protect a constitutional right [the right to private autonomy].[16] Such a duty was stated in conjunction with the principle of *social state* – a sort of new legitimacy to even out a structural imbalance in the bargaining power in contract law. Let us take a glimpse at the constitutional court's judgment.

In this case, we have two subjects of civil law, in particular, contract law: a businessman's daughter (natural person) who signed a contract as a surety, and a bank (juridical person) with which the daughter signed the contract. The mentioned businessman had arranged with the said bank a loan for his business of DM 100,000 (approximately €50,000) the guarantor for which was the daughter of the businessman – a 21 year old woman, with no higher education and working for the salary of only €575 per month (DM 1150) . Before signing the surety contract with the bank, the girl was assured by the bank official that signing this contract was 'just a formality' and would not impose any obligation consequences on her. As it sometimes happens with entrepreneurs, the business of the girl's father went bankrupt and the bank claimed a total of € 80,000 from the daughter under the surety contract that she had signed previously.

The legal action filed by the daughter went through all the instances of private law courts in Germany: the court of first instance – regional court (*Landgericht*), the Court of Appeal – a higher court (*Oberlandesgericht*) and the Federal Supreme Court in private law matters (*Bundesgerichtshof*). The *Landgericht* held that the surety contract entered into by the daughter was valid. She was thus ordered by the court to pay. *Oberlandesgericht* held that the bank had violated its duty to duly inform the daughter about the consequence of entering into such a surety contract. The court has thus held that she was not bound by the contract. The *Bundesgerichtshof*, however, overturned the decision of the *Oberlandesgericht* not accepting such a 'duty to inform' and reached a conclusion that any person of majority age is supposed to know the risks which signing surety contracts entails.

The girl filed a constitutional complaint with the Federal Constitutional Court of Germany (*Bundesverfassungsgericht*) appealing against the decision

---

16 BVerfGE 89, 214 [*Bürgschaft*].

of the *Bundesgerichtshof* stating that the latter violated her constitutional right to private autonomy (Article 2 (1) of German Constitution) and neglected the principle of the social state stipulated in Articles 20 (1) and 28 (1) of the Constitution of Germany. The Federal Constitutional Court satisfied her claim ruling that '...in cases where a structural imbalance in the bargaining power has led to a contract which is exceptionally onerous for the weaker party, the private law courts are obliged to intervene on the basis of the general clauses (§ 38 (1) and 242 of the Civil Code (*Bürgerliches Gesetzbuch* (BGB)) concerning, respectively, good morals and good faith. This obligation is based on the duty to protect the constitutional right to private autonomy in conjunction with the principle of the social state.'[17]

B) The Debate over 'Constitutionalisation' of Private Law

Following the case-law of the German Federal Constitutional Court, one may deduce that the academic discussion over 'constitutionalisation' of private law comes down to the degree to which constitutional rights may be evoked in the claims of private individuals against one another. The most audacious, yet not quite correct, conclusion that one may assume from the decisions of the German FCC is that constitutional provisions of fundamental rights are a higher law directly applicable in the private relationships and that no mediation of civil law rules (civil and commercial codes, special civil laws, etc) is needed. Developing this bold assumption further, one may fancy the idea that any legal dispute of private law may be directly brought in front of the constitutional court, neglecting the well-thought structural division of civil courts, administrative courts, labour courts, etc.

Of course, such an assumption is far-reaching. However, looking back at the reasoning in the *Handelsvertreter* and *Bürgschaft* cases, private lawyers fear that the central institute of civil law – private autonomy has been intruded upon. Because of the historical division of law into public and private and the abstention of a State from authoritative uniform regulation of private relations of the persons, civil contracts, freely entered into, are considered as the source of legal norms that govern relationships between the individuals in the same manner as other norms of legal acts. Now, the validity of such civil contracts is no longer a matter of civil law regulation, but is a subject of a constitutional review – a phenomenon, previously inconceivable for the private lawyers.

In the *Handelsvertreter* case, the FCC rebalancing the parity of a constitutional right of freedom of profession against private autonomy puts forward constitutional rights as a benchmark of further political decisions. Classically,

---

17 Olha Cherednychenko '*Fundamental Rights, Contract Law and the Protection of the Weaker Party. A Comparative Analysis on the Constitutionalisation of Contract Law, with Emphasis on Risky Financial Transactions*' – a PhD – thesis defended at the Utrecht University Institute for Legal Studies (the Netherlands) in 2007. To be published by Sellier, European Law Publishers, (p. 3).

it is up for the legislator to decide what social and economic balance should be achieved in a society. If this process is now subjected to the supervision of the Constitutional Court in the light of checking this balance with the fundamental rights, then it means nothing more but what Mattias Kumm refers to as a *'Total Constitution'.*[18]

Another fear for the private law may rise from the fact that subjecting civil litigation to the constitutional review may result in the latter's assessing and interpreting the very private law concepts, such as, for example, 'contract', or 'property', or 'tort', etc. Thus, the whole doctrine of private law is at risk to be revised from the angle of constitutional law and therefore the autonomy of private law can gradually evaporate.

A different danger constitutes a threat to the entire culture of the continental legal system that has a written law in the form of codifications as its primary source of law, as opposed to the Anglo-American system of law based on the legal precedent. Using constitutional law technique of balancing the interests stemming from the fundamental rights rather than the tools of conventional civil law threatens to renounce the respective private legislation and constitutes a danger of future opportunities to avoid the contract.

Having such arguments in mind, one may surely come to the conclusion that 'German private law is, indeed, 'already applied constitutional law'.[19] However, there are reasons to believe that 'private law is special and should be exempted from constitutional scrutiny'.[20] The substantive argument lies in the understanding that private law regulates the relationships among individuals while public law regulates the relationships between an individual and a State. Private autonomy in private law means that unlike in public law, individuals may discriminate socially in the way they want to and not be held responsible for this in front of the Constitutional Court. When applying constitutional rights to the private relations setting, it merely means that the autonomy interest of the *other* party should also be taken into consideration and the reciprocal limits of each other's rights are to be established. Such a balance is usually achieved by private law (civil or commercial codes, etc). However, if civil litigation is brought in front of the Constitutional Court, the relevant constitutional rights guarantees 'take into account the principle of private autonomy as a countervailing concern'.[21] A constitutional court, in such a case, merely assesses whether the legislator managed to strike the balance between the competing interests. If the existing private law managed to maintain such a balance then one may say that the relevant rules of private law indeed can be justified within the constitutional rights framework. If not, then whether directly or indirectly, but substantively

---

[18] Mattias Kumm, '*Who is Afraid of the Total Constitution? Constitutional Rights as Principles and the Constitutionalisation of Private Law*', German Law Journal, Vol. 07 No. 04 [2006], 341-346.

[19] Ibid, 361.

[20] Ibid, 359.

[21] Ibid, 362.

the balance between the competing constitutional rights is reached through the appropriate interpretation of civil law provisions by the relevant civil law courts in the light of constitutional rights.

II The Effect of EU Fundamental Freedoms on Private Relationships in the EU

So far we have explored the justifications found within national legal orders to the effect (direct or indirect) given to constitutional rights in private law. The phenomenon of 'constitutionalisation' of private law, however, transcends the boundaries of solely national law and presents itself also in the supranational legal orders, such, for example, as the European Convention of Human Rights legal order, or the EU legal order.

We shall avoid discussing here the mechanisms through which the European Court of Human Rights gives effect (horizontal effect) to European Convention rights in private law disputes (through: 1) the imposition of the positive obligation on the State-party to the Convention 2) review of national courts decisions in private litigation through the 'lance' of Convention rights). Instead, we shall take a look at the European private law and the impact that the European Community freedoms (free movement of goods, services, persons and capital) may have on it.

A) Case-Law of the European Court of Justice

In the previous section we have seen, from the example of the case-law of the German Federal Constitutional Court, the mechanisms through which constitutional rights are made effective both vertically (situations of public law: State – individual person) and horizontally (situations of private law: individual person – individual person). The justification for such an effect of constitutional rights is the one that constitutional rights form an *objective system of values* of a society that needs to be protected by all the branches of State power (including the courts); and a doctrine of the *obligation* of the State *to protect*.

Let us now remember one of the purposes that the EU Member States once agreed to achieve when by means of public international law tools – international agreements, they gave up a part of their national sovereignty to a supranational body. That purpose was and still is, as stipulated in Article 2 of the Treaty of Amsterdam, the establishment of the common market. Not indulging into the difference between 'common market' and 'internal market' – terms that the ECJ uses interchangeably, although 'common market' is a wider term than 'internal market' and includes also common commercial policy and competition policy, let us take a look at Article 14 of the Treaty establishing the European Community (TEC) which refers to the internal market as '...an area without internal frontiers in which the free movement of goods, persons, services and capital is ensured in accordance with the provisions of this Treaty.'

One of the primary reasons of membership in the European Union for many States remains a free and unrestricted access to another States' goods – a factor that, undoubtedly, increases the economic activity of a particular Member State as well as the Union as a whole, as one market power. To ensure the principle of free movement of goods, the Treaty set out the following goals:

1) to establish a customs union which shall cover *all trade in goods* and which shall involve the *prohibition* between Member States *of customs duties on imports and exports* and of *all charges having equivalent effect* (a), and the *adoption of a common customs tariff* (b) in their relations with third countries. (Article 23 TEC);
2) to eliminate quantitative restrictions on imports (Article 28) and exports (Article 29) and all measures having equivalent effect;
3) to adjust any State monopolies of a commercial character so as to ensure that no discrimination regarding the conditions under which goods are procured and marketed exists between nationals of Member States (Article 31 TEC).

As far as the principle of free movement of persons is concerned, the Treaty secures it in the provisions of the Articles 39-42 (workers) and Articles 43-48 (freedom of establishment). Thus, the basic rights of private persons and legal entities includes the right to freely enter/leave/reside in a Member State for the purposes of work/establishment/provision of services; the right to be treated in a hosting Member State without discrimination on the grounds of nationality.

Are the fundamental freedoms of the EU so 'fundamental' that they can be considered akin to fundamental rights on a national level? If so, what is the effect of the EU four freedoms on the private law of the Member States? Let us take a look at the example that illustrates the complexity of the situation on the supranational, EU level.

On Friday, 12 June 1998 at 09.00 heavy goods vehicles were not able to use the usual for them Brenner motorway and were immobilised until Saturday 13 June 1998 15.30 when the motorway was reopened. Among those vehicles were five lorries of the international transport undertaking *Schmidberger*, which, because of the closed Brenner motorway, were not able to transport freely timber from Germany to Italy and steel from Italy to Germany.[22] On the said dates, the Brenner motorway was closed as a result of a demonstration that was carried out on that segment of road by the Transitforum Austria Tirol, an association to protect the biosphere in the Alpine region. This association duly notified the Innsbruck provincial government of their demonstration and a press conference was convened disseminating the information on the closure of the Brenner motorway for the time period of 12.06-12.06.1998. On 3 June 1998, the Direc-

[22] Case C-112/00 *Schmidberger* [2003] ECR I-565, para 16.

torate of security for Tyrol issued an order that the demonstration was not to be banned. Thus, the demonstration was lawful as a matter of Austrian law.[23]

Schmidberger brought an action before the Innsbruck Regional Court seeking damages of ATS 140,000 against the Republic of Austria claiming the latter has exercised a restriction of free movement of goods by allowing the environmental demonstration. The Republic of Austria held that a permission to hold a demonstration was lawful and granted on the constitutional basis of the freedoms of expression and assembly, '...since fundamental rights are inviolable in a democratic society.'[24] Innsbruck Regional Court dismissed the action. Schmidberger appealed to the Innsbruck Supreme Court, which referred the case to the European Court of Justice for a preliminary ruling under the Article 234 TEC.

As we see, the two interests at stake in this case are the EC freedom of movement of goods guaranteed to the private transport company and the fundamental rights of freedom of expression and assembly guaranteed to the environment protectors, and which cannot be restricted without due justification. We should bear in mind that on the EU level there exists no fundamental right akin to that of Article 2(1) of the German Basic Law, the right to private autonomy (a general freedom to act in so far as such an action is not prohibited by 'lawful proportionate statutory law'). On the EU level, unless a specific behavior falls under a fundamental right, it may not be necessarily protected by fundamental rights. In the *Schmidberger* case, were the ECJ to consider a lawful peaceful demonstration (as a result of the exercising of the constitutional rights of freedom of assembly and expression) as a measure having equivalent effect (Article 28 TEC) and justify its direct application that would give rise to the turf question of the reconciliation of fundamental rights and fundamental freedoms.[25] We shall see further that the solution found by the ECJ is similar to the constitutional doctrine of '*Schutzpflichten*' of Germany.

It is convenient to group the judgments of the ECJ according to the degree to which they give an answer to the following questions, relevant to the topic of influence of fundamental freedoms on private actors within the EU:

a) cases that deal with the problem of triangular situations, duty of the state to protect and 'indirect third party effect' (*Commission v. France, Schmidberger, Dansk Supermarked, Clean Car*[26]);

---

23 Ibid, para 13.

24 Ibid, para 17.

25 'The case thus raises the question of the need to reconcile the requirements of the protection of fundamental rights in the Community with those arising from a fundamental freedom enshrined in the Treaty and, more particularly, the question of the respective scope of freedom of expression and freedom of assembly, guaranteed by Articles 10 and 11 of the ECHR, and of the free movement of goods, where the former are relied upon as justification for a restriction of the latter.' (Case C-112/00 *Schmidberger* [2003] ECR I-565, para 77.)

26 C-265/95 *Commission V. France* [1997] ECR I-6959; Case C-112/00 *Schmidberger* [2003] ECR I-565; Case 58/80 *Dansk Supermarket v. Imerco* [1981] ECR 181; Case C-350/96 *Clean Car Autoservice v. Landeshaupt-*

b) cases the judgments in which define what the 'state sphere' is (*Pharmaceutical* Cases and *Buy Irish* Case[27]);
c) cases that point at 'direct third party effect' and equal treatment cases (*Angonese, Defrenne II,* to a certain extent *Walrave* and *Bosman*[28]).

The reason why it is quite possible to detect from the reasoning of the ECJ in *Schmidberger* and *Commission v. France* that EC fundamental freedoms are subject to state protection against private individuals' infringement is the following one: Article 10 of the TEC states that 'Member States shall *take all appropriate measures*...to ensure fulfilment of the obligations arising out of this Treaty [...]. They shall *facilitate* the achievement of the Community's tasks. They shall *abstain* from any measure which could jeopardise the attainment of the objectives of this Treaty.'[29] Paragraph 30 of *Commission v. France* and paragraph 57 of the *Schmidberger* judgment state that '...as an indispensable instrument for the realisation of a market without internal frontiers, Article 30 *does not prohibit only measures emanating from the State* which, in themselves, create restrictions on trade between Member States. It also applies where a Member State *abstains* from adopting the measures required in order to deal with obstacles to the free movement of goods *which are* not *caused by the State*.'[30] This means that if the State fails to prevent the obstacles to free movement of goods (such '*obstacles*' being an individual's act (as opposed to a State's act), for example, manifestation of the environment protestors in *Schmidberger* exercising their constitutional rights to freedom of expression and assembly; or, criminal actions by the French farmers – private actions punishable under French Criminal law) that are created by actions of private individuals on its territory aimed at products originating in other Member State – this is likely to obstruct intra-Community trade in the same way as a positive act [of a State] (paragraphs 31 and 58 of the *Commission v. France* and *Schmidberger* respectively). Consequently, it is a *duty* of the Member State to *protect* (through adoption of all necessary and appropriate measures[31]) a fundamental freedom (to ensure that fundamental freedom is respected on its territory[32]). Thus, we can assume that the State needs to protect a private person's interest that arises from the freedom of goods against another person's right to private autonomy. This is true, however, in the constellation

mann von Wien [1998] ECR I-2521.

27 Joined Cases C-266 and 267/87 *The Queen v. Royal Pharmaceutical Society of Great Britain, ex parte Association of Pharmaceutical Importers* [1989] ECR 1267; Case 249-81 *Buy Irish* [1982] ECR 4005.

28 Case C-281/98 *Roman Angonese v. Cassa di Risparmio di Bolzano SpA* [2000] ECR I-4139; Case 43/75 *Gabrielle Defrenne v. Sabena* [1976] ECR 455; Case 36/74 *Walrave & Koch v. Association Union Cycliste Internationale* [1974] ECR 1405, 1418; C-415/93 *Bosman* [1995] ECR I-4921/5063.

29 Emphasis added.

30 Emphasis added.

31 Paras 32 and 59 of the *Commission v. France* and *Schmidberger* respectively.

32 Ibid.

when preference to the fundamental freedom (freedom of goods in this case) is given over the individual's behaviour which is punishable by national law (as was the case in *Commission v. France*) – a situation opposite to that in *Schmidberger* where the government of Austria undertook all appropriate and available measures to reduce the impact on Community trade.[33]

As far as balancing the EC fundamental freedom against the fundamental right (the one protected by national constitutions as well as the ECHR) is concerned, it is difficult to do so as they are qualitatively different and no court would run the risk of 'subordinating a fundamental human right to a Community economic freedom'.[34] Thus, the balancing of rights takes place, which means that none of them enjoy an absolute protection.

So far, we have explored the cases that did not involve discrimination on grounds of nationality. The judgment in *Angonese* affirms the direct applicability of Article 39 TEC between private individuals.[35] Article 39 (2) TEC (former Article 48) states that 'freedom of movement [for workers] shall entail the abolition of any discrimination based on nationality between workers of the Member States as regards to employment, remuneration and other conditions of work and employment.' In this case, Mr. Angonese, an Italian national whose mother tongue is German and who is resident in the province of Bolzano, Italy, went to study in Austria for 4 years. Upon his studies, he applied to take part in a competition for a post with a private bank in Bolzano, the Cassa di Risparmio.[36] One of the conditions for entry to the competition was possession of a special certificate of bilingualism (Italian and German) that Bolzano required for access to a managerial career in the public service.[37] However, the only way it was possible to obtain such a certificate was to have passed an examination held only in that province. Other certificates, attesting the knowledge of the languages, were not valid for that purpose of employment. From the date of the competition advertisement posted, it was not possible for Angonese to have obtained the necessary certificate to qualify for the job. His other certificates were not accepted as a valid proof of his skills in languages.

Although the tasks of achieving a uniform common market within the EU are assumed to be carried out by the Member States, the ECJ in paragraph 30 in *Angonese* stated that '...the principle of non-discrimination set out in Article 48

33 'Moreover, it is not in dispute that the isolated incident in question [the situation in *Schmidberger* case] *did not* give rise to a general climate of insecurity such as to have a dissuasive effect on intra-Community trade flows as a whole, in contrast to the serious and repeated disruptions to public order at issue in the case giving rise to the judgment in *Commission v. France*, cited above.' (para 88 of *Schmidberger* case; emphasis added).

34 Coppel and Neill in J. Insensee, *Handbuch des Staatsrechts* Volume V, Heidelberg, C.F. Müller Juristischer Verlag, 1992; 669, 690

35 Supra note 29, *Angonese*, para 36.

36 Ibid, para 5.

37 Ibid, para 6.

[now Article 39 TEC] is drafted in general terms and *is not* specifically addressed to the Member States.'[38] Moreover, citing its previous judgment in *Defrenne v. Sabena*[39] the ECJ restated in paragraph 34 that '...the prohibition of discrimination applied equally to *all agreements* intended to regulate labour collectively, *as well as to contracts between individuals...*'.[40]

The ECJ treats a discriminatory action differently as the non-discriminatory one. There is an undoubted social aspect in Article 39 TEC, which is akin to the fundamental right envisaged by Article 141 TEC, an article that has a horizontal direct effect in relationships of private law in Member States (especially employment relationships).[41]

Another important issue raised in *Angonese* is the question of what amounts to the 'sphere of State'. In *Angonese,* the ECJ restated its previous position in *Walrave*[42] and *Bosman*:[43] '...the abolition, as between Member States, of obstacles of freedom of movement for persons *would be compromised* if the abolition of State barriers could be neutralised by *obstacles resulting* from the exercise of their legal autonomy by *associations or organisations not governed by public law...*'.[44]

The ECJ does not indulge itself much by trying to figure out where the dividing line 'public-private' should be in the discrimination cases. Rather, the line of logic here is the obstacle to free movement, which is caused by the private autonomy behaviour of private associations that somehow have the character of

---

38 Emphasis added.

39 Supra note 29.

40 Ibid, para 34, emphasis added.

41 Article 141 TEC (emphasis added): 1. Each Member State shall *ensure* that the principle of equal pay for male and female workers for equal work or work of equal value *is applied*. 2. For the purpose of this Article, 'pay' means the ordinary basic or minimum wage or salary and any other consideration, whether in cash or in kind, which the worker receives directly or indirectly, in respect of his employment, from his employer.

Equal pay without discrimination based on sex means:

a) that pay for the same work at piece rates shall be calculated on the basis of the same unit of measurement;

b) that pay for work at time rates shall be the same for the same job.

3. The Council, acting in accordance with the procedure referred to in Article 251, and after consulting the Economic and Social Committee, shall adopt measures *to ensure the application* of the principle of equal opportunities and equal treatment of men and women in matters of employment and occupation, including the principle of equal pay for equal work or work of equal value.

4. With a view to ensuring full equality in practice between men and women in working life, *the principle of equal treatment shall not prevent any Member State from maintaining or adopting* measures providing for specific advantages in order to make it easier for the underrepresented sex to pursue a vocational activity or to prevent or compensate for disadvantages in professional careers.

42 Supra note 29, *Walrave*, para 18, emphasis added.

43 Supra note 29, *Bosman*, para 83.

44 Supra note 29, *Angonese*, para 32.

a State because of their dominant market position and which are, thus, empowered to promote protectionist measures.

III Conclusion

We have examined the current case-law of the EU regarding the balance of fundamental rights and EU fundamental freedoms. To understand the mechanism of how fundamental rights can be relied upon in private law litigations, we took the German concept of *Grundrechtilche Schutzpflichten* – duties of the State to protect – as an illustrative example. The cited above decisions of the ECJ show the direct applicability of Article 49 TEC in private law litigations and the questions that indirect effect of fundamental freedoms on private persons may raise in the context of their balance with the fundamental rights guaranteed by the constitutions of the Member States as well as by the European Convention of Human Rights.

CHAPTER 12

Conflict with International Law as a Ground for Invalidity of Community Acts

Pavel Svoboda

Globalization – economic, technological, cultural and political – leads to legal globalization, driven by the increasing need to integrate the existing legal orders at the national as well as international levels. Responding initially to the economic needs, the process gained momentum in both public and private law. Now, against the background of rising international terrorism, attention is being turned to the legal aspects of security policy. One of the inevitable questions in this context is the relationship between international and European law, in particular, the validity of Community acts giving effect to the rules of international law. The original rule of primary European law defining the grounds on which such acts can be declared invalid does not meet the present requirements. The European Court of Justice and the Court of First Instance ('the Court') has noted this situation and responded accordingly.

1 Sources of Legality of Community Acts

The legality of Community acts stems from two sources:

1) the rule of law. The European Community is *'a Community based on the rule of law, inasmuch as neither its Member States nor its institutions can avoid a review of the question whether the measures adopted by them are in conformity with the basic constitutional charter, the Treaty'* (ECJ judgment in case 294/83 *Les Verts*, para 23[1]). In the French original of this judgment, the expression '*Community based on the rule of law* ' is even more intensive: '*communauté de droit*' – community of law;
2) presumption of validity. Secondary community acts are presumed to be valid unless the contrary is proved (15/85 *Consorzio Cooperative d'Abruzzo*).

Procedural Framework

Typically, (in)validity of Community acts[2] comes under review in annulment proceedings (Article 230 of the Treaty establishing the European Community – 'EC Treaty' or 'Treaty'; Article 146 of the Euratom Treaty, incidental proceedings (Article 241 of the EC Treaty and Article 156 of the Euratom Treaty), and preliminary ruling proceedings (Article 234 of the EC Treaty and Article 150 of the Euratom Treaty). For general information on these procedures, the reader

* As.Prof. JUDr. Pavel Svoboda is an Ambassador – permanent representative of the Czech Republic to the Council of Europe and Associate Professor in European law at the Faculty of Law, Charles University, Prague. The author is aware of the fact that some of the core judgments quoted in this article are still subject to review by the European Court of Justice.

1 Cf. 314/85 *Foto-Frost*, para 16; C-314/91 *Weber v. Parliament*, para 8; T-222, 327, 329/99 *Martinez*, para 48; ECJ Opinion 1/91, para 21.

2 In addition to invalidity, Community acts may be declared null and void (7/56 *Algera*) if they are seriously and manifestly defective (15/85 *Consorzio Cooperative d'Abruzzo*, paras 10 and 11). However, nullity constitutes a ground for inadmissibility of applications for annulment (1 & 14/57 *Tubes de la Sarre*).

can refer to many excellent publications. The following text will therefore address only the main topic of this article.

Grounds for invalidity

The grounds on which a Community act can be declared invalid are enumerated in an exhaustive list in Article 230 (2) of the EC Treaty: (i) lack of competence, (ii) infringement of an essential procedural requirement, (iii) infringement of the Treaty or of any rule of law relating to its application, and (iv) misuse of powers. In a narrow sense, they might all be included under the catch-all phrase in (iii) – 'infringement of the Treaty or of any rule of law relating to its application', since they all refer to the Treaty. Nevertheless, the ECJ has always interpreted them very broadly to cover all possible situations that, in practice, can invalidate an act.

Though the Treaty seems to define these grounds explicitly for the purpose of annulment proceedings, a reference to them appears in Article 241 of the EC Treaty concerning incidental proceedings, and they are cited by the ECJ when ascertaining the validity of acts in preliminary ruling proceedings. Specifically enumerated grounds thus gradually came to be accepted as general grounds, invoked whenever the validity of secondary Community acts and external treaties comes under review (73-74/63 *Internationale Credieten*; 21-24/72 *International Fruit Company*, para 6).

The grounds are applied in the area of external relations, i.e. the EC/EU's international relations. Here, the law oscillates between the international and European systems of law, the basic premise being that Community law should be applied with due respect for international law (C-286/90 *Poulsen*).[3] It logically follows that consistency with international law must be a criterion for validity of acts in this area. For more than thirty years now, the ECJ has constantly held that *'the jurisdiction of the Court cannot be limited by the grounds on which the validity of* [Community] *measures may be contested'* (21 & 24/72 *International Fruit Company*). Later on, the Court specified *'the jurisdiction of the Court to give preliminary rulings under* [Article 234] *of the Treaty concerning the validity of acts of the Community institutions cannot be limited by the grounds on which the validity of these measures may be contested'. 'Since such jurisdiction extends to all grounds capable of invalidating these measures, the Court is obliged to examine whether their validity may be affected by reason of the fact that they are contrary to a rule of international law'.*[4] The Court thus made it clear that when giving preliminary

[3] In annulment proceedings, the Court has annulled some acts on the grounds of lack of competence (of the Commission to conclude an agreement with the United States regarding the application of their competition laws; C-327/91 *France v. Commission*), improper legal basis (chosen for the EEC-United States agreement on government procurement; C-360/93 *Parliament v. Council*), and a breach of the principle of non-discrimination (in the Framework Agreement on Bananas; C-122/95 *Germany v. Council*; C-368/94 *Portugal v. Council*).

[4] Case 162/96 *Racke*, paras 26, 27, referring to 21-24/72 *International Fruit Company (III)*, para 5.

rulings, it will not be limited by the grounds for invalidity in Article 230 of the EC Treaty, but will review the legality of Community acts also in the light of international law.

However, this statement lost some of its relevance some years later, when conflict with international law was explicitly accepted as a reason for reviewing the validity of a regulation in annulment proceedings (Article 230 of the EC Treaty) in case T-306/01 *Yusuf* (pending in C-415/05 P *Yusuf*).[5] In case T-306/01 *Yusuf*, the CFI reviewed the validity of a Community regulation giving effect to a Security Council resolution that left no room for discretion on the part of the EC (e.g. Regulation No. 881/2002), i.e. where the source of the potential invalidity of the regulation could only be the unlawfulness of the Security Council resolution. The CFI notes that, in general, the Court has no authority to call in question, even indirectly, the lawfulness of a Security Council resolution in the light of a Community sanction regulation, e.g. in the case of alleged human rights violations. Such review would – in the Court's own opinion – be inconsistent with (i) Articles 25, 48 and 103 of the United Nations Charter[6], (ii) Article 27 of the 1969 Vienna Convention on the Law of Treaties ('Vienna Convention')[7], (iii) Articles 5, 10, 297 and Article 307 (1) of the EC Treaty, and (iv) Article 5 of the EC Treaty (T-306/01 *Yusuf*, para 270[8]). However, the Court considers itself competent to examine three aspects of validity of the implementing Community regulation:

5 For details, see e.g. Eeckhout P., International Law and EU Law, lecture at the Annual European Law Conference 2006. The case concerns 'smart sanctions' reflecting the global nature of terrorism, which is no longer linked to a particular country, but to individuals worldwide. A Swedish national Ahmed Ali Yusuf, was affected by Regulations No. 467/2001 and No. 881/2002, giving effect to Security Council resolution 1333 which ordered the freezing of the assets of the Taliban and its associates. T-306/01. See also T-253/02 *Chafiq Ayadi*; T-315/01 *Kadi*; C-84/95 *Bosphorus*.

6 Article 25 of the United Nations Charter: *'The Members of the United Nations agree to accept and carry out the decisions of the Security Council in accordance with the present Charter.'* Article 48 of the United Nations Charter: *'1. The action required to carry out the decisions of the Security Council for the maintenance of international peace and security shall be taken by all the members of the United Nations or by some of them, as the Security Council may determine. 2. Such decisions shall be carried out by the Members of the United Nations directly and through their action in the appropriate international agencies of which they are members.'* Article 103 of the United Nations Charter: *'In the event of a conflict between the obligations of the members of the United Nations under the present Charter and their obligations under any other international agreement, their obligations under the present Charter shall prevail.'*

7 According to Article 27 of the Vienna Convention, a State may not invoke the provisions of its internal law as justification for its failure to perform a treaty.

8 *'As has already been explained, the resolutions of the Security Council at issue were adopted under Chapter VII of the Charter of the United Nations. In these circumstances, determining what constitutes a threat to international peace and security and the measures required to maintain or re-establish them is the responsibility of the Security Council alone and, as such, escapes the jurisdiction of national or Community authorities and courts, subject only to the inherent right of individual or collective self-defence mentioned in Article 51 of the Charter.'*

- possible violation of the peremptory norms of international customary law (*jus cogens*)[9] by the Security Council (T-306/01 *Yusuf*, para 278[10]), since these norms take precedence over the law of the United Nations, including Security Council resolutions. Therefore, international treaties conflicting with *jus cogens*, whether existing (Article 53 of the Vienna Convention) or new (Article 64 of the Vienna Convention) become null and void. Here, the Court indirectly – with reference to the invalidity of a Community act – assumes the competence to decide whether a legal act of lesser force conflicts with *jus cogens* as a norm of supreme force;[11]
- ascertaining whether the rules on formal and procedural requirements and jurisdiction imposed in this case on the Community institutions were observed; and
- ascertaining whether the Community measures at issue were appropriate and proportionate in relation to the resolutions of the Security Council which they put into effect (T-306/01 *Yusuf*, paras 268-9[12]).

---

9 In Article 53 of the Vienna Convention, *jus cogens* is defined as a peremptory norm of general international law, *'a norm accepted and recognized by the international community of States as a whole as a norm from which no derogation is permitted and which can be modified only by a subsequent norm of general international law having the same character'*. The ICJ defines such norms as *'intransgressible principles of international customary law'* (ICJ Advisory Opinion, Legality of the Threat or Use of Nuclear Weapons, ICJ Records 1996, p. 226, para 79; cf. Opinion of Advocate General F. G. Jacobs in C-84/95 *Bosphorus*, para 65).

10 *'In this connection, it must be noted that the Vienna Convention on the Law of Treaties, which consolidates the customary international law and Article 5 of which provides that it is to apply 'to any treaty which is the constituent instrument of an international organisation and to any treaty adopted within an international organisation', provides in Article 53 for a treaty to be void if it conflicts with a peremptory norm of general international law (jus cogens), defined as 'a norm accepted and recognised by the international community of States as a whole as a norm from which no derogation is permitted and which can be modified only by a subsequent norm of general international law having the same character'. Similarly, Article 64 of the Vienna Convention provides that: 'If a new peremptory norm of general international law emerges, any existing treaty which is in conflict with that norm becomes void and terminates'.'*

11 This leads to another – retrospective – question concerning the autonomy of Community law: Considering that in T-306/01 *Yusuf* the ECJ recognized the primacy of *jus cogens* over Community law, wasn't the Court right already in 1963, when it held that *'the Community constitutes a* new legal order of international law' (26/62 *Van Gend en Loos*) rather than a fully independent and separate legal order, as the Court's only slightly later expression 'its own legal order' (6/64 *Costa*) would suggest?

12 *'The institutions and the United Kingdom ask the Court as a matter of principle to decline all jurisdiction to undertake such indirect review of the lawfulness of those resolutions which, as rules of international law binding on the Member States of the Community, are mandatory for the Court as they are for all Community institutions. Those parties are of the view, essentially, that the Court's review ought to be confined, on the one hand, to ascertaining whether the rules on formal and procedural requirements and jurisdiction imposed in this case on the Community institutions were observed and, on the other hand, to ascertaining whether the Community measures at issue were appropriate and proportionate in relation to the resolutions of the Security Council with they put into effect. It must be recognised that such a limitation of jurisdiction is necessary as a corollary to the*

2 Conditions for Reviewing the Legality of a Community Act in the Light of International Law

Nevertheless, the conditions under which a Community act may be declared unlawful with reference to a breach of international law, are strict: The Court may only review the legality of an international act, which meets the following conditions: (i) the international legal act must be binding on the Community, (ii) directly applicable, and (iii) the breach must be manifest.

International legal act binding on the Community

The question whether an international act is binding on the Community has been examined by the Court in the context of sanction regulations giving effect to Security Council resolutions, since the EC itself is not a signatory of the UN Charter:[13] Security Council resolutions are binding on members of the United Nations, including all EU countries (under Articles 25 and 41 of the UN Charter), as well as on non-members of the United Nations (under Article 2 (6) of the UN Charter),[14] or adopted to fulfil the commitment to carry out a Security Council decision.

However, is the EC as such – without its Member States – competent to adopt a sanction regulation giving effect to a Security Council resolution, where there is no room for the EC's discretion (e.g. Regulation No. 881/2002 against the Taliban and Al-Qaeda network), considering that the EC as such is not a member of the United Nations? In the case of trade sanctions, yes, since the EC, though not directly bound by the UN Charter and thus not required to carry out Security Council decisions in accordance with Article 25 of the Charter (T-306/01 *Yusuf*, para 242), must respect international law in the exercise of its powers (Article 307 of the EC Treaty; C-286/90 *Poulsen*, para 210 above; C-162/96 *Racke*, para 210; 41/74 *Van Duyn*, para 22). As a result, the EC has the following duties:

i) A negative duty – duty not to impede – the duty of EC institutions not to impede the performance of the obligations of Member States stemming from the Charter (T-306/01, para 247; see also 812/79 *Burgoa*, para 9). It is based i.e. on the following facts:
- Founders of the EC – members of the United Nations – have conferred the responsibility for the maintenance of international peace and security on the Security Council (Article 24, para 1 of the Charter[15]), and thus

principles identified above, in the Court's examination of the relationship between the international legal order under the United Nations and the Community legal order.'

[13] E.g. restrictions on trade with Libya – Council Common Position No. 93/614/CFSP and subsequent Council Regulations No. 3274/93 and No. 3275/93.

[14] *'The Organisation shall ensure that states which are not Members of the United Nations act in accordance with these principles so far as may be necessary for the maintenance of international peace and security.'*

[15] According to Article 24, para 1 of the United Nations Charter signed on 26 June 1945, members of the United Nations *'confer on the Security Council primary responsibility for the maintenance of international*

could not transfer to the Community more powers than they possessed (para 245; the Roman legal principle *nemo ad alium plus juris transfere potest quam ipse habet,* applied to international law!),
- Members of the United Nations must ensure that their obligations under the UN Charter (Article 103 of the Charter[16]), including Security Council resolutions (Article 25 of the Charter[17]) prevail over their other commitments stemming from international law, including the European Convention on Human Rights and the EC Treaty,
- As members of the United Nations, EU Member States are required by Article 48 (2) of the Charter to carry out Security Council decisions *'directly and through their action in the appropriate international agencies of which they are members';*

ii) a positive – active duty (T-306/01, para 248): The powers of EC Member States in the area of trade policy have been completely transferred to the EC, thus becoming the exclusive powers of the EC; consequently, no EU Member State can give effect to the sanctions on a national basis. This is proven by the existence of Article 301 of the EC Treaty, inserted in the Treaty exactly for this purpose. Otherwise, Member States would have to invoke Article 297 of the EC Treaty and take measures for the protection of international security. In fact, the EC actually used this avenue to join the GATT 1947 (para 253). The legal basis for the sanction regulation is thus EC law, and not international law (para 257).

Naturally, this does not apply to sanctions imposed by the EC/EU on its own Member State. Such sanctions are subject to special rules under Article 7 of the EU Treaty and Article 309 of the EC Treaty.

2.1 Direct Applicability

An act in international law is *'capable of conferring rights on citizens of the Community which they can invoke before the courts,'* i.e. directly applicable (cf. 21-24/72 *International Fruit Company (III)*, para 8; cited in 9/73 *Schülter,* para 27; however, the Court refuses to recognize direct applicability of the WTO Agreement).

---

peace and security, and agree that in carrying out its duties under this responsibility the Security Council acts on their behalf.'

16 Article 103 of the UN Charter: *'In the event of a conflict between the obligations of the Members of the United Nations under the present Charter and their obligations under any other international agreement, their obligations under the present Charter shall prevail'.* Unlike the rules commonly applied to successive treaties, this applies equally to earlier and later treaties (Article 30 of the Vienna Convention, cf. ICJ judgment in *Nicaragua v. United States,* ICJ Reports 1984, p. 392, para 107).

17 Confirmed by the ICJ in *Libya v. United States,* ICJ Reports 1992, p. 16, para 42, and in *Libya v. United Kingdom,* ICJ Reports 1992, p. 113, para 39.

2.2 Manifest Breach of an International Rule

The third condition for invoking a breach of international law as a ground for unlawfulness of a Community act is that the breach must be manifest: '... *because of the complexity of the rules in question and the imprecision of some of the concepts to which they refer, judicial review must necessarily, and in particular in the context of a preliminary reference for an assessment of validity, be limited to the question whether, by adopting* [a regulation suspending the application of the Cooperation Agreement between the EEC and former Yugoslavia] *the Council made manifest errors of assessment concerning the conditions for applying these rules'* (C-162/96 *Racke*, para 52); here, the Council is treated very generously.

Exhaustive nature of the list in Article 230 (2) of the EC Treaty

As shown above, literal interpretation of Article 230 (2) of the EC Treaty inevitably leads to the conclusion that the list of grounds for invalidity of a Community act is exhaustive. If this is really the case, it means that one or more of the grounds on this list may be understood as covering conflicts with international law. However, if international law is not concerned, it is necessary to find – another interpretation or a legal ground prevailing over the literal meaning that suggests that the list in Article 230 (2) is exhaustive.

In any case, the possibility to declare a Community act invalid with reference to a conflict with international law is a logical consequence of the rule that European law must be applied with due respect for international law.[18] This rule is implicit in Article 300 (7) of the EC Treaty, which provides that external EC agreements are binding on EC institutions and on Member States, thus implying a relationship between international law and primary EC law. That is why in the hierarchy of the legal sources of Community law, legal acts concerning external relations take a central position between primary and secondary law, to show that Community acts must be compatible with the rules of international law.

Therefore, can any of the grounds cited above – (i) lack of competence, (ii) infringement of an essential procedural requirement, (iii) infringement of the Treaty or of any rule of law relating to its application, and (iv) misuse of powers

---

[18] Cf. e.g. 41/74 *Van Duyn*, para 22: limitations of the freedom of movement v. the principle of international law according to which a state is precluded from refusing its own nationals the right of entry; 89, 104, 114, 116, 117 ,125/85 *Ahlström v. Commission*, paras 15-23: anti-trust law (principle of extraterritoriality) v. sovereign jurisdiction of states over their own territory; C-268/90 *Poulsen*, para 9: EC fisheries law v. international law of the sea; T-115/94 *Opel Austria*, paras 90-95: conclusion and entry into force of the Agreement creating the European Economic Area (EEA), in particular the ban on frustrating the object and purpose of international treaties: an EC regulation, adopted one week after the Community entered into the EEA Agreement, withdrew tariff concessions for imported gearboxes, the producer of which received state aid in Austria (then a non-EU country), C-162/96 *Racke*: suspension and termination of an external treaty and customary international law, Cooperation Agreement with former Yugoslavia.

– be understood as including conflict with international law? We believe not, and this negative view is supported by the Court's refusal to let its jurisdiction be limited by the explicit grounds for invalidity. Admittedly, what really interests the Court is whether the reasons for annulment, as presented by the applicant, are convincing, rather than how they are classified, but this does not mean that the Court can ignore the purpose and spirit of Article 230 (2) of the Treaty. Any interpretation of the enumerated grounds, no matter how broad, must at least fit in the framework of primary EU law.

If conflict with international law cannot be included under any of the cited grounds for invalidity, it follows that the ECJ has called in question the exhaustive nature of the list in Article 230 (2) and introduced a new fifth ground – conflict with international law.

Is it thus possible to deduce, in the light of Article 220 of the EC Treaty, that the list in Article 230 (2) is demonstrative? The ECJ could certainly justify this by reference to its general task, which is to *'ensure that in the interpretation and application of this Treaty the law is observed'* (Article 220 of the EC Treaty), but it has not done so. In the absence of a definition of 'law' for the purposes of Article 220, the term may be understood as including public international law.[19] On the other hand, Article 230 (2) of the EC Treaty undeniably is a special clause, as opposed to the general Article 220; accordingly, Article 230 (2) as a *lex specialis* should take precedence.

The Court's extension of the list of legal grounds for reviewing legality of certain legal acts is not unprecedented in European law. The well-known *Cassis de Dijon* judgment examining the relationship between an exhaustive list of exemptions from the restrictions on free movement under Article 30 of the EC Treaty and so-called imperative reasons of public interest has been discussed by many authors, but still we are more used to seeing this practice in the area of freedoms related to the EC internal market rather than in the procedural area. However, there is no denying that, even though the Court might be said to engage in 'quasi-legislative' activities (probably exceeding its powers), it is doing so for a good and useful purpose, responding to legal globalization and developments in international law, a process which could have hardly been foreseen by the Founding Fathers in the wake of the Second World War.

[19] However, it is to be stressed that the Court's decision declaring an act invalid has only intracommunity effect, i.e. does not apply to the other (non-EU) party and does not affect the validity of the act in international law.

CHAPTER 13

"Euro-amendment" to the Czech Constitution

Lenka Pítrová

In late autumn 2001,[1] the Czech Parliament approved a 'euro-amendment' to the Czech Constitution that came into force on 1st June 2002. This constitutional amendment made the legislative changes necessary for the Czech Republic to comply with the obligations and exercise the rights of membership in the European Communities and the European Union. This amendment was to allow for the ratification of the fundamental treaties upon which the European Union is built. It was also to incorporate the principles of the relationship between Czech law and the distinctive system of Community law as well as the relationships between national and Communitarian 'constitutional' bodies into the Czech constitutional legal order.

The role of the Czech Parliament in preparation of this draft amendment was very important. It is necessary to remark that it was not the first attempt to amend the Constitution within the context of the forthcoming accession of the Czech Republic to the European Union. In April 1999, the Government approved a draft amendment to the Constitution, the aim of which was the modification of the Czech legal order in order to enable the Czech Republic's membership into NATO. This amendment should have also accelerated preparation of the Czech Republic for accession to the EU. This draft in particular contained a provision enabling the Government to speed up the process of approximation by giving power to the Government to adopt Decisions with the legal power of the law (statute), the so called European Decision of the Government (with the *ex post* 'veto' right of the Parliament). This transfer of legislative powers to implement EC legislation by governmental decisions was inspired by the Spanish pre-accession experience[2] (*decretos legislativos*). Nevertheless, this idea of shifting wide scope legislative powers to the Government did not find the necessary political support in Parliament and the draft was rejected. The Parliament expressed clearly its will to participate actively in the process of transposition of European legislation to the national legal system.

The new draft amendment to the Constitution was therefore prepared in co-operation with the representatives of all parliamentary political parties. That should ensure political consensus over the text. The draft was based not only on the political consensus of the political parties but also on the comparative work of legal experts and it was presented to the Parliament in spring 2001. The general purpose of this draft was:

1) to solve transparently relationship between international law and national law;

---

* JUDr. Lenka Pitrova, CSc. is senior Legal Adviser, Vice-director of the Parliamentary Institute, Office of the Chamber of Deputies of the Czech Parliament, Prague, Czech Republic.

1 Constitutional Act No. 395/2001 Coll. of 18 October 2001 amending Constitutional Act of the Czech National Council No. 1/1993 Coll., the Constitution of the Czech Republic, as amended. The draft constitutional law was adopted on 3rd July 2001 by the House of Deputies, on 19th October by the Senate and it was signed by the president on 30th October 2001.

2 Law No. 47/1985.

2) to create constitutional conditions for the integration of the Czech Republic into international institutions to which powers of the constitutional bodies are transferred.

1 Relationship Between International and National Law

Firstly, it was necessary to formulate at the general level a relationship between national law and international law. In Article 1 the following text was added, reading:

'(2) The Czech Republic comply with the obligations arising for it from international law.'

This general provision expresses explicitly the postulate that the Czech Republic will thenceforth comply with obligations arising from international agreements, as any other democratic state. The draft formulation of this article was influenced by the Polish Constitution 1997 (art. 9) and the Swiss Constitution 1999 (art.5 (4)). The expression 'obligations' should be interpreted as inclusive of general rules and principles of international law.

The key provision concerning the relationship between national law and international law before the revision was Article 10 of the Czech Constitution 1993. This article created quite a unique model combining dualistic and monistic approaches to this relationship. By this provision, only one category of the international agreements was regarded as 'directly applicable' in the national legal system and only these agreements were given the force of law. This category of agreements is, from the point of view of individuals, the most important one; these are agreements on fundamental rights and freedoms. The scope of this provision has been interpreted by the Constitutional Court. All other international agreements (irrespective of the fact they confess rights or impose obligations) had to be transposed by legislation or at least a reference clause (provision) inserted into national legislation to become enforceable. The new wording of Article 10 after having been vividly discussed in the Parliament has in fact cancelled the above-mentioned dichotomy of special regime for agreements on fundamental rights as well as the necessity to transpose international agreements by legislation. This revolutionary change in the Czech constitutional law happened in one sentence forming the new Article 10:

'Promulgated international agreements, the ratification of which has been approved by the Parliament and by which the Czech Republic is bound, constitute part of legal order; if an international agreement makes provision contrary to a law (statute), the international agreement is applied.'

The constitutional amendment simultaneously defined which agreements concluded by the Czech Republic must be regarded as being part of the legal order and having precedence over laws (statutes):

'Article 49
The approval of both Chambers of Parliament is required to ratify international agreements
a) regulating the rights and duties of persons,
b) that are contracts of alliance, peace, or other political purpose,
c) under which the Czech Republic assumes membership in an international organisation,
d) that are economic contracts of a general nature,
e) on other matters, the regulation of which is reserved for a law.'

There are three conditions under which these international agreements should have the two above-mentioned consequences, i.e. shall be regarded as being part of the legal order and having precedence over laws (statutes).

The first condition shall be an approval of such agreements by the Parliament before their ratification. Without this approval, international agreements could not be given precedence over laws (statutes). Through this procedure, the control of the national parliament over concluded international agreements is also strengthened. The second condition of the internal effect of international agreements shall be their promulgation, i.e. their publication in the Official Collection of International Agreements. A postulate of the rule of law that the sources of law should be accessible for citizens shall be thus fulfilled. The third condition of internal applicability of international agreements is that they are binding for the Czech Republic. This condition is regulated by the Vienna Convention on the Law of Treaties. A logical consequence of this priority of the international agreements forming part of the national legal order over the laws (statutes) is their precedence in application by the national courts (see below).

The new provision of Article 10 does not explicitly mention Community law. But even if Community law constitutes 'a separate legal order, which provisions belong neither to international law nor to the municipal law of the Member States'[3], this general formulation allows us to interpret the relationship between national and Community law in the light of the principles of direct effect, direct applicability and priority.

The relationship between international and national law is solved by the constitutions of European states in different ways representing monistic, dualistic or mixed model. Nevertheless, the aim of all the concepts is to enable it to absorb international obligations into national law. In some states, international agreements are given constitutional or even potentially over-constitutional character. (This applies to the monistic model of the Dutch Constitution as well as the dualistic Austrian approach where it depends on hierarchy of a recep-

[3] Case 6/64 *Costa v. ENEL* ECR 585.

tion norm). The concept embodied in the new Articles 10 and 87 of the Czech Constitution ranks the Czech Republic among the states which give the international agreements priority over the laws (statutes), such as France, Greece, Belgium, Luxembourg, Switzerland and Poland. Some other states, such as Germany, Hungary, partly Austria, Italy, and the United Kingdom transpose international agreements by legislation, having in practice precedence over national laws (statutes).

2 Transfer of Sovereign Rights

The cornerstone of the 'euro-amendment' is an integration Article 10a enabling transfer of powers to the international institutions including the European Union (even if this is not explicitly mentioned):

'Article 10a
(1) some powers of bodies of the Czech Republic may be transferred to an international organisation or institution under an international agreement.'

This provision is reminiscent of the integration provisions inserted in the Constitutions of some Member States and it is nearly identical with art. 24(1) of the German Basic Law. Ratification of the agreement transferring sovereign rights to the international institution requires, as in many constitutions of the Member States, approval by qualified majority in both Chambers of the Parliament. According to the newly inserted art. 39(4):

'(4) The approval of a three-fifths majority of all Deputies and a three-fifths majority of Senators in attendance is required to pass a constitutional act and to approve the ratification of an international agreement stipulated in Article 10a (1).'

As the accession to the European Union required broad political and national consensus, the constitutional amendment opened also the possibility of a referendum, the holding of which is in the case of accession to the European Union supported by all parliamentary political parties. According to the Article 10a (2):

'(2) The approval of the Parliament is required to ratify an international agreement stipulated in paragraph (1), unless constitutional law provides that approval awarded in a referendum is required for ratification.'

Once again, it is the Parliament that plays an important role in drafting the Act on Referendum. As to the senator's initiative on the draft Act on Referendum on the accession to the EU, the Government did not support this draft mainly because of the fact that it dealt only with monothematic referendum. In reaction, the Government submitted its own draft Act containing both general legislative framework for a referendum and particular conditions enabling a referendum on the accession to the EU. In October 2002 a Constitutional Act providing for an ad hoc referendum on EU accession was finally passed and the referendum was held on 13-14 June 2003.

3 Relations Between the Government and the Parliament

Newly formulated Article 10b of the Constitution indicates political will for greater involvement by the national Parliament in EC law making and in EC/EU affairs after accession. This provision is clearly inspired by the Protocol on the Role of the National Parliaments in the European Union inserted into the Amsterdam Treaty:

'Article 10b

(1) The Government informs the Parliament regularly and in advance of issues related to obligations issuing from the Czech Republic's membership in an international organisation or institution stipulated in Article 10a.

(2) The Chambers of Parliament make statements on the decisions of such an international organisation or institution, that are being prepared as provided by their rules of procedure.

(3) The act on the principles of conduct and relations of both Chambers mutually and in external relations may entrust the competence of the Chambers under paragraph (2) to a joint body of the Chambers.'

The mechanism of exerting parliamentary influence and scrutiny is based upon a due and timely supply of information and documents. It gives the two chambers the possibility to adopt resolutions (in accordance with their rules of procedure) on the issues of their interest. In the case of the European Union, it enables the Parliament to have its word in legislation under preparation. This provision could be compared to the parliamentary control under Article 88-4 of the French Constitution. It does not go that far to give the Parliament the power to mandate ministers (as it happens in Denmark) or to use parliamentary 'reserve' (as in the UK).[4] Nevertheless, it does not mean that the role of the national parliament could not be further strengthened in the provisions of the Rules of Procedure or in the Act on the principles of conduct and relations of both Chambers mutually and in external relations. The possibility to establish a joint body of the two Chambers, which would deal especially with European affairs, has been left open. It could probably be a joint committee for European affairs. It is necessary to note that the existence of such a joint committee in the two chamber systems is relatively rare (Spain and Ireland) and the question remains to whom such a body would be responsible. The general formulation of

[4] Laursen F., Pappas S.A.: 'The Changing Role of Parliaments in the European Union', European Institute of Public Administration, Maastricht 1995.

this provision will allow the Parliament (if there is political will) to exert scrutiny and influence also in the 'virgin territory' under the second and third pillar of the European Union.[5]

4 Preliminary Control (*contrôle préalable*) by the Constitutional Court

As soon as the international agreement becomes part of legislation, the ratification of which has been approved by the Parliament and by which the Czech Republic is bound, there is nothing to prevent its internal application. As the respect of the constitutional rules is an eminent interest of every state, the possibility of conflict between constitutional rules and international agreements should be avoided. Originally the Czech Constitution did not contain any provision regulating the control of constitutionality of the international agreements. The following provision of Article 87 (2) was inserted reading:

'(2) The Constitutional Court also passes decisions on the conformity of an international agreement under Article10a and Article 49 with the constitutional order, such being before ratification thereof. Until such time as the Constitutional Court makes a decision an agreement cannot be ratified.'

In Article 89, paragraph (3) was added, reading:

'(3) A decision of the Constitutional Court whereby, in accordance with Article 87 (2), unconformity of an international agreement with the constitutional order is pronounced, prevents ratification until such time as the unconformity is eliminated.'

By these provisions, the Czech Constitutional Court has gained a new competency of preliminary control of the constitutionality of international agreements. This contrôle préalable of French origin is nowadays successfully applied not only in France but for example also in Germany, Spain, Portugal and Poland.

In accordance with a draft amendment to the Act on the Constitutional Court,[6] only qualified subjects, i.e. the Chamber of the Parliament; a group of at least 41 Deputies or 17 Senators and the President of the Republic may bring a proposal before the Constitutional Court to decide about international agreements' conformity with the constitutional order.

Precedence in application

The autonomy of the Community legal order, the necessity for its uniform interpretation and application in all Member States implies that Community provisions have precedence over national legislation in case of conflict. Since

[5] Craig P., Harlow C., Lawmaking in the European Union, London 1998, p. 209 et seq.

[6] Act No. 182/1993 Coll.

national courts are under obligation to apply Community rules alongside the provisions of national law, it is likely that conflict will result from this simultaneous application. The European Treaties contain no explicit provisions regarding the solution of such cases. Only a few national legal systems provide for conflict rules to solve such conflicts. The amendment to the Czech Constitution not only provides that the provisions of the international agreements have precedence over existing national laws and regulations, it also specifies that every national court, in cases within its jurisdiction, must apply international agreements and must set aside any conflicting provision of national law (whether prior or subsequent to the international agreement provision). The new Article 95 of the Czech Constitution provides that:

> *'Article 95*
> *(1) In his decision-making, a judge is bound by the law and any international agreement constituting part of legal order; he is entitled to assess the conformity of another legal regulation with the law or with such international agreement.*
> *(2) Should a court conclude that the law that is to be applied in the settlement of a matter contravenes the constitutional order, it shall submit the matter to the Constitutional Court.'*

Even if this provision refers to the precedence of the international agreements in general and it is only with difficulty that one can equate Community measures with the latter, this solution is not unique. German Basic Law[7] is even less precise and refers to the precedence of the general rules of international law. The Italian Constitution only provides that: 'Italian legal system conforms to the general principles recognised by international law'.[8]

It is clear that these constitutional texts form a rather meagre basis for the obligation that the national courts should give precedence to Community law over national law in case of conflict between the two. Furthermore, there are the Member States whose Constitutions contain no provisions in this respect. Therefore, I do not find the critique of the euro-amendment of the Czech Constitution according to which it should explicitly provide that the same precedence applies to measures enacted by the institutions set up under international agreements and that the conflict between an existing Community rules and national law should be explicitly mentioned adequate.

It must be stressed that even in the case where the constitutional provision is so explicit (e.g. Dutch Constitution[9]), doubts might subsist as to precise consequences. If the sole legal basis for precedence or supremacy of the Community law over national law were national law itself, this principle would be at the mercy of any next constitutional amendment. The ground is not therefore referenced to the national legal order but the Community legal order itself.[10]

---

7 Art. 25 German Basic Law.

8 Art. 10(1) Italian Constitution.

9 Art. 66 and 67 Dutch Constitution.

10 See Mathijsen P., A Guide to the European Union Law, London 1999, p. 40 et seq.

CHAPTER 14

The Enlargement of the European Monetary Union and its Perspectives in the New Member States

Michal Tomášek

When on May 1st, 2004 ten new Member States[1] joined the European Union, a new question arose as to when these countries would be able to join Stage Three of the EMU and when they would be able to introduce the single currency. When Slovenia joined on stage Three of the EMU on 1 January 2007 and when Bulgaria and Romania joined the EU on the same day, eleven new Member States have a derogation within the meaning of Article 122 of the EC Treaty but no special status as regards Stage Three of the EMU[2]. After 1 January 2007, twelve EU Member States were provided with a derogation according to Article 122 of the EC Treaty, i.e. eleven new Member States and Sweden which was given the status of a Members State with a derogation by a decision of the EU Council of May 1998.

As far as the new Member States are concerned, Article 4 of the Act concerning the conditions of accession provides that 'Each of the new Member States shall participate in Economic and Monetary Union from the date of accession as a Member State with a derogation within the meaning of Article 122 of the EC Treaty'. Thus, the new Member States are committed by the EC Treaty and by their Accession acts to adopt the euro, which implies that they have to strive to fulfil all the convergence criteria.

1 Nominal and Real Convergence Criteria

Legally speaking, a Member State can (and must) join Stage Three of the EMU when it fulfils all the five convergence criteria. However, more and more experts, particularly from the economic areas, are putting in doubt the sustainability of the convergence criteria under the present economic development. They argue that these criteria were elaborated in the early 1990's under a different macroeconomic situation in Europe and that they do not reflect present economic trends. Whatever a reaction on such arguments may be, a pragmatic answer is that the convergence criteria are a part of primary Community law as they are anchored in the EC Treaty. Any modification of such criteria should be subject to the amendment of the EC Treaty under the provisions of Article 48 of the EU Treaty.

Nevertheless, economists agreed that convergence criteria as they are established in the Articles 104 and 121 of the EC Treaty do not sufficiently reflect the real economic situation, in particular, countries with a very divergent economic development from the old Member States, i.e. real economic situation of new Member States. A notion of 'real convergence criteria' was established long ago in order to describe important macroeconomic parameters like economic growth, GDP per capita ration to an EU average or inflation rate. To join Stage

* Prof. JUDr. PhDr. Michal Tomášek, DrSc. Is Professor of European Law at the Charles University in Prague, Member of the Scientific Board of the Czech Banker's Association, Czech Republic.

1 Cyprus, Czech Republic, Estonia, Hungary, Latvia, Lithuania, Malta, Poland, Slovakia and Slovenia.

2 Special status was granted to Denmark and to the United Kingdom.

Three of the EMU, any new Member State would thus be evaluated as well according to 'real convergence criteria', not only according to 'nominal convergence criteria' as provided for by the EC Treaty.

EU enlargement brought about other phenomena not completely new as far as the convergence criteria are concerned. The question is how to apply convergence criteria in different parameters to a Member State. The answer is definitely not simple. Theoretically, any Member State has to strive to fulfil all the five convergence criteria. But an unofficial statistic proves that in the first wave of EMU countries in 1998, the average fulfilment of convergence criteria was 3 : 2[3] and there are even serious doubts concerning the accession of Greece in 2001. It is very likely the European Central Bank and other EU authorities will be quite prudent as far as the new Member Sates are concerned in order particularly not to undermine the already fragile budgetary discipline in the euro area.

2 Price Stability

According to the Article 121 (1) of the EC Treaty, first indent, the achievement of a high degree of price stability is the first and most important monetary criterion for a Member State to join Stage Three of the EMU. This criterion means that a Member State should have a price performance that is sustainable and an average rate of inflation, observed over a period of one year before the examination, that does not exceed by more than 1.5 percentage points that of, at most, the three best performing Member States in terms of price stability[4]. When the euro was introduced in the twelve EU Member States, a discussion started about an interpretation of this criterion. One of the arguments was that the euro area inflation is to be taken as one area. Such an approach would substantially change the logic of this criterion because the wording of the EC Treaty speaks about 'states'. Inflation should be thus calculated on country base regardless to participation in the euro area.

Over the period of one year before October 2006, the reference value was 2.8%. It was calculated by adding 1.5 percentage points to an unweighted arithmetic average of the inflation rate of the three best performing Member States – Finland: 1.2%, Poland 1.2 and Sweden: 1.5%. The following table shows inflation development in new Member States as evaluated in 2006:

[3] For example, Belgium with its internal debt of 122.2% instead of 60% threshold or Italy with its internal debt of 121.6% instead of 60% threshold.

[4] Price stability calculation should be performed in conformity with Council Regulation (EC) No 2494/95 of 23 October 1995 concerning harmonized indices of consumer prices (OJ L 277) in later amendments.

Cyprus	2.3
Czech Republic	2.2
Estonia	4.3
Hungary	3.5
Latvia	6.7
Lithuania	2.7
Malta	3.1
Poland	1.2
Slovakia	4.3

Source: European Central Bank

Over the past two years, the inflation rate has been relatively low in most of the new Member States. From close to 10% in 1997, the weighted average rate of inflation declined to around 2% in 2002, where it remained until early 2004. After the accession to the EU, inflation rose markedly, mainly in response to EU entry-related increases in indirect taxes and administered prices, rapid growth in domestic demand and rising energy prices. In response, central banks in some countries have increased official interest rates in order to counter the growing risk of inflation.

3 Long-term Interest Rates

According to Article 121 (1) of the EC Treaty, fourth indent, the durability of convergence achieved by the Member State and of its participation in the exchange-rate mechanism of the European Monetary System being reflected in the long-term interest-rate levels. This criterion means that, observed over a period of one year before the examination, a Member State has had an average nominal long-term (ten years) interest rate that does not exceed by more than 2 percentage points that of, at most, the three best performing Member States in terms of price stability.

Over the period of one year before October 2006, the reference value was 6.2%. It was calculated by adding 2 percentage points to an unweighted arithmetic average of the long-term interest rates of the same three countries entering the calculation of the reference value for the criterion on price stability – Finland: 3.7%, Poland: 5.2% and Sweden: 3.7%. The following table shows long-term interest rates in new Member States as evaluated in 2006:

Cyprus	4.1
Czech republic	3.8
Estonia	4.3

Hungary	7.1
Latvia	3.9
Lithuania	3.7
Malta	4.3
Poland	5.2
Slovakia	4.3

Source: European Central Bank

During the past three years, long-term interest rates were on a broad downward trend in new Member States. This development reflected mainly low inflationary pressures, market perceptions as regards to the EU and the euro area participation and, for some of the new Member States, with the exception of the Czech Republic and Slovenia, the growing credibility of monetary policy. Long-term interest rates in Poland and in Hungary stay well above the reference value. In Hungary, the increase in long-term interest rates was mainly due to continuing fiscal imbalances. In Poland, long-term interest rates increased in 2003, mainly due to rising inflation and growing fiscal uncertainty.

Long-term interest rates are sometimes presented as an example of the obsolete performance of such a convergence criterion. While in the early 1990's, when this criterion was established, interest rates in general were considerably high and a trend was to reduce them. Nowadays interest rates are low enough to influence a ten year- average in order to allow in a matter of fact everyone to reach the threshold. The table above clearly shows that a large majority of new Member States would not have any problems with the present reference value of 6.2%.

4 Exchange Rates

According to the Article 121 (1) of the EC Treaty, third indent, the observance of the normal fluctuations margins provided for by the exchange-rate mechanism of the European Monetary System, for the last two years, without devaluing against the currency of any Member State. This criterion means firstly, that a Member State has been integrated in the exchange-rate mechanism (ERM), at present ERM II[5], for the last two years. Secondly, that a Member State has respected the normal fluctuation margins provided for by the ERM II without severe tensions for the last two years before examination. In this point, a question occurred recently on the definition of 'normal fluctuation margins'. It is well known that original 'normal fluctuation margins' under ERM I from March 13, 1979 were + 2.25%. After speculative attacks on some ERM I currencies, the Ecofin extended 'normal fluctuation margins' in August

5 Exchange rate mechanism – ERM II replaced the former ERM I, established March 13, 1979, from January 1st 1999.

1993 up to + 15%. Such an extension definitely weakened this criterion and in 1998, preparing the first wave of Stage Three of the EMU, no Member State had a problem fulfilling this criterion. After the ERM II was established on January 1st, 1999, only two Member States with a derogation, Denmark and Greece, joined this mechanism. Denmark opted for a narrow fluctuation margin of + 2.25%. When Greece joined the Stage Three of the EMU on January 1st, 2001, some experts within the ECB argued that the wording 'normal fluctuation margins' in the EC Treaty should be interpreted as a fluctuation margin for Denmark because nobody else was there and thus a fluctuation margin of + 2.25% could have been considered as normal. Such an approach was refused by new Member States even before their accession to the EU. The criterion of exchange rates thirdly means that a Member State has not devaluated its currency's bilateral central rate against any other Member State's currency on its own initiative for the period of the last two years before examination.

Since May 1st, 2004, all new Member States, with the exception of The Czech Republic, Hungary and Poland, were joining the ERM II as follows:

Member state	***ERM II M ERM II participant since***
Estonia	28 June 2004
Cyprus	2nd May 2005
Lithuania	28 June 2004
Latvia	2nd May 2005
Malta	2nd May 2005
Slovakia	28 November 2005
Slovenia	28 June 2004[1]

[1] Until 31st December 2006 before introducing the euro from 1st January 2007

The following table shows exchange rate stability in new Member States outside the ERM II as evaluated in October 2006:

Country	***Maximum downward deviation***	***Maximum upward deviation***
Czech Republic	0.5	10.2
Hungary	14.6	1.4
Poland	0.6	11.2

Source: European Central Bank

The Czech Republic adopted in 1998 an inflation-targeting framework. Since May 1st, the Constitution (Art. 98)[6] and consequently the Act on Czech National

6 Constitutional amendment of 27 November 2001, Constitutional Act no. 448/2001 Collection of Laws of the Czech Republic.

Bank[7] stipulated that the primary objective of the central bank should be to maintain price stability. The inflationtargeting framework had been preceded by a change in the exchange rate policy in May 1997, when the Czech Republic abandoned the fixed peg of its currency and shifted to a (managed) floating exchange rate regime. Inflation targeting has not been very successful so far. An original inflation target was abandoned in spring 2002 and the price index returned to it in May 2004. Monetary policy of the Czech National Bank is considered to be more restrictive than necessary for its inflation targeting.

The monetary policy of Hungary used to be based on the crawling peg regime until 2001 using mini devaluations of the Hungarian forint. In July 2001, the Hungarian central bank adopted a new monetary regime using the euro as a benchmark with a unilateral central rate established by the Hungarian National Bank. A standard fluctuation band of + 15% is observed around this unilateral central rate. Furthermore, the monetary policy of Hungary adopted in 2001 an inflation-targeting framework. The inflation targets for 2001, 2002 and 2003 were not maintained. In order to maintain the unilateral fluctuation band, the Hungarian Central Bank devaluated the forint by 2.26%. Other devaluations are likely in its unilateral system before joining the ERM II. Hungarians could very probably follow the policy of Greece. Greek central bank devaluated the drachma in 1998 and then revaluated it in 2000 in order to join the euro in 2001.

Until 1998, the monetary policy of Poland was based on the crawling peg regime combined with inflation-targeting. Because it was difficult to achieve both monetary goals, Poland adopted a system of floating in 2001. A slow-down of the Polish economy at the end of the 1990's led to a reduction of interest rates, which was a trend until the summer of 2004. Inflation-targeting was relatively successful; nevertheless, some analysts consider the Polish Central Bank monetary policy to be quite restrictive. The exchange rate of the Polish zloty against the euro has shown a high degree of volatility with maximum downward deviation of 20.9% exceeding a standard fluctuation band of more than 5%. Before joining the ERM II, the Polish National Bank is likely to adopt a floating regime.

Assuming from the above description of monetary policies of individual new Member States outside the ERM II, it is clear that there is not a unique approach to reach the goals of exchange rate stability under the ERM II. The three new Member States outside the ERM II have chosen a floating regime with some specific features like inflation-targeting in the Czech Republic or Poland or inflation-targeting combined with slight devaluations in Hungary.

---

7 Act on Czech National Bank no. 442/2000 Collection of Laws of the Czech Republic.

5 Public Deficit

According to the Article 104 (2) of the EC Treaty, the Member State does not fulfil the requirements for fiscal discipline in order to join Stage Three of the EMU if the ratio of the planned or actual public deficit to GDP exceeds a reference value of 3% (unless either the ratio has declined substantially and continuously and reached a level that comes close to the reference value or (alternatively) the excess over the reference value is only exceptional and temporary and the ratio remains close to the reference value).

The following table shows public deficit in new Member States as evaluated for 2006:

Cyprus	- 1.9
Czech Republic	- 3.5
Estonia	+ 2.5
Hungary	- 10.1
Latvia	- 1.0
Lithuania	- 0.6
Malta	- 2.9
Poland	- 2.2
Slovakia	- 3.4

Source: European Central Bank

With regard to the budgetary performance of the ten new Member States, one country – Estonia, recorded a financial surplus and other countries with a derogation recorded fiscal deficits. Of these eight new Member States, five – Cyprus, Latvia, Lithuania, Malta and Poland – meet the reference value according to Article 104 of the EC Treaty. Three countries – the Czech Republic, Hungary and Slovakia recorded deficits above 3% and are in an excessive deficit situation. Because Article 104 of the EC Treaty is designed for a declining trend of deficits, one can assume a declining trend in Slovakia. The question remains whether such a decline can be interpreted as 'substantial and reaching the level comes close to the reference value' in light of Article 104 of the EC Treaty. The Czech Republic and Hungary have recorded an increasing trend as compared with the preceding period.

6 Public Debt

According to Article 104 (2) of the EC Treaty, the Member State does not fulfil the requirements for fiscal discipline in order to joint Stage Three of the EMU if the ratio of gross public debt to GDP exceeds over the reference value of 60%, unless the ratio is sufficiently diminishing and approaching the reference value at a satisfactory pace.

The following table shows gross public debt in new Member States as evaluated for 2004:

Cyprus	64.6
Czech Republic	30.9
Estonia	4.0
Hungary	67.6
Latvia	11.1
Lithuania	18.9
Malta	69.6
Poland	42.4
Slovakia	33.0

Source: European Central Bank

As regards to public debt, three new Member States exhibited debt ratios above 60% of GDP: Cyprus, Hungary and Malta. Other new Member Sates have their debt ratios below the reference value. However, with regard to the provisions of Article 104, not only the reference value of 60% but a declining trend as well should be taken into consideration. Looking back at the period from 1996 to 2003, debt levels increased substantially in most of the new Member States. The highest increases in the debt ratio were recorded in Malta (increase of 31 percentage points), in the Czech Republic (increase of 25 percentage points) and in Slovakia (increase of 12 percentage points). The major reasons for the rise in debt ratios were largely to primary deficits and substantial deficit-debt adjustments. In Latvia, Lithuania and Slovakia the debt ratio appears to have stabilised. In Estonia, the debt ratio is projected to decline slightly. In the Czech Republic, it is forecast to increase but remain below the 60% reference value. In Cyprus and Malta, where the debt already exceeds the 60% reference value, it is expected to rise further.

Further substantial consolidation is thus required in most of new Member States in order to achieve lasting compliance with the fiscal criteria as required by the EC Treaty and by the Stability and Growth Pact[8]. There is a strong case for the consolidation of deficits particularly in the Czech Republic, Cyprus, Hungary, Malta or Poland, where primary deficit ratios would result in debt ratios rising above 60% reference value.

8 Council Regulation (EC) No 1466/97 of 7 July 1997 on the strengthening of the surveillance of budgetary positions and the surveillance and coordination of economic policies and Council Regulation (EC) No 1467/97 of 7 July 1997 on speeding up and clarifying the implementation of the excessive deficit procedure.

After an evaluation of the above-described convergence criteria and of their performance by individual new Member States, one can approach to and answer the question of how many new Member States can join Stage Three of the EMU. By the end of 2004, the performance of the five criteria can be shown as follows:

Country	***Inflation***	***Interest rates***	***Exch. rates***	***Public deficit***	***Public debt***
Cyprus	Yes	Yes	Yes	Yes	No
Czech Rep.	Yes	Yes	No	No	Yes
Estonia	Yes	Yes	Yes	Yes	Yes
Hungary	No	No	No	No	No
Latvia	No	Yes	Yes	Yes	Yes
Lithuania	Yes	Yes	Yes	Yes	Yes
Malta	No	Yes	Yes	Yes	No
Poland	Yes	Yes	No	Yes	Yes
Slovakia	No	Yes	Yes	No	Yes

The table above should obviously be taken with a reserve. Some data is relative, like public debt which is about to increase in some new Member States. A compliance with exchange rate criterion requires a formal participation in the ERM II met only by Estonia and Lithuania.

7 Real Economic Criteria

Assuming from the above shown data, for example, Lithuania could become an EMU participant very easily and very soon. However, things do not work that simple. Coming back to previous pages of this article, it should be repeated that not only nominal convergence criteria but real convergence criteria as well are to be met by any new Member State in order to join Stage Three of the EMU. As mentioned above, several real convergence criteria in economic terms can be applied but this is more a matter of an economic analysis than of a legal paper. Nevertheless, GDP per capita in purchasing power can be considered as a most important real convergence criteria. It is an indicator of a country's total production and expenditure and is therefore a way of measuring and comparing the degree of economic development of any country. The purchasing power standard reflects differences in national price levels that are not taken into account by exchange prices. The following table shows GDP per capita in new Member States in purchasing power as a percentage of EU average for 2006.

Cyprus	91%
Czech Republic	75%
Estonia	55%
Hungary	64%
Latvia	46%
Lithuania	51%
Malta	75%
Poland	51%
Slovakia	57%

Source: Eurostat

Regardless of a relatively good performance of nominal convergence criteria, it is very difficult to imagine an integration of any EU new Member State into Stage Three of the EU when such a country degree of economic convergence measured by GDP per capita is extremely low. Coming back to the case of Lithuania, performing all the convergence criteria in terms of the EC Treaty, it is unlikely this country could be absorbed by the EMU when its GDP per capita does not reach close to the EU average. It would be definitely harmful for any national economy to adopt the euro when purchasing price levels and GDP per capita product stay far below the level of euro area countries. A question can rise to what extent is the level of GDP per capita sustainable to absorb the euro in any new Member State. A threshold for sustainability for a new Member State to join the Stage Three of the EMU lays somewhere at 75% of the EU average. There is the precedent of Portugal which joining -- Stage Three of the EMU in 1998 with its GDP per capita of 75% of the EU average or of Greece joining -- Stage Three of the EMU in 2001 with its GDP per capita of 74%. Furthermore the EU funds are at present not in a condition to equilibrate any difference in GDP per capita below a threshold of 75% of the EU average. At present only three Member States, Cyprus, the Czech Republic and Malta could possibly join Stage Three of the EMU at least in terms of GDP per capita. But Cyprus and Malta do not fulfil some of nominal convergence criteria. The enlargement in 2004 of ten new Member States included into the statistics at least seven or eight Member States with a very low GDP per capita, which led to a decline of the EU average. If there is an average of the EU 15 old Member States, the reference figure would be even higher and the values for new Member Sates less favourable. The enlargement of the EU in 2007 with Bulgaria and Romania with their GDP per capita of 30% of the EU 25 Member States average reduced the average of EU 27 Member States for 2007, which will make real convergence criteria of GDP per capita even weaker.

8 Conclusions

The accession of the then new countries to the EU was an important milestone in a process that will lead to the future adoption of the euro by these new Member States. The euro will go east and south and the road to the adoption of the euro is embedded in a well- defined institutional framework. How far are the new Member States on this road towards the euro? The countries that joined the EU in 2004 have shown impressive economic growth rates and have made great strides in reducing inflation. They belong to the most dynamic economies in the EU, having gone through profound structural changes, For example, they have taken thorough measures to reform their product and labour markets, and some new Member States, in some respects, may be even more advanced than other, old EU countries. They have become more integrated with the euro area, with the major part of their trade now occurring with the euro area and tight financial links: as a matter of fact, the share of the new ten Member States in the total external trade of the euro area stands around 11%, compared with around 14% for the United States and 3% for Japan. In addition, the transition process has brought their economic structures closer to those of the euro area. At the same time, while remaining a diverse group in many respects, the new Member States still display distinct economic characteristics that differ from the euro area. Their income-per-capita and productivity levels are still low relative to the euro area, which may have an impact on their inflation rates.

The new Member States are confronted on the road to the euro with two particularly important economic challenges: price stability and fiscal policy. Price stability is an essential requirement for the successful monetary integration process. Inflation rates in many new Member States have picked up recently to an average of almost 5%, following increases in food and energy prices and indirect tax changes. The challenge for the new Member States is to contain inflation and inflation expectations in an environment of rapid catching-up. Besides solid macroeconomic policy frameworks and prudent wage policies, progress in structural reforms is conductive to price stability by improving the supply side of the economy and enhancing the growth potential. The second challenge is the need to achieve sound fiscal positions. Fiscal deficits are on average high or even very high in a number of new Member States and mostly despite very high economic growth. The governments are confronted with competing expenditure demands, including public investment in infrastructure and the need to strengthen the effectiveness of public administration and the judicial systems. This, however, should not be seen as an excuse for delaying fiscal consolidations, but as an additional reason to design and implement a credible consolidation path based on durable and growth-enhancing structural reforms. It is important to bear in mind that fiscal consolidation in the new Member States becomes increasingly important in the course of the monetary integration process, and it is essential for the smooth participation in the ERM II and the eventual adoption of the euro.

CHAPTER 15

Aspects of the New Neighbourhood Policy of the EU

Kateryna Karpova

The external relations policy of the EU, a wide-spread range of activities with third countries, gained a new dimension when the EU was enlarged in 2004 and new frontiers appeared between the EU and non-Member States. It seemed to be of high importance to have specific, intensified relations with the neighbouring countries. The most important challenges were to regulate the interrelations between the EU and its new neighbours and to intensify cooperation in the fields of common interest with the eastern neighbours.[1] In 2003, the Commission defined the concept of a European Neighbourhood Policy (ENP) in its basic document *'Wider Europe – Neighbourhood: A New Framework for Relations with our Eastern and Southern Neighbours'*,[2] filling in the details in the *Strategy Paper on the ENP* (2004)[3] and in *the Regulation of the European Parliament and of the Council* (2006) (known as *Financial Instrument*)[4]. Bilateral *Action Plans* for most of the neighbouring countries describe the concrete objectives and instruments which will be applied.

I Definition and the Aims of the ENP

The ENP is destined for 16 countries, which are in a 'neighbourhood relation' with the EU: geographic proximity and potential threats resulting from instability in these countries are also dangerous for the EU. The geographical dimension means 'immediate neighbourhood either by land or by sea'[5].[6] Stability and security are closely linked to one another. Therefore, countries which are strategically of particular interest to the EU have been included in the category of neighbouring countries.[7] This is likely to be the reason why Azerbaijan and Armenia belong to this group, although they have no immediate land or maritime border with the EU. A general definition of the ENP as such is the sum of the policies aiming to promote the countries mentioned, helping them to achieve their own stability.

Four important aims are characteristic of the ENP:

1) the aim of transformation: promoting the rule of law-based political systems;

* Kateryna Karpova, M.A., Dipl. Jurist, M.A. (Kiev), M.A. (Erfurt), Ph.D. Candidate at the University of Regensburg, Germany.

1 Deutsche-Aussenpolitik. Foreign Policy in Dialogue, Vol. 7 – Issue 19, p. 7, http://www.deutsche-aussenpolitik.de.

2 COM(2003) 104 final.

3 COM(2004) 373 final.

4 Regulation (EC) No 1638/2006 of the European Parliament and of the Council of 24 October 2006, OJ of 9 November 2006 L 310/1.

5 European Commission, European Neighbourhood Policy, The Policy: What is the European Neighbourhood Policy?, http://ec.europa.eu/world/enp/policy_en.htm.

6 COM(2003) 104 final, p. 3.

7 The strategic aspect has been underlined for the 'South Caucasus engagement' of the EU by the Communication from the Commission to the Council on ENP of 2005 (COM(2005) 72 final, p. 2).

2) the aim of development: promoting economic, social and cultural welfare;
3) the aim of guaranteeing peace: resolving regional conflicts by peaceful means;
4) the aim of integration: intensifying relations between the EU and the neighbouring countries.

II Aims More in Detail

1) *The aim of transformation* means to assure a political-legal system in the neighbour country based on democracy and the rule of law. These principles are fundamental values shared by the EU and Member States, values which are important factors of legal and political stability and therefore indispensable for neighbour countries as parties of the EU.

The rule of law is closely connected with the protection of the fundamental rights of the individual. Liberty, human dignity and fundamental rights are the ideological basis of a democratic regime. Transformation is mainly concentrated on the realization of these values. It is evident that political transformation necessarily includes economic transformation, both expressions of liberty. Furthering the transformation to a free market economy is therefore an essential part of the neighbourhood policy.

It is consequent that neighbour relations are not fully realizable within authoritarian systems such as that of Belarus. Furthering the democratization process in this country is an aim of EU policy, in particular by supporting civil society,[8] while full contractual links could only be established after democracy has been completely established on the basis of free and fair elections.[9]

2) *The aim of economic, social and cultural development* consists of a large spectrum of measures. It is essential to reach enhanced preferential trade relations.[10] The establishment of Free Trade Areas with neighbouring countries is the first priority. Beyond that, cooperation in many other fields such as energy,[11] transport, environment, research and technology are envisaged.[12] Cooperation in the energy sector is of the highest importance given the fact that the EU is the largest oil and gas importer in the world, while neighbouring countries such as Russia, Azerbaijan, Algeria, and Libya are rich in natural resources.[13]

---

8 See Wolfgang Benedek, Civil Society and Good Governance in Societies in Transition, 2006.

9 COM(2004) 373 final, p. 4.

10 COM(2004) 373 final, p. 14.

11 See the Green Paper of the EU Commission of 8 March 2006 'A European Strategy for Sustainable, Competitive Secure Energy' (COM (2006) 105 final).

12 COM(2004) 373 final, p. 17-19.

13 See Steve Wood, The European Union and its Neighbourhood: Interests, Values and Public Opinion, Osteuropa Institut München, 2006, http://www.oei-muenchen.de/ext_dateien/eu_und_neighbourhood_wodrev3.ppt#7.

The new enhanced agreement, which is about to be negotiated with the Ukraine, will introduce such a Free Trade Area.[14] For this, the further removal of import and export restrictions is necessary, as already initiated by the existing Partnership and Cooperation Agreement.[15] Restrictions on services should also be eliminated. Furthermore, the investment climate and the environment for companies must be ameliorated.[16] Law approximation to EU concepts in fields such as company and competition law will facilitate the links to the EU internal market. Membership in the WTO, politically supported by other EU countries, will be possible when the WTO conditions are fulfilled.[17] Developments in numerous other fields such as energy, transport, competition policy and intellectual and industrial property rights are also important as complementary to economic advance.[18]

The European Neighbourhood Policy has great potential to tackle both economic and social challenges in the neighbour countries. Economic and social issues interact with each other. Improvement in the social sphere necessitates work on economic development, employment and social policy as such. Aspects such as reducing poverty, assuring employment, improving the effectiveness of social assistance and national welfare systems play a crucial role for the evolution of a self-sufficient society.[19]

Cultural and educational aspects are essential in neighbourhood relations: enhancing the interconnection between the EU and its neighbours also means promoting mutual understanding of each other's culture and values.[20] Therefore, it is necessary to encourage the mobility of students and teachers within the existing EU educational programmes such as Tempus and Erasmus Mundus.[21]

3) Stability largely depends on the absence of regional conflicts in the neighbourhood area. The ENP must contribute to *the prevention of conflicts as well as to their resolution* if they break out. Until now, the EU's role in conflict resolution has been rather modest.[22] Conflict resolution is more efficient with collective

---

[14] See EUROPA, Press Room, Press Releases, EU-Ukraine start negotiations on new Enhanced Agreement, 2 March 2007, http://www.europa.eu/rapid/pressReleasesAction.do?reference=IP/07/275&format=HTML&aged =0&language=EN&guiLanguage=en.

[15] Title III of Partnership and Cooperation Agreement (PCA) with the Ukraine, 1998; see also Action Plan 2005, Ukraine, 2.3.

[16] COM(2004) 373 final, p. 16.

[17] Europa, Press Releases, http://europa.eu/rapid/pressReleasesAction.do?reference=IP/06/1184&format =HTML&aged=0&language=EN&guiLanguage=en.

[18] See Action Plan 2005, Ukraine, 2.2.; 2.3.5.; 2.5.

[19] COM(2004) 373 final, p. 14.

[20] COM(2004) 373 final, p. 19.

[21] COM(2004) 373 final, p. 20.

[22] COM(2006) 726 final, p. 4.

efforts. In order to avoid conflicts, regional cooperation is very helpful. Existing regional cooperation on the EU's eastern borders as well as in the Mediterranean area shall be further developed into a good relationship with the EU. This can intensify the capacity to avoid conflicts. The ENP also has to enable the countries involved to face better the key threats of today: terrorism, proliferation of weapons of mass destruction and organised crime.[23]

4) *The ENP's aim of integration* is to intensify the dialogue with the EU in all fields covered by the bilateral agreements as well as by the *Action Plans*. Approximation of laws to EU concepts is foreseen by the agreements not as a strict obligation but as a legally binding promise to endeavour to achieve this. This is a basis for strengthening cooperation with the EU in the area of the economy and the numerous other fields of common interest. While entry to the EU is not linked to neighbourhood relations, close cooperation within the ENP can lead to EU membership. The ENP should also respect the regional cooperation existing before the entry of Central and Eastern Europe countries into the EU. The ENP should find appropriate means to uphold these former links and integrate them, in an adequate way, to further EU-neighbour relations.

III Geographic Extension

The ENP is applicable to the following countries: Algeria, Armenia, Azerbaijan, Belarus, Egypt, Georgia, Israel, Jordan, Lebanon, Libya, Moldova, Morocco, the Palestinian Authority, Syria, Tunisia and Ukraine.[24] There is a specific relationship with the Russian Federation by way of the four common spaces referred to by a *Strategic Partnership*.[25] These spaces are: a common European economic space, a common space of freedom, security, and justice, a common space for research and education and a common space of external security. Within these spaces, cooperation is intensified and liberalisation will be increasingly realized.[26]

That many Mediterranean countries are included into the ENP is the result of the specific EU Mediterranean Partnership Program (Barcelona process).[27] It

---

23 European Security Strategy, A secure Europe in a better world, Brussels, 12.12.2003, p. 3-5, http://www.consilium.europa.eu/cms3_fo/showPage.ASP?id=266&lang=EN&mode=g.

24 See European Commission, EU in the World, European Neighbourhood Policy, Partners, http://ec.europa.eu/world/enp/partners/index_en.htm.

25 Officially agreed at the May 2003 EU – Russia Summit; see Russia's Strategic Partnership with Europe, http://www.twq.com/04spring/docs/04spring_lynch.pdf.

26 Communication from the Commission to the Council and the European Parliament on relations with Russia, COM(2004) 106, 09/02/04, 1. Introduction.

27 See European Commission, European Union in the World, External Relations, Euro-Mediterranean Partnership/Barcelona Process, http://ec.europa.eu/external_relations/euromed/index.htm.

should be noted that a series of South-Eastern Europe countries are not defined as neighbour states but are covered by the South-Eastern Europe stabilisation and association process: Bosnia and Herzegovina, Croatia, the Former Yugoslav Republic of Macedonia, Albania, Montenegro and Serbia, including Kosovo.[28]

IV Instruments of the ENP

The main instruments to be used for the realisation of the ENP are:

1) contractual means;
2) EC-related instruments which are known from the internal EC order, such as regulations, and
3) soft law.

1) *Contractual means*: the classic instrument to regulate matters between subjects of public international law is a treaty, characterized by legal equality of the partners. This is an instrument of coordination.

The ENP uses the bilateral treaty[29] as a basic instrument. The treaty obligations constitute legally binding relations with reciprocal obligations. The Partnership and Cooperation Agreements are such treaties.[30] They give stability for the time period in which the treaty is in force. After the expiration of the treaty, a new agreement must be made to prolong the obligations. For that purpose, this instrument is not flexible enough to adapt to all the changes and new challenges, which might appear in a period of 10 years for example in relation to the Partnership and Cooperation Agreement Ukraine-EU. The treaty remains in force even after its expiration, to be extended each year for a further year if negotiations on a new agreement fail. Thus, continuity is assured.

The contents of the treaty cannot be modified without a revision of the treaty. Adaptations are possible to a certain extent through the institutions established by the treaty: in particular, the Co-operation Council, the Parliamentary Co-operation Committee and other corresponding committees foreseen by the treaty. The treaty obligations are often formulated in general terms, which leave space for discretionary decisions developing the objectives of the treaty further. Within the treaty, there are usually dispute resolution mechanisms and mechanisms for interpretation. A complete change of the treaty is only possi-

28 See EUROPA, Summaries of legislation, The stabilisation and association process, http://europa.eu/scadplus/leg/en/lvb/r18003.htm.

29 This includes treaties with one neighbour state on the one side and the EC with all Member States on the other side.

30 The Association Treaties concluded in the context of the Mediterranean Partnership (Barcelona Process) as well as the corresponding agreements in the South-East Europe Program are to be qualified in the same way.

ble through a new treaty or a reform treaty, which replaces the old mechanism either totally or only in part.

2) Another type of instrument in this context is *the legal acts of EC law*. For example, in October 2006, a European Community regulation on general provisions establishing a European Neighbourhood and Partnership Instrument was adopted.[31]

It is evident that such European Community instruments are not applicable to third states. They do not create extra-territorial effects. They establish internal EU mechanisms, which can be used by the EU institutions for regulating relations with neighbour countries. The binding effect covers the EU institutions' action, attributing them specific competences to use with effect to third countries. These effects are the application of assistance with grants of financial subsidies or political support. Obtaining these benefits depends on the fulfilment of certain conditions. There is an element of reciprocity in this relationship.

The regulation as a normative act of the European Community deploys its binding force only within the Community legal order, addressed to the supranational institutions and authorising them to contact third state subjects, not in order to unilaterally impose obligations on them, but to make proposals for support. They are free to accept them in order to obtain financial and other benefits. Thus, the regulation creates and provides the details of how the instrument is to be used in relation to third states with regard to voluntary action.

Going back to the specific content of the European Neighbourhood Policy Instrument, the following must be outlined. Assistance to neighbour countries is a core of the ENP. For a more efficient policy in this respect, it seems useful to establish a single instrument replacing a number of existing instruments and thus ensure coherence, simplifying programming and management of the assistance.[32] This instrument shall be used for the 'development of an area of property and good neighbourliness'.[33] The range of application shall cover the EU as well the countries listed in the Annex of the Regulation (in Eastern Europe: Belarus, Moldova, the Russian Federation and Ukraine).

This assistance shall promote cross-border and trans-regional cooperation as well as enhanced cooperation and progressive economic integration between the EU and partner countries.[34] In particular, fulfilment of the treaty obligations resulting from Partnership and Cooperation Agreements, association and other agreements shall be furthered, as will the efforts of these countries to attain good governance and appropriate social and economic development.[35]

---

[31] Regulation (EC) No 1638/2006 (note 4).

[32] Regulation (EC) No 1638/2006, L 310/2 (16).

[33] Regulation (EC) No 1638/2006, Art. 1.

[34] Regulation (EC) No 1638/2006, Art. 1.2, Art. 2 and 6.

[35] Regulation (EC) No 1638/2006, Art. 2.1; see also the detailed list of nearly 30 types of measures to be applied in the framework of the assistance through the European Neighbourhood Policy Instrument in Art. 2.2 of the Regulation.

The principals relevant for the use of the assistance instrument are complementarily, partnership and co-financing. This means that assistance shall be complementary to projects of the partner country, which are about to be implemented on a national, regional or local level.[36] The principle of partnership means close cooperation between the EU Commission and the beneficiaries. Partnership in this context is an open concept, which includes public authorities, economic and social partners, civil society and other bodies.[37] Co-financing means that the assistance, in principle, shall not be the only financial source of help, but a mere support to the beneficiary who shall mainly use public funds or its own finances.[38]

The object of financing shall be *compatible* with Community policies and values and *coherent* with other financial aid from the Community, the European Investment Bank[39] or EU Member States. Furthermore, *coordination* is close cooperation with Community institutions in order to strengthen the operational effectiveness of the assistance and to harmonise it with the existing policies and procedures of the Community.[40]

Of particular importance in this context is cross-border cooperation, which shall be carried out by multi-annual programmes. Programming is essential in this context and therefore defined in a very detailed manner in Art. 9 of the Regulation. Management, in particular in joint forms ('shared management'), with the cooperation of joint managing authorities[41], is also important.

To summarise, it can be said that the Regulation on the European Neighbourhood Policy Instrument is a technically well-structured instrument, which is able to further efficiency of assistance and to promote the substantive aims of ENP.

3) A third type of instrument is *soft law,* which is of non-normative character: the large majority of legal and political documents have no binding force but give recommendations, make proposals, announce benefits under certain conditions regarding behaviour and so on.[42] These *soft law* relations are often more efficient than strict legal rules, which do not possess enough flexibility. Flexibility is necessary for the modalities of action and *soft law* is neither formalized nor strictly bound to rules of a determined content. Furthermore, the subtlety of such actions allows rapid adaptation to unforeseen changes of the political and factual situation. *Soft law* is able to generate guiding effects, which can be even

36 Regulation (EC) No 1638/2006, Art. 4.1.

37 Regulation (EC) No 1638/2006, Art. 4.2.

38 Regulation (EC) No 1638/2006, Art. 4.4.

39 See the Activity Report 2006 of the EIB http://www.eib.org/publications/annual-report-2006.htm?

40 Regulation (EC) No 1638/2006, Art. 5.1-4.

41 Regulation (EC) No 1638/2006, Art. 10.

42 See Matthias Herdegen, Internationales Wirtschaftsrecht, 5th ed., 2005, §2/ 9.

more efficient than normative acts. *Soft law* can be repealed easier and substituted by different methods than normative acts.

The *Action Plans* are examples of *soft law* with the effect of providing efficient guidance. Without normative force, they strongly influence the third state's behaviour: they are based on the idea of reciprocity. Fulfilling a certain task paves the way for financing or co-financing projects. The financial incentive is of great effect and can go beyond the observance of legal rules. The *Action Plans*, examples of highly influential *soft law*, play a crucial role in developing the relationship between the EU and its neighbourhood. Today there are twelve ENP *Action Plans* with EU neighbours.[43] Both the EU and its neighbours have mutual interests and engagements. The goals of an *Action Plan* are the same for each neighbour country but measures to be taken are different, corresponding to the particular political, economical, social and other situations in each country.

The *Action Plan* covers a time period of 3 to 5 years. If the *Action Plan* is completed, the EU is ready to conclude a *Neighbourhood Treaty* (as it has been called by the *Strategy Paper*[44]). It seems possible for example to qualify the next coming agreement between the EU and Ukraine with enhanced cooperation as such a *Neighbourhood Treaty*.

V Principles of the ENP

There are various principles characteristic of the ENP:

1) A principle of *common interest* can be found in the fact that EU actions concerning neighbour countries have the finality to support the neighbour country and to contribute to its political, legal and economic development. The development of this country is in the interest of both parties: to help the country as well as to ensure strategic security within the region. A well-developed neighbour is more stable, a better trade partner, without political tensions which could have negative cross-border effects, and is more prepared to establish cross-border cooperation, perhaps even more prepared to create an integrated area with the neighbour.

The neighbourhood concept connects the neighbours with their own interests. The situation of one neighbour often affects the other neighbours, so that they necessarily have a common interest in the shared impact a critical situation can have on them.

2) The second principle is that of *'coherence and efficiency'*.[45] Specific aspects of this principle are:

---

43 See European Commission, EU in the World, European Neighbourhood Policy – Reference documents, http://ec.europa.eu/world/enp/documents_en.htm#5.

44 Strategy Paper, COM (2004) 373 final, p. 5.

45 COM (2004) 373 final, p. 6.

a) substantive coherence;
b) functional coherence (synergy) and
c) functional complementarity.

a) *Substantive coherence* means that the content of policies within the EU and also towards third countries as partners have the same orientation and are based on the same values. There are strong affinities in EU and third state activities.

b) On the *functional* level, *coherence* means that one activity is able to promote two or more objectives. Thus, this principle requires the choice of the type of action that can promote both EU goals and the goals of the neighbour countries.

c) Furthermore, efforts should be made under the principle of *functional complementarity*, to coordinate activities on the Community side and on the neighbour country's side, which could lead to the intended result where both activities are combined. Complementarity would also mean that the EU carries out its own task by way of the participation of the neighbour country. Cross-border cooperation between the EU and neighbour countries could be a model for such 'combined' activity.

3) A principle of *'joint ownership'*[46] intends to express a shared inner concern to realise a common task, in awareness of common values and substantive priorities, voluntarily pre-determined by an agreement between the EU and its partners.[47]

Reciprocity is, to a certain extent, inherent in 'joint ownership'. The degree of commitment to common tasks and common values corresponds to the desire of the neighbour countries to integrate with the EU.

4) A forth principle is that of *state promotion*: the modernisation of the neighbour state is a fundamental objective which includes political transformation in particular, the deepening of democracy, the implementation of the rule of law[48], the full establishment of the free market system and an increase of economic power.

5) A fifth principle is that of *value promotion*: values are the ideological basis of state and society. Good governance needs a stable standard of values rooted in the society. These values are common to the EU and Member States but also have to be expanded to include third states; the neighbour countries. Promoting

---

46 COM (2004) 373 final, p. 8.

47 Ibid.

48 See Rainer Arnold, Le principe de l'État de droit dans les nouvelles Constitutions de l' Europe centrale et orientale, in: Protection des droits de l'homme: la perspective européenne. Mélanges à la mémoire de Rolv Ryssdal, édité par Paul Mahoney, Franz Matscher, Herbert Petzold, Luzius Wildhaber, 2000, p. 65-78.

these values is a characteristic feature of the ENP. This is not a unilateral value transfer against the will of the third state, but a voluntary process of acceptance of values, which is based on the recognition of their importance for the individual. Good governance necessarily comprises an anthropocentric dimension,[49] which can only be reached by reference to values.

As has already been pointed out, the principle of state promotion refers essentially to democracy and the rule of law, institutional values connected not only to the state, but also to the individual. Democracy means political self-determination of the individual and therefore has an important fundamental rights dimension. The rule of law is also destined to ensure the position of the individual in relation to the public order and thus to assure his/her liberty. Institutional values form part both of the state values and the individual's values.

6) The ENP is also characterized by the principle of *differentiation*. This policy is common for 16 neighbour countries[50] with clearly diverging geographical location, political conditions, standards of economic development, degrees of reform implementation and with varying relations with the EU and other neighbour countries.[51] Therefore, the *Action Plans* are differentiated and adapted to each partner's situation.[52] The principle of *differentiation* is complemented by a principle of *uniformity* in the basic structures of the ENP. This means that the ENP is and must be a coherent policy with common basic orientations and goals. Thus, uniformity and differentiation must be adequately combined.

7) The principle of *added value* means that the ENP must be used in such a way that clear advantages, which can be gradually increased,[53] can be expected. An intensified degree of integration will be linked to the degree of correspondence with EU intentions.[54] Agreed priorities are the orientation lines for the neighbour country in this context. The ENP offers, with its objectives and instruments, an efficient system for such gradual deepening of integration into the EU, even without the prospect of membership.

8) The principle of *monitoring* means that monitoring bodies, often composed of the EU, Member States and representatives of the neighbour country, will control all steps taken by neighbour countries in fulfilling the relevant commitment. Monitoring is the basis for advancing the links between the EU and the partner country.

---

49 See Kateryna Karpova, Comparative Aspects of Fundamental Rights in Germany and Eastern Europe: the example of Ukraine, University of Örebro, International Conference on: New Dynamics in Comparative Law, 23-24 May 2007, publ. in preparation.

50 See above sub 5.

51 COM (2004) 373 final, p. 8.

52 Ibid.

53 Ibid.

54 Ibid.

VI Evaluation

Experience of the ENP has been limited. An initial overall assessment was delivered by the EC Commission in December 2006,[55] drawing some general conclusions and evaluating the implementation of *Action Plans* in seven of the 16 neighbour countries.

A good number of countries involved are in the process of transformation; for them the relevant *Action Plan* is an anchor point (for example in Morocco) or a central point of reference (as for Moldova). This means that the ENP is a dynamic vehicle of modernisation, which includes the acceptance of modern legal and political maxims, such as democracy, the rule of law and fundamental rights.

The ENP refers to a great variety of states, geographically near and distant, with diverging political, economic, social and cultural situations. *Action Plans* therefore must be clearly differentiated. Despite this differentiation, basic concepts and 'overall trends'[56] are common, which shows a positive tendency: the wish to cooperate intensively, to meet freely agreed conditions for deepening policies and to complete transformation.

It is encouraging that political dialogue and cooperation with ENP countries as such has increased significantly. In part, considerable progress has been made in realizing the rule of law and justice reform. Specific border problems, such as the Transnistria question are about to be resolved.[57] Although huge problems remain there, in areas of political tensions such as Israel and Palestine, the ENP gives support to resolving peace-threatening problems.[58] Reform and institution building are promoted by the ENP in Palestine, which lays the groundwork for the construction of an independent state. Economic progress has been promoted by the ENP, which helped and helps to transform the former system into an efficient free market and to increase the economic potential of the partner countries. Human rights are also a highly important issue for the ENP; progress in this field has been made but significant deficits in certain countries must be admitted[59].[60] Financial assistance in the framework of the

---

[55] SEC(2006) 1504/2, Overall Assessment (COM(2006) 726 final).

[56] SEC(2006) 1504/2, p. 2.

[57] See EUROPEAN PARLIAMENT, MEPs denounce and fully reject Transnistria referendum on independence / South Ossetia – MEPs call for a peaceful resolution to the conflict, 26.10.2006, http://www.europarl.europa.eu/news/expert/infopress_page/030-11950-293-10-42-903-20061020IPR11906-20-10-2006-2006-false/default_en.htm; also see Joint Motion for a Resolution, 25.10 2006, http://www.europarl.europa.eu/sides/getDoc.do?type=MOTION&language=EN&reference=P6-RC-2006-0539

[58] European Commission, European Union in the World, External Relations, The Middle East Peace Process, http://ec.europa.eu/external_relations/mepp/index.htm#1.

[59] See Rainer Arnold / Kateryna Karpova, The ENP and the Promotion of the Rule of Law in Neighbouring Countries: the Case of Ukraine, in: The European Neighbourhood Policy: A Framework for Modernisation?, European University Institute, http://www.eui.eu/LAW/Events/ENP/Presentations.shtml

[60] SEC(2006) 1504/2, p. 4-5.

ENP is 'policy – driven', that means it supports the reform process in these countries. It is evident that financial funding alone will not 'buy the reform'.[61]

As a summary, it can be said that the first overall assessment can be described as broadly positive; considerable progress has been made through the ENP but this policy aims for mid or even long-term success. As for the Ukraine, the negotiations for a new Enhanced Agreement have begun, which will establish a Free Trade Area with the EU.

On the basis of the first period's success and the acceptance of its methods of functioning by the countries concerned, it seems that the ENP will be successful in the future as well and live up to its full potential. The application of the ENP, especially the impact of the New Enhanced Agreements, as in negotiation with Ukraine, make ENP partner countries able to participate in the EU's internal market by introducing increasingly free movement of goods, persons, services and capital.

The final step, accession to the EU, will come closer at an advanced stage of the ENP. Accession to the EU is neither promised nor excluded by the ENP. However, it can be said that the ENP experience contributes to finding new forms of close integration with the EU, even without formal membership.

61 SEC(2006) 1504/2, p. 6.